CHILDREN AT HOME AND IN DAY CARE

CHILDREN AT HOME AND IN DAY CARE

(K.) Alison Clarke-Stewart
University of California, Irvine
Christian P. Gruber
Western Psychological Services, Los Angeles
Linda May Fitzgerald
University of Illinois, Chicago

 LAWRENCE ERLBAUM ASSOCIATES, PUBLISHERS
1994   Hillsdale, New Jersey   Hove, UK

Lawrence Erlbaum Associates, Inc., Publishers
365 Broadway
Hillsdale, New Jersey 07642

Cover design by Mairav Salomon

Library of Congress Cataloging-in-Publication Data

Clarke-Stewart, Alison, 1943–
    Children at home and in day care / K. Alison Clarke-Stewart,
Christian P. Gruber, and Linda May Fitzgerald.
        p. cm.
    Includes bibliographical references and index.
    ISBN 0-8058-1484-1 (c)
    1. Child development. 2. Child psychology. 3. Day-care cen-
ters.I. Gruber, Christian P., 1948–   . II. Fitzgerald, Linda May.
III. Title.
HQ772.C555   1994   93-38962
305.23'1--dc20   CIP

Books published by Lawrence Erlbaum Associates are printed on
acid-free paper, and their bindings are chosen for strength and dura-
bility.

Printed in the United States of America
10 9 8 7 6 5 4 3 2 1

CONTENTS

    PREDICTORS

8   COGNITIVE DEVELOPMENT: DAY CARE   123
    AND BEYOND

9   SOCIAL COMPETENCE   152

10 SOCIABILITY WITH MOTHER   175

11 COMPLIANCE   183

12 PEER RELATIONS   196

13 CONCLUSION   228

    APPENDIX   243

    REFERENCES   256

    AUTHOR INDEX   271

    SUBJECT INDEX   276

PREFACE

Psychologists have always been interested in how children's development is related to their early experience. From their first studies of "maternal deprivation" to their latest investigations of "within-family variance," psychologists have probed the effects of children's early lives. While researchers have been tracking down answers to questions about early experience, however, the questions have kept one step ahead of them. In the beginning, it seemed enough to ask about the mother's influence on the child. Later it was found necessary to include the father, and still later, siblings. But even as psychologists broadened their search to include the whole family, the ecology of early childhood shifted; children's everyday experiences more and more came to include those outside the family—in nursery school and day care, with nannies and peers. Today, in this society, even the youngest children live in complex worlds of home and beyond.

In this book, we take a look at the complex worlds of contemporary preschoolers. The question we pose is how the components of these worlds contribute to children's development. Do mothers have as significant an influence on children who spend time every day with another caregiver as they do on children who are home all day? How predictive of development are children's experiences in nonfamilial caregiving environments? Do experiences in these other environments have the same links to development as similar experiences at home? Does knowing about children's experiences in both home and day-care environments increase our ability to predict their development? The answers to these questions are not readily available in the existing research literature. Nevertheless, they are important to those who would understand the context of child development, either as a window into human development or as a reflection of contemporary childhood. In this book we report on a study that provides some answers to these questions.

The study was supported by a grant from the Bush Foundation, supplemented by funds from the Spencer Foundation and the Foundation for Child Development. We express our appreciation to these Foundations and to the following people: to Janellen Huttenlocher and Susan Levine for providing original assessments of language development; to the research assistants who collected the data (Margaret Ellis Snow, Linda Espinosa, Julie Spielberger, Harry Piotrowski, Kathy Cornell, Bonnie Umeh, Laima VanderStoep, Constance Filling Hevey, Lynn Barker, Janna Dresden, Carol Walcer Finder, Barbara Roth Luskin, Miriam Rabban, Anita Wolfe, Jeffrey Rosenberg, Susan Giannino, Carol Draeger, Richard Rogers, Phyllis Barnum, Jane David, Susan Mulford, Brenda Spiga, Therese Chappell, Meredith Spencer, and Betsi Tom); to the research assistants who coded the data (Saba Ayman-Nolley and Katina Kay Kostoulas); and to the research assistants who assisted in data reduction (Grant Blank, Mark Bjerknes, Andrew Norton, and Ted Scharf).

K. Alison Clarke-Stewart
Christian P. Gruber
Linda May Fitzgerald

1

Background: Children's Experiences and Their Effects on Development

THE CONTEMPORARY CONTEXTS OF CHILDHOOD

Today the majority of preschool children in the United States spend at least some time in a setting in which they are cared for by someone other than their parents—the result of a major social change in adult roles in this society. Since the mid-1960s, the number of women employed in jobs outside the home, including the mothers of young children, has increased dramatically. Today about 60% of the mothers of preschool children are working (U. S. Bureau of the Census, 1992). They have gone to work in order to maintain or improve the family's standard of living, because rising costs and high inflation have created a need for increased income in most families. They have also gone to work because they want careers, because they like their jobs, because they want to get out of the house and meet people and have new and interesting experiences, and because the feminist movement has made it easier for them to work and created the expectation that they would. Even among those mothers who currently are at home, as many as one third would prefer to work if acceptable day care were available for their children.

It is this increase in maternal employment that has led to the change in children's early experiences. Although fathers are more involved in day-to-day child care now than they were a generation ago, this does not compensate for the decreased availability of care by working mothers. Only about one quarter of the mothers who work are able to coordinate their schedules with their partner's so that the father can take care of the children while the mother is at work. The rest must make some other arrangement for the daily care of their children.

Some families have relatives—grandparents, aunts, older siblings—available for this task. But the trend observed in all Western societies toward smaller and smaller families has clearly increased parents' need to find child care outside the family. Because most families in the U.S. now have only two children who are relatively close to each other in age, there are often no older siblings available to provide care for younger brothers and sisters. Nor are there as likely to be aunts or cousins who could provide child care, because now families have smaller networks of relatives and those relatives are less likely to live nearby. Even if they live nearby, moreover, female relatives are more likely to have jobs of their own and are therefore less likely to be available for child care.

The increased use of nonparental child care has also coincided with changes in beliefs about appropriate roles for parents and children. Over the past few decades, there has been a marked move away from the traditional notion that parents should devote their lives to their children, making sacrifices in their own comfort and personal lives to ensure that their children have it better than they did. In one survey of parents in the 1970s (Yankelovich, Skelly, & White, Inc., 1977), all parents viewed themselves as less self-sacrificing than parents were in the previous generation. Of those interviewed, 43% reflected the attitudes of a "new breed" of parents, who reject conventional notions of marriage, religion, thrift, and toil. These "me generation" parents were less child-oriented and more self-centered than their parents were and were raising their children to eat, play, dress, and do as they pleased. The goal for both parents and children in these families was personal fulfillment, a goal that freed parents from feeling that childrearing was their exclusive duty and led them to want and expect supplementary child care for their children.

As a consequence of all these changes, then, the number of young children who are in some form of day care has increased markedly. Since the 1960s, the number of preschool children in day care has more than doubled. The fact that so many children are spending so much time in child-care settings unlike those in which their parents and grandparents were reared has led to concerns among parents and among psychologists, as well, who wonder about the effects of these alternative environments on children's well-being and development.

Many have feared that being in day care will harm children. They paint a gloomy picture of day care as reflected in unstable babysitters, unsafe day-care homes, and overcrowded day-care centers, and point to the dangers of institutional rearing revealed in early studies of children in orphanages and asylums (e.g., Spitz, 1946; Spitz & Wolf, 1946). They suggest that children in day care might suffer the same fate, being deprived of maternal love and adequate stimulation. Of course children in day care are not deprived of maternal love or even maternal care in the way these institutionalized youngsters were; they have that love and care before they are placed in day care and continue to experience it at the end of every day. What is more, the retarded children in institutions were deprived of much more than maternal love. They had little affection or attention from anyone. Attendants were few and always changing; they could not give individual children continuous, consistent, warm, or responsive care. The physical surroundings were poor, with minimal health care, inadequate food, and little that was interesting to look at or play with. There were no programs of education or exercise. Few day-care facilities today have conditions as extremely depriving as these, but still these studies raise questions that must be addressed.

These questions include the following: What is the nature of the attention children receive from their caregivers in day care and what is the significance of their daily separations from their mother? Researchers have demonstrated the ill effects of lengthy separations from parents for children's immediate and long-term emotional well-being (e.g., Robertson & Robertson, 1971), but the effects of briefer, more frequent separations are not so clear. Nor is the effect of having multiple caregivers in day care. The research on residential institutions suggests that children who have only a changing cast of caregivers to rely on do not fare well. But if children have the continuing presence of the mother at home every night, is harm done by having multiple caregivers in the daytime? How many adult caregivers can be involved before it becomes too much? What does it mean if these caregivers are unrelated to the family and if their styles of interacting with the child are different from the parents' and from each other's?

We must also address the issue of what effect being in day care has on children's intellectual development. Can children be given enough stimulation to ensure their intellectual growth in a day-care facility with a large group of children and few caregivers or in a home-care arrangement with a disinterested caregiver? What aspects of the day-care environment are critical for providing such stimulation of development?

And what about children's social development? Most often, when children are in day care, they are in a setting with a group of other children. Children behave quite differently with peers and with adults. Will children who spend many hours with peers be more sociable with other children? Will they be more aggressive toward them? Will they be withdrawn and passive? Will they conform to normal adult standards for socially acceptable behavior, such as courtesy and cooperation?

Clearly, there are many worrying questions. It was these questions that motivated our study.

FORMS OF DAY CARE

Day care may occur in the family's own home or someone else's, in a home setting or a center, with an unpaid relative or a paid care provider, with a friendly neighbor or a professional nanny. The child may be in a setting with one other child or many, in a facility run by a church, a community organization, the government, the school district, or an individual entrepreneur, in a program that stresses education, social skills, or play. The quality of care in these settings can range from merely "custodial," with minimal standards of safety and no program of stimulation, to "developmental," with frequent and fond attention from adult caregivers, a safe and interesting physical environment, and the opportunity to play with other children in a program of enriching educational experiences.

Table 1.1 shows the distribution of the major types of care arrangements currently being used by working mothers of preschool children in the United States. About one quarter of the families in which mothers work manage to cover child care by juggling the parents' schedules or by taking the child along to work. Another one quarter use other relatives—aunts, grandmothers, older siblings. Care by relatives is especially common for infants, for poor children, and for children whose mothers work part time. A small number of families use a nonrelated caregiver who comes to or lives in their home—a neighbor, a friend, a paid or unpaid babysitter, nanny, housekeeper, maid, live-in student, au pair, or undocumented worker. Again, this form of day care is relatively more common for infants. About one quarter of the children whose mothers work are cared for by a nonrelated provider who looks after a number of children, perhaps including her own, in her home. This "family day care" arrangement is the most common type of care for 1- and 2-year-olds whose mothers work full time.

Day-care centers are used relatively rarely for infants and toddlers; only 16% of the infants of working mothers are in centers. But for 3- and 4-year-olds whose mothers work full time, centers are the day-care arrangement of choice. About one third of the 3- and 4-year-olds whose mothers work are in centers. In addition, many children whose mothers are not employed attend day-care centers or nursery schools; currently about half of all 3- and 4-year-olds in the United States attend some kind of center program.

TABLE 1.1
Primary Child-Care Arrangements Used by Employed Mothers for Their
Children Under 5 Years of Age

	Percent Using the Arrangement	
Type of Care	For Infants and Toddlers (%)	For Preschool Children (%)
Parents themselves	25	23
Another relative	27	21
Nonrelated in-home provider	7	5
Day-care home	26	18
Day-care center	16	33

Note. Statistics based on data from the National Center for Education Statistics (1992) and the U. S. Bureau of the Census (1990, 1992).

Care in the Child's Home

Care by a provider (most often a relative) in the child's own home while the mother is at work may be a common form of day care, but it is the one about which we know least. It simply has not been studied—perhaps because it is so private, or because it varies so much from home to home, or because it is a family affair, or because it seems to be so much like care by the mother. In-home care is distinct from other more formal kinds of day care in allowing the child to remain in a familiar, secure place, and in giving the mother, to some extent, the opportunity to monitor the behavior of a caregiver who, if not one already, becomes like one of the family. In-home care keeps siblings together and allows the caregiver to provide each child with individual attention. It does not, however, offer the professional expertise of a day-care center staff or the opportunity for the child to interact with peers.

Care in a Day-Care Home

In day-care homes the care provider may or may not be related to the child; she[1] may or may not be trained in early childhood education. The number of children in the day-care home may range from 1 to 6 (family day-care home) or 6 to 12 (group day-care home). The basis for this arrangement varies from an informal agreement about shared caregiving between friends to a formal, supervised network of licensed day-care homes. Most home providers work alone, but 40% have partners or helpers (Kisker, Hofferth, Phillips, & Farquhar, 1991). Day-care homes are usually located near the child's home, and, therefore, they are easy to get to and are in a familiar neighborhood where people are likely to share the parents' values and circumstances. The mother may have more control over what happens to her child in a day-care home than she would in a day-care center because she can give instructions to a day-care home provider that she would not be able to give a day-care center teacher. Studies show that parents using family day care are more likely to have a close personal relationship with the care provider than are parents using center care. They talk to the care provider more and say that they would "keep in touch" with her after the child leaves the day-care home (Pence & Goelman, 1987). A day-care home provider is usually flexible about taking children of different ages and this form of care offers the child an opportunity to interact with a handful of children of different ages rather than a large group of agemates. The day-care home provides new experiences for the child while at the same time providing continuity with the kind of family care the child is used to—in a home setting with a "mother figure." A day-care home pro-

---

[1]Throughout this book, we use the feminine pronoun to refer to caregivers in day care, because they are almost always women.

vider, like an in-home caregiver, can devote individual attention to the children she is looking after. Most day-care homes tend to be informal, unprofessional, and short lived. Slightly more than half of the home providers in the national Profile of Child Care study (Kisker et al., 1991) said they were providing child care so they could earn money: one third said they were doing it so they could stay home with their own children; one fifth said they were doing it as a business; and one third said it was because they liked children.

Day-Care Centers

A day-care center is the most visible and easily identified child-care arrangement, the one most people think of when they speak of "day care." A center may provide care for fewer than 15 children or more than 300. About one third of children in centers attend full time (at least 35 hours per week). They are usually divided into classes or groups according to their age. Most children in day-care centers are 3 or 4 years old. Teachers in the centers are almost inevitably women (97%) and under 40 years old (80%; Whitebook, Howes, & Phillips, 1990). Most have attended college. Compared to other day-care arrangements, centers are relatively stable and publicly accountable. They usually have some staff with training in child development and they offer children the chance to play with peers, often with educational materials. All other things being equal, the majority of parents prefer centers for their preschool children. They like them because of their convenience and because they offer the child learning experiences that change as the child gets older.

Currently, about half of the day-care centers in the United States operate for profit. Nine percent are in day-care chains (e.g., Kinder-Care, which now has more than 1,200 centers in more than 40 states and generates an annual income of over $200 million). But most for-profit centers are single-center, "mom-and-pop" operations. Most for-profit centers offer full-day care. That care may be excellent, educational, individualized, and stimulating— or it may consist of custodial care in a "baby warehouse." The level of quality in the center is very much linked to the state or county requirements for licensing. These centers have no eligibility criteria and will take anyone who can pay the fee, which is likely to be lower than some other kinds of day-care centers. Usually they are quite small, enrolling about 30 children, and are often located in converted stores or shops. Their clientele tend to be homogeneous and from the neighborhood in which they are located. They have less recreational space and equipment and fewer educational activities than other day-care centers (S. Kagan, 1991; Whitebook et al., 1990).

About 40% of day-care centers are run by private community or charitable organizations, churches, or cooperating parents. Those run by community or church organizations are usually for children from poor families.

They emphasize personal attention and affection from caregivers (who may be volunteers) rather than physical facilities. They are often located in old buildings, such as church or community halls, and have limited recreational facilities. They are unlikely to stress education.

About 10% of the day-care centers in the United States receive government funding. These centers offer families the widest range of services, from meals to medical attention, from toys to transportation, and all meet standards to ensure adequate physical facilities, equipment, staff, and educational programs. There is usually an emphasis on children's cognitive development in an environment offering books, music, blocks, sand, paints, puzzles, lessons, and conversation. Eligibility is restricted to low-income families. The parents are often involved in policymaking and may participate in auxiliary educational programs. The center staff may include student aides, community volunteers, and senior citizens as well as trained teachers and directors. The main goal is often preparing children for school.

In addition to these centers, a small number of centers are sponsored by employers—corporations, factories, hospitals, universities, or trade unions. Usually such centers are at a site near the company building, so that mothers can drop in to see their children during their breaks. These centers are relatively large (80 to 100 children on the average), with well-qualified and well-paid staff. They are likely to offer the full range of services: education, recreation, and health care in bright, cheerful, and well-equipped physical settings.

The tiniest number of centers are model research-and-demonstration centers. Despite their rarity, however, this is a significant kind of day-care center because much of the research on day-care effects has been done in this kind of facility. These centers, usually affiliated with universities, reflect what is currently thought to be optimal day-care practice. The physical environment is relatively spacious and stimulating. The educational curriculum is based on the latest in child development research as well as tried and true traditional nursery school activities. The focus is usually on language and intellectual development. The staff is ample, experienced, and extensively trained in child development. The teachers meet regularly with the researchers to talk about the program and the children. Teachers also make an effort to talk regularly with the parents, who tend to be from low-income or university student families. Classes are small, and an effort is usually made to keep children with the same caregiver and classmates while they are in the program.

Sometimes working mothers can adjust their schedules so that they need only part-time day care; sometimes they use a combination of arrangements. In these cases, part-day programs like nursery schools and pre-kindergarten classes can serve as day-care settings. Traditionally, nursery schools have been concerned with children's creative expression and social adjustment and have offered children an opportunity for enriched play as they choose freely from a lavish buffet of blocks, dolls, dress-ups, puzzles, books, paints, and pets, with assistance, advice, comfort, and instruction provided by the teacher as needed. In the past two decades many nursery schools have also shifted to a more developmental curriculum, rather than simply providing these opportunities for free expression and exploration.

As this overview shows, day care comes in many shapes and sizes. It is a phenomenon of great magnitude and great diversity. It is an integral part of the life of most children in this country before they ever set foot in a schoolyard. What is more, it is unlikely that the significance of day care will diminish in the near future. There are no signs that mothers, en masse, are leaving the work force for full-time housework or that fathers are relinquishing their jobs to provide child care. For these reasons, it is essential that we think about the potential influence of day care on children's development in as probing and detailed a way as possible. It was with this in mind that the study described here was undertaken.

As background for that study, several relevant areas of research must be reviewed. These areas include the following: research documenting children's experiences in these different contexts—in day-care settings and at home; studies comparing the development of children in day care with the development of children at home; and research relating children's development to their experiences in day care and at home. The results of research in these areas are summarized next.

DIFFERENCES IN EXPERIENCES AT HOME AND IN DAY CARE

There are, of course, many ways in which being in day care is different for children from being at home with mother. There are differences in the number of children in the setting, the level and content of the caregiver's training, and the frequency of formal educational activities. These differences are reflected in the children's experiences in the two different kinds of environment. Children in day care, studies have shown, spend more of their time interacting with other children (Rubenstein & Howes, 1979, 1983; Siegel-Gorelick, Ambron, & Everson, 1981b) and have less frequent conversations with adults than children at home (Cochran, 1977a; W. Hayes et al., 1983; Prescott, 1973; Tizard, Carmichael, Hughes, & Pinkerton, 1980). Children in day care, in one study, for example, were three times as likely to talk to another child as to an adult (Sylva, Roy, & Painter, 1980). Not only is the frequency of interaction with adults different in the two kinds of environment, so is the nature of the interaction. Compared to mothers, caregivers in day care were found to be less directive and authoritarian, less critical and restrictive, more likely to help, suggest activities, make tasks into games, respond to children's initiation of play, and mediate interactions with other children (Cochran, 1977a; Hess, Price, Dickson, & Conroy, 1981;

Howes & Rubenstein, 1981; Prescott, 1973; Rubenstein & Howes, 1979, 1983; Tizard et al., 1980). At home, in these studies, mothers' "teaching" was likely to be casual and informal; children had more free time and time alone and learned from exploring household objects, helping mother, performing real-life tasks, and seeing real live role models—not from explicit lessons. Conversations with mothers were longer, included more complex utterances, offered children more opportunities to ask questions and express opinions, and were more "inductive" than conversations with caregivers in day care. In day care, conversations were more likely to be "deductive" and convergent, taking the form of teacher questions and child answers (Cochran, 1977a; Prescott, 1973; Tizard et al., 1980; Wittmer & Honig, 1989).

These differences between children's experiences at home and in day care are especially marked for children who are in center care, because centers have more children, more trained caregivers, and more educational equipment and activities than home day-care arrangements (Kontos, 1992; Kontos & Dunn, 1993). But even when children are in home day care—with a babysitter or nanny or in a day-care home—research suggests, their experiences differ from those of children at home with their mothers. Children in day-care homes in the National Day Care Home Study (Stallings, 1980) spent about half their time interacting with other children, and interactions with home care providers were less emotional, responsive, and social than interactions with mothers (Rubenstein, Pedersen, & Yarrow, 1977; Siegel-Gorelick, Ambron, & Everson, 1981a; Stith & Davis, 1984).

These studies provide useful information about children's experience in day care, but they are somewhat limited. For one thing, a number of the studies (Cochran, 1977a; Tizard et al., 1980; Sylva et al., 1980) were done outside the United States, and therefore may not accurately represent day care in this country. For another thing, many of the studies focused on just one or two contrasting settings and the researchers often used different selection criteria for identifying subjects within the settings. These studies, therefore, paint the outline of differences between settings in broad strokes, but they do not provide the detailed comparisons needed to advance our knowledge.

DIFFERENCES BETWEEN CHILDREN AT HOME AND IN DAY CARE

Researchers have been more interested in studying differences in developmental outcomes for children who are in day care compared with those who are at home with their mothers. In a number of studies, they have found that children with experience in day care during the preschool years have advanced cognitive and language development and achievement relative to children who are at home (Andersson, 1989; Burchinal, Lee, & Ramey, 1989; Clerkx & Van IJzendoorn, 1992; Cryan, Sheehan, Wiechel, &

Bandy-Hedden, 1992; Garber & Hodge, 1989; Golden et al., 1978; Gullo & Burton, 1992; Larsen & Robinson, 1989, for boys; Osborn & Millbank, 1987; H. Robinson & N. Robinson, 1971; J. Robinson & Corley, 1989; Rubenstein & Howes, 1983; Rubenstein, Howes, & Boyle, 1981; Taylor, 1976; Thornburg, Pearl, Crompton, & Ispa, 1990, for African-American children; Winnett, Fuchs, Moffatt, & Nerviano, 1977; and see reviews by Belsky, 1984; Clarke-Stewart & Fein, 1983; C. Hayes, Palmer, & Zaslow, 1990). This difference is not always found (e.g., Ackerman-Ross & Khanna, 1989; Cochran, 1977b; Peaslee, 1976; Thornburg et al., 1990; Vandell & Corasaniti, 1990), but there is a substantial body of research suggesting that the intellectual development of children who attend relatively high-quality day-care centers, nursery schools, or early childhood programs in the preschool years is advanced over the development of children from comparable family backgrounds who do not.

In a number of studies, children who attended day-care programs were also observed to be different in their social behavior. They were more self-confident, outgoing, assertive, verbally expressive, self-sufficient, and comfortable, and less distressed, timid, and fearful in new situations (Cochran, 1977b; Fowler, 1978; J. Kagan, Kearsley, & Zelazo, 1978; Lally & Honig, 1977; Moskowitz, Schwarz, & Corsini, 1977; Schwarz, Krolick, & Strickland, 1973). They were more independent of their mothers in such situations; they went farther away and spent more time away and out of the mother's sight (Wynn, 1979). They exhibited more social skills and initiated more interaction in play with unfamiliar peers (Herwig, 1989; Wille & Jacobson, 1984; Wynn, 1979). They knew more about social rules (Siegal & Storey, 1985). Like the differences in intellectual competence, differences in social competence appeared frequently, although not invariably, in these studies (no differences were found by Golden et al., 1978; Lamb, Hwang, Broberg, & Bookstein, 1988; Schenk & Grusec, 1987; Winnett et al., 1977, for example).

Researchers have also found that, in addition to being more independent and outgoing, children in day care are sometimes less polite, agreeable, and compliant with their mother's or caregiver's requests; louder and more boisterous, more irritable and rebellious, more likely to swear and have temper tantrums, and more likely to have behavior problems than children who are not or who have not been in day care (Fowler, 1978; Rabinovich, Zaslow, Berman, & Heyman, 1987; Robinson & Corley, 1989; Rubenstein & Howes, 1983; Rubenstein et al., 1981; Thornburg et al., 1990). With peers, day-care children have been observed to be more aggressive and to engage in more negative interactions than children who have not attended day care (Bates et al., 1991; Haskins, 1985; Thornburg et al., 1990; Wille & Jacobson, 1984)—although this finding, too, is not inevitable (e.g., Hegland & Rix, 1990).

But these studies of children's social and cognitive development include an unspecified range of day-care settings, settings that offer widely different conditions and qualities of care, and, as we have already mentioned, differences in development are not found in every study or every day-care setting. To understand the source of the differences in development that do occur, it is necessary for researchers to explore these differences in day-care conditions. It is to such studies that we turn next.

PREDICTORS OF DEVELOPMENT

Features of Day-Care Settings That Predict Development

In recent research, investigators have begun to connect the conditions and qualities of day care with differences in children's development. They have probed within the monolith of day care to examine children's experiences in different day-care programs and linked these experiences to differences in development. A number of investigations have documented significant associations between global indexes of day-care quality and children's cognitive development as assessed by tests of intelligence and language ability (Howes, 1988; Phillips, McCartney, & Scarr, 1987; Phillips, Scarr, & McCartney, 1987; Schlieker, White, & Jacobs, 1991; Whitebook et al., 1990) and social development as assessed by ratings of sociability, considerateness, compliance, and self-regulation (Howes, 1990; Howes & Olenick, 1986; Howes & Stewart, 1987; Phillips, McCartney, & Scarr, 1987; Phillips, Scarr, & McCartney, 1987; Vandell, Henderson, & Wilson, 1988). But global indexes hide a myriad of relations and are not helpful for uncovering specific connections between children's experiences and development. More useful are those studies in which researchers have examined the predictability of separate components of the day-care environment.

Physical Environment.   Studies of particular features of the day-care environment have revealed, first, that children's behavior and development are linked to aspects of the physical setting. Children do better, the results of these studies suggest, in day-care settings that are neat, clean, safe, and orderly, in settings that are organized into interest areas and oriented toward children's activities (Holloway & Reichhart-Erickson, 1988; Howes, 1983; Prescott & David, 1976), settings that have varied, age-appropriate, educational toys, materials, and equipment (Connolly & Smith, 1978; Goelman & Pence, 1987a; Holloway & Reichhart-Erickson, 1988; Howes & Rubenstein, 1985). Children are more likely to do constructive, mentally challenging things with building materials, to have interesting and mature conversations in play using dramatic props, to cooperate with peers in social games like checkers and pickup sticks (Phyfe-Perkins, 1980; Sylva et al., 1980), and having a variety of materials adds to the range of children's experiences. Simply adding novel materials to preschool classrooms or having more varied materials accessible, however, does not necessarily lead to cognitive gains; toys alone were not a direct promoter of development in two studies (Golden et al., 1978; Rubenstein & Howes, 1979). It was in combination with teachers' behavior that materials were more likely to be related to children's advanced development (Busse, Ree, Gatride, & Alexander, 1972; Ruopp, Travers, Glantz, & Coelen, 1979).

Caregivers' Qualifications and Behavior.   Not surprisingly, then, studies of day care also show quite consistently that the performance of children in day care is predicted by the caregivers' behavior. For one thing, children's social and intellectual development has been found to be related to the amount of attention they receive from the caregiver. Children whose teachers talked to them more were found to be advanced in communication and language skills and to score higher on intelligence tests (Carew, 1980; Rubenstein & Howes, 1983; Ruopp et al., 1979; Phillips, McCartney, & Scarr, 1987; Phillips, Scarr, & McCartney, 1987; Whitebook et al., 1990). Even more closely related to children's performance and development is the quality of the attention the caregiver offered. Children whose caregivers were stimulating, educational, and respectful, who offered the children "intellectually valuable" experiences, especially language mastery experiences, had more advanced social and intellectual skills (Carew, 1980; Golden et al., 1978; McCartney, 1984; Phillips, Scarr , & McCartney, 1987). Children spent more time working on a task, played at more complex levels, and did better on tests of intelligence and achievement when their teachers were more positive and responsive to their questions, less physically affectionate, critical, and directive, and used positive rather than negative reinforcement (Fagot, 1973; Miller, Bugbee, & Hybertson, 1985; Rubenstein & Howes, 1979; and see Phyfe-Perkins, 1981). Children were more socially competent if teachers encouraged their self-direction and independence, cooperation and knowledge, self-expression and social interaction (Miller & Dyer, 1975; Schweinhart, Weikart, & Larner, 1986).

Some studies also show that caregivers who behave in more stimulating and positive ways have certain common background characteristics. Caregivers with more training in child development were more positive, involved, interactive, helpful, talkative, and didactic, and less authoritarian toward the children in their care (Arnett, 1989; Berk, 1985; Fosburg et al., 1980; Howes, 1983; Kinney, 1988; Klinzing & Klinzing, 1974; Lazar, Darlington, Murray, Royce, & Snipper, 1982; Ruopp et al., 1979, Tyler & Dittman, 1980; Whitebook et al., 1990). Teachers who had more professional experience were more responsive, accepting, positive, and playful (Howes, 1983; Kontos & Fiene, 1987). But this relation is not always found; in the National Day Care Study (Ruopp et al., 1979), teachers with more extensive experience were observed to provide less stimulating and educational interaction than caregivers with less experience, and in the National Day Care Home

Study (Fosburg et al., 1980; Stallings, 1980), caregivers with more experience were not markedly different from caregivers with less experience.

Educational Program.   Studies of day-care components have also shown that children in more educationally oriented day-care programs— with prescribed educational activities such as lessons, guided play sessions, story reading, teaching of specific content, and more direct teacher instruction—differ from those in less educationally oriented programs. In these educational programs children have been observed to spend more time in constructive and complex play with materials and with peers and to score higher on intelligence and achievement tests (Ferri, 1980; Fowler, 1978; Goelman & Pence, 1987a; Goodman & Andrews, 1981; Johnson, Ershler, & Bell, 1980; Lazar, Hubbell, Murray, Rosche, & Royce, 1977; McCartney, 1984; Miller & Dyer, 1975; Sylva et al., 1980; Tizard, Philips, & Plewis, 1976; Winnett et al., 1977). When children spent their time in the day-care center just playing around with other children they experienced less "rich" play and were less competent in social and cognitive ways (McCartney, 1984; Phillips, McCartney, & Scarr, 1987, Phillips, Scarr, & McCartney, 1987; Sylva et al., 1980). On the other hand, having too much structured activity, too much academic pressure, also predicts less advanced development (Hirsh-Pasek, Hyson, & Rescorla, 1990; Miller & Dyer, 1975; Sylva et al., 1980).

Other Children.   Often the reason children spend their time in day care just playing around with other children is that the class is large or that the ratio of adults to children is low. These day-care variables have also been found to predict children's behavior and development. When the adult-child ratio was experimentally reduced (e.g., from 1:4 to 1:10 or 1:12, in one study), children experienced less contact with the caregiver, had fewer of their questions answered, engaged in shorter conversations, were subject to more prohibitions, and spent more time playing with and talking to peers (Asher & Erickson, 1979; Smith & Connolly, 1980). The same effect has been observed in correlational studies. In day-care classes with more children per caregiver, it has been found that each child experienced less interaction with the teacher and the interaction was of lower quality than in classes with fewer children per caregiver; the classroom climate was less likely to be facilitative of social stimulation, positive in affect, or responsive to the child's needs, and was more likely to be restrictive and negative in tone (Howes, 1983; Whitebook et al., 1990). In day-care programs with more children in a class, children have been found to be less cooperative, less talkative, and more hostile with their peers; their play was less complex; they had more conflicts, and spent more time in aimless activity (Ruopp et al., 1979; Smith & Connolly, 1980; Sylva et al., 1980). Significant associations showing the detrimental effect of low adult-child ratios and high class sizes for children's behavior and development have been found in a substantial number of studies (Holloway & Reichhart-Erickson, 1988; Howes, 1983,

1987; Howes, Rodning, Galluzzo, & Myers, 1988; Howes & Rubenstein, 1985; Lamb, Sternberg, Knuth, Hwang, & Broberg, 1991; Phillips, McCartney, & Scarr, 1987; Phillips, Scarr, & McCartney, 1987; Ruopp et al., 1979; Smith & Connolly, 1980; Sylva et al., 1980; Whitebook et al., 1990).

The time a child spends interacting with another child or children in day care, however, has been found not to be negatively related to the child's social and intellectual competence (McCartney, 1984); it was even positively related to the child's level of play in one study (Rubenstein & Howes, 1979). This is probably especially likely if the other child is older: Children have been observed to play more maturely with older children in day care (Siegel-Gorelick et al., 1981b). There is some suggestion that children in classes with a heterogeneous age mix behave more competently than those in homogeneous groups. In mixed-age preschool classes, children have been observed to exhibit fewer dominance activities (hitting, kicking, demanding objects), more language (asking questions, conversing, imitating), more cooperation (offering objects), and more altruism (helping, giving), and to increase in persistence, flexibility, intelligence, and positive response to a stranger (Beller, 1974; Bizman, Yinon, Mivtzari, & Shavit, 1978; Logue, 1989).

We see, thus, that there is a substantial body of research linking qualities of the day-care environment with children's behavior and development. Perhaps that would be sufficient to answer our questions about day-care "effects." Unfortunately, however, day care is only half the picture. Children not only attend day care of different kinds and qualities, they also have families of different kinds and qualities. Perhaps the observed differences in children's behavior were affected by characteristics of their families as well as—or instead of—by their experiences in day care. Researchers have generally not observed their day-care subjects at home to explore this issue. The possible links between children's experiences in day care and at home were a major concern in our study.

Features of Family Life That Predict Development

Although researchers have not studied the correspondences between children's experiences at home and in day care, they have performed numerous investigations of the influence of experiences at home for children who are not in day care. Another area of research that provides a background for our study, therefore, is research relating children's development to qualities and conditions in their families. In this research, as in the research on day-care quality, global indexes of the quality of care children receive at home have been found to predict their development. In the most comprehensive analysis of family variables predicting development, a six-site collaborative study using Caldwell and Bradley's Home Observation for Measurement of the Environment (HOME) Inventory, this global index of quality family care was found to predict higher levels of intelligence significantly and consistently across different sites and different preschool ages (Bradley et al., 1989; A. W. Gottfried, 1984). In other research, too, this measure has been associated with more advanced intelligence (Yeates, MacPhee, Campbell, & Ramey, 1983), for 4-year-olds, even when the contribution of mother's IQ was controlled statistically. Moreover, the HOME Inventory has also been correlated with advanced verbal abilities (Broberg, Hwang, Lamb, & Bookstein, 1990) and social skills with familiar peers and unfamiliar adults (Lamb et al., 1988).

But we can glean limited information about the processes of environmental influence from global indexes alone. We need to know how the components of family care are associated with children's development, and whether these associations parallel those just discussed for day-care environments.

Physical Environment.   Studies of the predictiveness of different components of family care suggest that, as in day-care settings, the physical environment in the home is related to children's development. One of the two most highly and consistently predictive subscales in the collaborative HOME study was the variety of toys the child had at home (Bradley, 1986; Bradley et al., 1989; A. W. Gottfried, 1984). Organization of the physical environment was not highly related to children's intelligence in this study, but it was found to be one of the few scales that predicted intelligence for adopted 7-year-olds in the Colorado Adoption Project (Coon, Fulker, DeFries, & Plomin, 1990).

Parents' Behavior and Background.   The other major predictor of development in the collaborative HOME study was the mother's involvement with the child—watching, talking, encouraging, playing, teaching (Bradley, 1986; Bradley et al., 1989; A. W. Gottfried, 1984). The mother's involvement predicted children's levels of intelligence consistently across time and place, and after it was removed in regression analyses, relations with the other subscales of the HOME were no longer significant. Extending this association, it has also been demonstrated that when mothers interacted and talked more frequently with their young children, the children had better peer relations (MacDonald & Parke, 1984), more extensive early vocabularies (Huttenlocher, Haight, Bryk, Seltzer, & Lyons, 1991), and more positive moods (Stevenson-Hinde, Hinde, & Simpson, 1986). The father's involvement with the child, as well, has been found to be related to children's development, most clearly to intellectual development. The more time children spent with their fathers, the higher was their cognitive level (A. E. Gottfried, Gottfried, & Bathurst, 1987; Radin, 1976; Reis & Gold, 1977; Ruopp et al., 1979). We do not have such consistent evidence of the father's contribution to children's social competence; few investigators have studied this association. But in one study that included measures of social competence, children with more involved fathers were found to have higher personality maturity scores yet lower social skills observed with a friend at home or an adult visitor (Lamb et al., 1988).

When interactions with mother, as well as being frequent, are warm and affectionate and not hostile or rejecting, researchers have found that children's play with peers was less likely to be negative (Hinde & Stevenson-Hinde, 1986; Stevenson-Hinde et al., 1986). Children whose interactions with their mothers were more positive also were more compliant (Londerville & Main, 1981), socially competent, mature, self-reliant (Baumrind, 1967; Olson, Bates, & Bayles, 1984; Roberts, 1986), and intellectually competent (Barocas et al., 1991; Estrada, Arsenio, Hess, & Holloway, 1987; Jennings & Connors, 1989; Roberts, 1986). The warmth, affection, and nurturance shown by the father also were related to children's cognitive development, at least for boys and school-age children (Epstein & Radin, 1975; Honzik, 1967; Jordan, Radin, & Epstein, 1975; Radin, 1973, 1976).

Consistent relations with children's performance have also been found in research on maternal responsiveness. Mothers who were more verbally responsive (answering children's questions and responding to their requests) and responsive in play (not suggesting what to do but helping when help was needed) had children who performed better on assessments of intelligence and language (Barnard, Bee, & Hammond, 1984; Bradley et al., 1989; A. W. Gottfried, 1984; Levenstein, 1986; Olson, Bayles, & Bates, 1986) and play (Rubenstein & Howes, 1979). Their children were more compliant (Lay, Waters, & Park, 1989; Parpal & Maccoby, 1985), less moody (Stevenson-Hinde et al., 1986), and more self-confident and socially responsive (Levenstein, 1986).

Another significant predictor of children's development is parental control. In general, research suggests, children do better with moderate, "authoritative" control; when parents exert either no control or strict and restrictive control, their children do more poorly. The children's intellectual development, as measured by school-relevant performance, language, and IQ, was impaired by such extremes of discipline (Barnard et al., 1984; Epstein & Radin, 1975; Hess & McDevitt, 1984; Nelson, 1973; Radin, 1976; Roberts, 1986), and their social competence was limited; they were more withdrawn and dependent, more hostile and rejected with peers, more noncompliant and defiant with their mothers (Bates et al., 1991; Baumrind, 1967; Crockenberg & Litman, 1990; Fagot, 1991; Hinde & Stevenson-Hinde, 1986; MacDonald & Parke, 1984; Roberts, 1986; Silverman & Ragusa, 1990). Gentle, positive control was related to higher performance on intelligence tests (Scarr, Lande, & McCartney, 1989), more friendly behavior to peers at preschool (Stevenson-Hinde et al., 1986), and greater compliance (Crockenberg & Litman, 1990).

Not only is positive, responsive, and authoritative parental behavior linked to children's development, this style of discipline has also been found to be linked to parents' levels of education. In the collaborative

HOME study, for example, mothers with higher education were found to be higher on the total HOME Inventory and its subscales—responsivity, involvement, acceptance, and provision of play materials and varied stimulation (Bradley et al., 1989). Parents' education, as reflected in their socioeconomic status (SES), was linked to children's intelligence in this study, as it has been in many other studies (e.g., Ackerman-Ross & Khanna, 1989; Desai, Chase-Lansdale, & Michael, 1989; Goelman & Pence, 1987b; Honzik, 1967; Jennings & Connors, 1989; Laosa, 1982; Melhuish, Lloyd, Martin, & Mooney, 1990; Moss & Kagan, 1958; Nelson, 1973; Olson et al., 1984; Schlieker et al., 1991). However, it contributed little to the prediction of children's intelligence beyond what the HOME environment did (Bradley et al., 1989).

Educational Program.   Although most parents do not provide formal educational activities for their children at home, informal education does occur and this, too, has been found to predict children's development. Children whose parents offered them more varied and stimulating opportunities for intellectual development had higher levels of tested intelligence. In the collaborative HOME study, for example, the most predictive HOME scale included structuring the child's play periods and providing toys that challenged the child to develop new skills (Bradley et al., 1989; A. W. Gottfried, 1984). Also significantly related to intelligence was the scale that included reading stories to the child and providing the child with books. In other studies, similar links have been found. Carew (1980) observed that language mastery experiences initiated by the parent predicted children's IQ; Milner (1951) and Laosa (1982) found that how much mothers read to their children predicted children's achievement.

Other Children.   A final factor in the home environment that may influence children's development is the presence of other children. Family size has often been related to children's lower performance on tests of intelligence (e.g., Desai et al., 1989; A. W. Gottfried & Gottfried, 1984). But although coming from a large family may be detrimental for the child's development, having one or two siblings may have some benefits. It has been observed that children with siblings received more prosocial behavior and fewer agonistic overtures from peers (Pepler, Corter, & Abramovitch, 1982). It has also been observed that girls with brothers spent less time onlooking or unoccupied at preschool than girls with no brothers (Berndt & Bulleit, 1985), were rated by kindergarten teachers as more competitive, ambitious, and enthusiastic (Koch, 1955, 1956), and had higher scores on tests of quantitative abilities (Rosenberg & Sutton-Smith, 1966). But these results are not always found. Sometimes children with siblings have been found to do less well. With unfamiliar peers, researchers have found, children with siblings have more negative interactions (Easterbrooks & Lamb, 1979) and are less sociable and assertive (Snow, Jacklin, & Maccoby,

1981). In grade school, girls whose siblings included only brothers had lower IQ, reading, and achievement scores (Cicirelli, 1967). Simply having a sibling, apparently, is not consistently related to development.

Nor is birth order consistently predictive of differences in development: Advantages for firstborns have been observed in some studies for intellectual ability (e.g., A. W. Gottfried & Gottfried, 1984; Nelson, 1973; Rosenberg & Sutton-Smith, 1966), and for sociability and assertiveness with an unfamiliar peer (Snow et al., 1981). With familiar peers, however, children with younger siblings have been observed to be dominant but less talkative; children with older siblings to receive both more aggression and more prosocial behavior (Berndt & Bulleit, 1985); and the superiority of firstborns' intellectual ability has not always been confirmed (cf. Marjoribanks, 1976).

In this body of research on family predictors of development we see parallels with the day-care literature in several areas. Both in day care and at home, children's development is related to having more stimulating materials in the physical environment and to having interactions with the adults that are frequent, responsive, positive, and authoritative, to being cared for by adults who have higher levels of education and who structure the children's play and read to them. Parallels for the results concerning the effects of other children in the setting are less clear, although it does seem that a having large number of children in either venue is associated with lower performance.

Family Predictors for Children in Day Care.   But these studies of the predictability of children's development from family variables have for the most part included only children reared at home. If children in day care were included, researchers made no attempt to separate them from the home-reared children in their analyses of the influence of family factors. Therefore, we cannot answer the question of whether family predictions are comparable for home-reared and day-care children based on this research—despite the critical importance of this issue.

In only one study did researchers directly examine differences in prediction from family variables for children in day care and at home. In this study, by Ramey, Farran, and Campbell (1979), children from low-income families were randomly assigned to attend a model day-care center or not. The researchers found that day-care attendance did alter the predictiveness of some maternal factors. For children at home with their mothers, IQ was predicted by mothers' verbal interaction, involvement, and IQ; for children in day care, it was predicted by mothers' verbal interaction, accepting attitude, and organized HOME environment, but it was not predicted by the mother's IQ. But this was an unusual study, involving low-income mothers, a model day-care center, and an experimental design. No generalizations about the "normal" population can be drawn.

Family and Day-Care Predictors Combined

Although they have not probed the differences in predictiveness of family variables for children who are or are not in day care, researchers have recently begun to include assessment of family variables in their studies of day-care children. They have begun to acknowledge the need to consider both day-care and family predictors in a more integrated way. From these studies we are beginning to get a picture of how family and day-care variables are interrelated and of how both day-care and family variables may together predict children's development. The picture presented in these studies is still very dim, however, and the study to be described in this book sheds significant light on the subject.

Links Between Family and Day Care.   Researchers have shown that parents at higher socioeconomic levels are more likely to use day care (Melhuish, Moss, Mooney, & Martin, 1991) and to use day care of higher quality (Holloway & Reichhart-Erickson, 1988; Schlieker, White, & Jacobs, 1989-1990; Tizard et al., 1976), although this link was not found in all studies (Howes, 1988). Parents who sent their children to day-care or preschool programs were also likely to include fathers who were more involved in child care (Larsen & Robinson, 1987; Winnett et al., 1977) and mothers who were more remote from their children, even before they enrolled them in day care (Blurton Jones, Ferreira, Brown, & Macdonald, 1980; Melhuish et al., 1991). Parents using day care in one study were found to provide more stimulating home environments (A. W. Gottfried & Gottfried, 1984). In other research, parents who used higher quality day care were found to be more positive and sensitive (Owen & Henderson, 1989), more nurturing and less restrictive (Howes, 1990; Howes & Stewart, 1987); they expected their children to acquire developmental skills earlier (Holloway & Reichhart-Erickson, 1989).

Because of these differences in parents' attitudes, behavior, and SES, it is hard to separate the effects of family and day-care variables, and, indeed, difficult to establish that either environment is actually causing differences in children's development. Most researchers faced with this problem have tried to match their samples of day-care and home-reared children on the SES of the family or have controlled SES statistically in their analyses of day-care effects (e.g., Holloway & Reichhart-Erickson, 1988; Howes & Stewart, 1987; Owen & Henderson, 1989; Schlieker et al., 1991). A few researchers have examined day-care effects experimentally, randomly as-signing children to high-quality care (Garber & Heber, 1980; Ramey et al., 1979) or to different preschool programs (Miller & Dyer, 1975; Miller et al., 1985). A few have carried out experimental manipulations of day-care variables (Ruopp et al., 1979; Smith & Connolly, 1986). A few have used microanalytic techniques to examine minute-to-minute interactions be-tween children and their caregivers in an effort to observe processes of influence (Wittmer & Honig, 1988). These research strategies are not a complete solution to the causal conundrum that plagues research in this area, as it plagues research on family processes (see Clarke-Stewart, 1988). They do not eliminate the bias of self-selection from the research results we have already reported. They do, however, provide some preliminary evidence that day care can have direct effects on children—and on their parents. In several studies, for example, participation in high-quality day care has increased both children's intellectual skills and their parents' stimulation, play, and positive discipline at home (Edwards, Logue, Loehr, & Roth, 1987; Garber & Heber, 1980; Ramey et al., 1979). These studies have not, however, demonstrated the extent to which ordinary day care may affect children and their families.

Predictiveness of Family Versus Day-Care Variables.   Some researchers who have included both family and day-care variables in their studies have tried to compare the relative predictiveness of the two sets of variables. A number of them have found that family variables were more closely related to children's development than were day-care variables: Family variables were more predictive of development than whether or not the child attended day care, the type of day care attended, or the quality of the day-care program. Bates and his associates (1991) and Howes (1988) found that SES and parent discipline were more consistently and substantially related to children's adjustment to school or kindergarten than was prior day-care history. Desai et al. (1989) found that mother's verbal ability was more highly related to the children's language ability than was type of child care. Goelman and Pence (1987b) found that mothers' education accounted for about 15% of the variance in children's intelligence, whereas the type of child care and the quality of child care (caregiver's training) each accounted for less than 5%. Broberg et al. (1990) found that the quality of the HOME environment was more highly related to children's verbal abilities than the type or quality of day care. Melhuish et al. (1990) and Tizard et al. (1976) found that mothers' education was related to children's tested cognition, whereas type of day care was not. Wadsworth (1986) found that although preschool experience predicted children's verbal scores, its power was small compared to mother's education.

In several other studies, however, day-care attendance or quality was found to be as highly predictive of children's abilities as family variables. Children's intelligence and language were as highly predicted by an overall index of day-care quality as by parents' SES and values in a study done in Bermuda by Phillips, Scarr, and McCartney (1987). Children's social skills were more highly predicted by day-care quality (caregiver-child ratio) than by parents' SES and quality of care (HOME inventory) in a study done in Sweden by Lamb et al. (1991). Children's grades, work habits, compliance, emotional health, and relations with peers were more highly predicted by day-care history (length and amount of day care) than by family characteristics (SES, size, marital status) in a study in Texas by Vandell and Corasaniti (1990). And attendance at a model educational day-care center predicted children's intelligence more highly than did their mother's IQ or participation in a parent education program in research by Wasik, Ramey, Bryant, and Sparling (1990).

One reason for these inconsistencies in the predictiveness of family and day-care variables may be that researchers have used different measures in the two settings. This is a problem that can only be solved by using comparable measures of children's experiences in day care and at home. This solution was used by Howes (1990), who found that parental discipline predicted social adjustment in kindergarten for children who started day care after infancy more highly than did teacher discipline, whereas teacher discipline predicted adjustment in children who were enrolled prior to 12 months more highly than parental discipline. But clearly much more research to extend this finding is needed before we can draw a firm conclusion about the relative importance of home and day-care environments for children's development.

Predictiveness of Family and Day-Care Variables Combined.   We also need more research to explore the issue of the combined effects of home and day-care environments on development. A few researchers who have assessed both family and day-care variables have looked for combined effects using regression or path analyses. Their analyses show that the level of predictability of children's development is greater when both sets of variables are included—children did better when they received high-quality care, stimulation, and encouragement in both home and day-care settings (Goelman & Pence, 1987b; Holloway & Reichhart-Erickson, 1989; Laosa, 1982; Sternberg et al., 1991). They have also found that the positive effects of full-time high quality day care were greatest for children whose home environments were least advantageous (Jarvis, 1987; Scarr et al., 1989; Schlieker et al., 1991; Tizard et al., 1976) and have hypothesized that the negative effects of poor quality care would be greater for children from more advantaged families (Long, Peters, & Garduque, 1985). These findings and hypotheses need to be extended by applying multivariate analyses to data collected in a range of families and day-care settings.

WHY THE NEED FOR AN INTEGRATIVE STUDY

Thus, it is clear that although existing research provides a useful background and some hints about possible answers to our questions concerning the relative influence of home and day-care environments on young children's development, there are still serious gaps in our knowledge. First, much of the research is based on a limited selection of day-care environments, often university-based model day-care programs; there is a need for research that is descriptive of the normal variation of community child care obtained by a range of families. Second, the most comprehensive studies of community day care have been done in other countries (Bermuda, Canada, Sweden, England), which have different day-care policies and opportunities; there is a need for a comprehensive study of children's experiences and development in day care in the United States. Third, researchers have most often used as their measures of children's development standard tests of intelligence and language; there is a need for research that includes and compares the predictability of a variety of other indexes of development as well, such as behavioral indexes of the child's social competence, compliance, and relations with mother. Fourth, most researchers have not systematically documented the quality (or qualities) of either the day-care settings or the home environments of their subjects; there is a need for research that probes the qualities of both kinds of setting. Fifth, when researchers have included measures of home and day-care settings, they have most often used distal measures of the family environment (like SES) and day-care quality (like adult-child ratios) as proxies for children's experiences at home and in day care, rather than including comparable *in situ* observations of children's experiences at home and in day care. There is a need for research in which children's experiences in the natural ecologies of home and day care are observed in equivalent ways so that we may find out about the relative predictive power of family and day-care variables. Our study represents an effort to begin filling these needs.

2

An Integrative Study: Purpose and Design

The present study extends and improves upon existing research in a variety of ways that attempt to fill the gap in our knowledge about the relative effects of family and day-care experiences on young children. Its primary purpose was to explore the full range of children's experiences in a wide variety of settings and to examine how those experiences were related to the children's development. It was intended that the study would provide a quite comprehensive view of the contexts of contemporary childhood. To fulfill this aim we included a wide spectrum of measures—wider than had been used in previous studies—and analyzed these measures in a wide variety of ways, both simple and multivariate. The range of observations, variability of settings, and integration of measures across the broad contexts of family and day care make this study unique.

The primary and most distinctive variability provided in the study was in the range of day-care environments studied. This was no study of model day-care programs. Based on an original design that was modified when we began enrolling subjects and discovered the realities of the arrangements that parents created to fit their families' needs, the study ultimately included children in five different day-care arrangements: with caregivers who came to their homes, in family day-care homes, in nursery schools part time, in day-care centers full time, or—the popular arrangement, which we had not anticipated—in a combined arrangement of part-time nursery school and part-time in-home caregiver. No other study had incorporated this breadth of arrangements.

Within each of these types of care, in addition, a breadth of settings was included. We did not search out "model" day-care settings, but took them as they came, as parents found them—hoping, in this way, to increase the generalizability of our results over those of studies of specific, selected centers. We maximized the range of variability in the settings studied by limiting the sample to, at most, a few children in any individual setting, so that we would be assured of a wide range of experiences in day care that we could then link to children's development.

We made similar efforts to include wide variability in the kinds of families we studied. Our success in this area should not be exaggerated; we did not include families in the poorest neighborhoods of the city in which researchers might be exposed to danger, and we did not recruit single parents or families on welfare. Nevertheless, nearly 20% of the sample was from working poor families (unskilled or semi-skilled work at a near minimum wage). We also did not include families affluent enough for both parents not to be working. The socioeconomic variation in the study, although not including these extremes of income, was sufficient to permit the evaluation of differences attributable to family background. In addition, this variability made it possible to assess differential relations between setting characteristics and child outcomes in different socioeconomic groups.

The breadth of the measures included in the study created another kind of variability and further contributed to the study's power. The measures were of three distinct kinds, which each covered a range of important qualities. The first kind was natural observations: Each child was followed and observed for a number of hours and detailed and systematic records of behavior (both the behavior the child exhibited and the behavior to which the child was exposed) were made. Included at these times, too, were checklists that provided an account of the setting's physical characteristics. The second kind of measure consisted of interviews: Each caregiver and parent was presented with a structured set of questions ranging widely over their demographic characteristics, educational background, caretaking experience and practices, and curricular preferences. The third kind of measure included formal assessments of the child's performance. These measures were collected primarily during extended visits by the child and mother to a laboratory playroom, where it was possible to include observations in semi-structured situations as well as more conventional tests of children's cognitive and social functioning. This breadth of coverage helped ensure that the effects of day care could be assessed across the widest possible set of child outcomes and ultimately attributed to the narrowest and most distinctive set of independent factors.

Other researchers have, for the most part, used a simpler battery of assessments than we did. To measure child development they have most often relied on standard tests of intelligence and caregivers' ratings of sociability; to measure the environment of home or day care they have typically used distal measures like the SES of the parents and the level of education and training of the caregiver. In our study we went beyond these measures to probe children's behavior and experiences with a variety of original instruments. These instruments were behaviorally based; they involved actual observation of children's and adults' actions. They were replicated in various settings (the child's natural settings and a standard "laboratory" setting). They tapped a range of domains of development—intellectual, social, emotional—in ways that allowed a balanced comparison of day-care "effects" in these different areas.

Not just the variety of measures, but also the way in which they were used, helped provide new information in the study. Strong parallels were created in the use of the same measures in different settings: Identical observations were made in both day-care settings and the child's home; interview questions for the mother were also addressed to the father and the daytime caregiver; measures of the child's performance drew on comparable information from both home and laboratory assessments. This approach ensured that important effects could be considered regardless of the setting in which they occurred and ultimately that the relative contributions of different sorts of independent influences could be assessed (e.g., outcomes influenced by characteristics of the home and parents vs. those of the caregiver and day-care arrangement). It is only by using identical measures in different settings that cross-setting comparisons can legitimately be made. Few other researchers have observed children's experiences in both their day-care settings and home environments in comparable ways.

Variability in children's experience was also maximized by observing each child at three times of day: morning, afternoon, and the end of the day—wherever the child normally was at that time of day. For children who were at home with their mothers all day, this meant that they were observed alone with mother and possibly a sibling during the daytime and also at dinnertime with the entire family. For children in day care, this meant that they were observed in both their day-care and typical weekday home environments. Children in a combined care arrangement were observed in both their home day-care and center day-care environments and in their family environments as well. Spreading these three observations across the day allowed us to paint a representative picture of the child's total daily experience. Including observations of children at home with their entire families at the end of the day allowed us to compare the experiences the child had with mother and with father and to observe the effect of the presence of father and other family members on the child's interactions with mother.

The final feature of this study was the inclusion of a longitudinal design. Again, there was an effort to maintain breadth and parallel coverage. Both the observations and the laboratory-based assessments were repeated at two points in the study, about 1 year apart. This feature made it possible to look for relations with children's performance that were replicated across time, to address questions about cross-time predictions of development, and to go beyond analysis of simple differences in the level of outcomes to look at changes in outcome over time and increased exposure to day care.

DESIGN OF THE STUDY

The specific design of the study, in brief, was as follows. Children were selected to represent a variety of different daytime care arrangements: at home with their mother; with a caregiver (babysitter, nanny, housekeeper) in their own home; with a caregiver in the caregiver's home (family day-care home); in a nursery school or day-care center. At least 20 families using each of these kinds of care were recruited. No more than four children from any single day-care setting were included in the sample. The children in day care were in their first day-care arrangements, and had been there for less than 1 year when the study began. These children were then followed longitudinally for a little more than a year and observed at home, in their day-care environments, and in standard situations in a laboratory playroom. Parents and other caregivers were interviewed to supplement the observed information about the children's experiences and environments.

SUBJECTS

Recruitment and Enrollment

In deciding how to select subjects for the study we were confronted by two alternative strategies. One strategy was to try to eliminate the bias of self-selection by matching children in different kinds of day care according to their family backgrounds, for example, SES. This strategy would have had the advantage of allowing us to analyze day-care effects without the confounding factor of family background (and vice versa). The alternative strategy was to allow day-care and family characteristics to covary naturally, and then attempt to control for each statistically. Because we were interested in finding out about the "real world," of which natural variation is an integral part, we chose the second strategy. If highly educated parents were more likely to select nursery school rather than home day care for their children, for example, this was part of the ecology of early childhood, and, therefore, data for our study.

Having chosen to follow this strategy, our tactic in recruiting subjects was to locate all children through their parents, rather than using different recruitment methods for the different child-care groups (e.g., day-care centers for children in day care and newspaper advertisements for children at home). The names of parents of 2- and 3-year-old children were obtained from doctors, churches, child-care referral agencies, notices in supermarkets, and a purchased mailing list. All subjects were approached through a letter to the parents and then, for those who indicated their interest, by a follow-up phone call. In order to maximize the stability of the sample, we selected two-parent families who lived in relatively safe neighborhoods and in which the father was employed.

The sample that we recruited using these methods consisted of 150 children (2-year-olds and 3-year-olds in equal numbers). Our original plan was to recruit 25 children in each of six categories of care: only children at home with mother; children with siblings at home with mother; children with an in-home caregiver; children in day-care homes; children in centers part time; and children in centers full time. It turned out, however, that it was more difficult to find children to fit some of these categories than others, and many children would not fit into our neatly defined cells. Consequently, we modified the plan, created a new combined home-care/center-care category, and recruited 150 children with a minimum of 15 children in each category.[1] The children who were recruited were distributed across daytime care arrangements as follows: at home with mother (n = 48; 24 with and 24 without siblings under age 6 who were at home in the daytime), with a caregiver in their own home (n = 15), in a day-care home (n = 22), in a day-care center or nursery school program part time (n = 25), in a day-care center program full time (n = 25), in a combination of part-time center and part-time in-home care (n = 15). Thus, in the sample at the beginning of the study, 48 children were not in day care; 52 children were in home day care; and 65 children were in center day care.[2]

Attrition and Change

In the study, we visited each child nine times over a period of approximately 14 months. The visits were clustered into two parallel sets of assessments about 1 year apart (morning, afternoon, dinnertime, and laboratory visits). Not surprisingly, despite our best efforts, a number of subjects missed one or more visits. Other subjects dropped out before the study was complete, primarily because they moved away from the area. As a result, by the end of the first complete set of assessments, 3 months into the study, the size of the sample on which there were complete data was 144; by the end of the

---

[1]There were at least 15 children in each of these six specific categories (mother, in-home caregiver only, day-care home only, part-time center only, full-time center only, both in-home and center); there were at least 20 children in each of the five types of care (i.e., mother, in-home caregiver, day-care home, part-time center, full-time center).

[2]When we began this study, at the end of the 1970s, only about 50% of the mothers of 2- to 4-year-old children were in the work force (U. S. Bureau of the Census, 1982). By 1993, this number had increased to about 60%. Nevertheless, despite this increase in day-care usage, our data are not likely to be out of date. Mothers must still confront the same issues in deciding to go to work and in finding day care, and the kinds and quality of day-care facilities that are available have not changed. Parents and psychologists are still concerned about the possible effects of day care on development and still want to know whether the influence of parents is dampened by using day care. There is no reason to believe that a similar study conducted in the 1990s on a comparable population would yield substantially different results.

study, it was 127. Subjects who dropped out were evenly distributed across child-care arrangements (17% in mother care, 15% in home day care, and 16% in center day care). The only significant difference in the first-year outcomes between the subjects who dropped out and those who did not was that the children in mother care who dropped out scored lower on social cognition ($t = 2.8$, $p < .01$) and social competence with an adult stranger ($t = 2.3$, $p < .05$).

Over the course of the study, as children got older, the care arrangements of many children changed. Almost inevitably the change was from a home arrangement to a center arrangement. Twenty-one children who had been at home with mother in the first year of the study started nursery school or entered a day-care center in the second year, and 18 who had been in a home day-care arrangement switched to a center. As a consequence, for the second-year assessments, there were only 23 children who were not in any kind of day care, 6 who were in in-home care, and 7 who were in day-care homes. In Year 2, 39 children were in center programs part time, 31 were in center programs full time, and 22 were in a care arrangement involving a center part time and a home caregiver part time. All the children who were in center care at the first assessment stayed in centers, although many had different caregivers. Altogether, 75 children changed to a different caregiver over the year-long period; 20 of these children changed twice.

These data are interesting in their own right. They illustrate the natural progression of children's early care in the first 5 years of life—from home and mother, to another caregiver in a home setting, to a "school" type setting. They also demonstrate vividly the "instability" in children's experiences. In fact, this is probably an underestimate of that instability, because, in the beginning, when we were recruiting subjects for the study, we restricted our sample to those parents who said that they expected that their child's care arrangement would remain the same over the next year. How naive they, and we, turned out to be!

RESEARCHERS

The researchers who collected the data in the study were graduate students at the University of Chicago. Children were observed and tested by different researchers in each different setting; these researchers were blind to data on each subject collected in previous observations. Examiners, in laboratory and home assessments, also were blind to the child's care arrangement. Initial interviews of mothers were done by separate interviewers, so that researchers collecting observational data could be kept unaware of demographic and life history information about the child. The interviewers and observers were all women; the examiners included both men and women.

Training and Reliability of Observers

Observers were initially trained on videotaped observations until they were familiar with the coding system. Then they were trained in the field with families who were not in the study, until they reached a criterion of agreement with more experienced observers in which Cohen's Kappas between pairs of observers over all the behaviors reached .90 or better. Finally, formal reliability assessments of observation variables using actual subjects in the study were conducted during each year of data collection. Pairs of observers were sent to conduct 2-hour observations together on each of 12 visits. Correlations between the observers' totals for each observation variable were then calculated across the 12 visits. Table A.1 in the appendix lists these correlations for each observation variable. Variables that were not reliably observed were dropped from further analysis.

Training and Reliability of Examiners

The original team of four examiners worked with the investigator to devise the structured assessments by pilot testing with 12 children who were not in the study. Before data collection began these examiners had developed standardized procedures and coding and were implementing them with a high degree of consistency. Procedures were fully scripted and interexaminer agreement on all coding categories was higher than 90%. Several other examiners who participated later on in the study were trained by the original team to the same standards.

ANALYSES

In analyzing the vast array of data collected in the study, our overall goals were, first, to describe children's experiences in different environments and, second, to predict their development on the basis of these experiences. It has become quite common in contemporary research to rely solely on multivariate analyses, combining all independent and dependent variables into the fewest possible regression analyses. We believed that there was important information in this study at simpler, descriptive levels of analysis, that it was informative to look at the data at the level of means and frequencies, simple and partial correlations, as well as at the more compressed level of multivariate analysis. Consequently, we have presented a variety of kinds of analyses in this book, proceeding from simple to multivariate levels. The organization we have followed in presenting these analyses is to begin with the analyses of observations of children's experiences in different settings. In chapter 3 we discuss the methods we used for making those observations and the variables we created to represent children's experiences; in chapter 4 we discuss the analyses showing what the experiences were and how they differed according to the setting; and in chapter 5 we discuss the links between the observations of children's experiences at home and in day care. In the next set of analyses we examined the relations between children's experiences and their developmental levels in different domains. Chapter 6 presents the methods we used for assessing children's abilities and behavior in the different domains, and the following chapters (7 to 12) treat the results of linking experience and development for each domain in turn.

3

Methods of Documenting Children's Experiences

We designed our study to obtain varied and extensive information about children's experiences. To accomplish this goal, we used two major methods of data collection, which are described in the first two sections of this chapter. The first involved direct observations of the children's behavior in their homes and in their day-care settings. The second involved extensive and parallel interviews conducted with the children's parents and daily caregivers. The third and last section of this chapter presents descriptive statistics drawn from the interviews and so documents the major demographic characteristics of the sample.

OBSERVATIONS

To find out about children's daily experiences and environments, it is important to cover the child's entire day. Often researchers simply visit families when it is "convenient" for the parents, and thus miss important aspects of the child's life—like that chaotic time at the end of the day when everything seems to happen at once. In this study, an observer visited each child at three different times—in the morning, the afternoon, and at dinnertime. The first three visits occurred within a period of 1 to 2 months at the beginning of the study (mean age of the children = 37 months). The same schedule of visits was repeated 1 year later. These visits took place wherever the child normally was at the time—at home or in a day-care setting. Each visit lasted approximately 2 1/2 hours. The dinnertime visit at home was scheduled at a time when the whole family including the father was together, typically beginning about 1 hour before dinner and lasting until the child's bedtime.

During the visits, the observer worked to be as inconspicuous and unobtrusive as possible while she kept a running record of the child's naturally occurring experiences. She made her observations following a technique developed by Clarke-Stewart (1973). This technique consists of recording by hand in a stenographer's notebook codes representing behavior directed to the child in the left column of the notebook and codes representing the child's behavior in the right column. The codes are simply abbreviations for a limited set of behaviors that have been agreed upon in advance. For example, the code for *affectionate tactual contact*—hugging or kissing—was "atc"; the code "v" (*verbalization*) was used to indicate any utterance directed to the child; "vd" was the code for a *verbal demand* made to the child; and an *appropriate response* by the caregiver to the child was indicated with the code "apr." Behavior was recorded continuously on successive lines of the notebook, and 10-second intervals were indicated with a mark at the sound of an earphone beeper. Thus, this method of observing provides a continuous record in real time of behavior directed to and from the child. Observations using this technique were recorded for approximately 2 hours (720 10-second intervals) during each visit.

The behaviors coded included all the social interactions in which the child participated, all the physical encounters the child had with peers or adults, and all play and learning activities in which the child engaged. Each utterance (a sentence, or speech burst, separated by pauses) directed to the child or made by the child was coded on the spot into teaching, demanding, offering a choice, reprimanding, or responding. The length of behaviors having some duration (touching, hugging, helping, playing, reading, singing, crying, watching TV) was preserved by indicating in the notebook record when they started and when they stopped. Behaviors to which the child was not attending, or that were not deliberate attempts to gain the child's attention, were not recorded.

Taking seriously the goal of observing children's naturally occurring experiences, observers followed children wherever they went: not only to the family living room, but also to the park with a nursery school class, to the bathroom in which a group of day-care home children were engaged in water play, even to a neighborhood street carnival. In all these settings, the observer focused on the individual child's experience, not on giving an overview of the classroom or living room from the caregiver's or a casual viewer's perspective. For example, although a teacher might spend 15 minutes reading a story to the class, our focused observation of the target child might reveal only two brief episodes of attention to the story, broken by periods of watching other children playing outside on the playground or playfully poking another child sitting nearby.

Each handwritten record of observation behavior codes was then typed into a computer file and put into a standard line-by-line format. First-level variables were then created using a string-search program. These variables were taken directly from the observation behavior codes, without *a priori* combination or manipulation. Second-level variables were created by (a) combining variables that were conceptually clustered and infrequent (e.g., combining the frequency of all different types of peer behavior directed toward the child into a variable of "peer interaction" or "sibling interaction"), and (b) forming ratios (e.g., calculating the proportion of maternal behavior toward the child that was physical or the proportion of maternal talk to the child that was didactic). First-level variables that were not included in any combined second-level variables and that were of low frequency were dropped. To make variables comparable across different lengths of observation, behavior frequencies were converted to a baseline of 720 10-second intervals (2 hours). Morning and afternoon observations were combined if a child was in the same setting during both these observations, so that for each year's observations each subject ended up with only one daytime observation in each child-care setting (own home, day-care home, or day-care center/nursery school).

In this chapter we discuss the observation variables that best reflected the child's experiences at home and in day care. (The entire set of observation variables is described in Table A.1 in the appendix.)

The first observation variable was an index of the amount of interaction the child had with the adults in the setting (e.g., the caregiver in the day-care observations, the parents at home) during the observation. It gave a quick indication of how much attention the child was receiving in the setting. That variable was the amount of verbal interaction directed by the adult to the child:

Talk
The number of utterances made by the adult to the child.

But the adult's verbal interaction could be directed either to the child alone or to a group of children that included the child. In order to distinguish between the experiences of children at home with a single adult and children in settings with more than one child, we divided the adult's utterances into the following two variables:

One-to-One Talk
The number of utterances by the adult that were directed to the child alone.
Talk to Group
The number of utterances by the adult that were directed to the child as part of a group.

These broad quantitative variables were not expected to be as revealing of the child's experiences as variables that focused on the quality of the interaction the child had with the caregiver. The areas of interaction we assessed were those that had been linked to child development in the research described in chapter 1. One important aspect of the quality of the child's experiences, and one that we expected to differentiate between experiences in day care and at home, was the educational content of the adult's conversations with the child. To assess this aspect of the child's experiences we identified a number of different variables:

Teaching
The number of utterances the adult directed to the child that were informative, didactic, or explanatory in content.
Teaching, Proportion
The proportion of the adult's utterances to the child that were didactic in content.
Teaching One-to-One
The number of didactic utterances the adult directed to the child that were directed to the child alone.
Teaching Group
The number of didactic utterances to the child that were directed to the child as part of a group.
Giving Lesson
The number of 10-second periods in which the adult was giving the child a lesson: a nonplayful interaction in which the focus was on teaching something.
Giving Object
The number of times the adult gave an object to the child.
Showing Object
The number of times an adult or peer showed an object to the child.
Child Imitating
The number of times the child imitated the action of an adult or a peer.
Reading or Singing
The number of 10-second periods in which the adult read, sang, or recited rhymes to the child. (Reciting occurred half as often as reading or singing.)

A second important dimension of the quality of interaction with the adult was the adult's discipline of the child. The variables that we used to tap this dimension were as listed here:

Control
The number of 10-second periods in which the adult physically controlled, forced, or punished the child.
Demands
The number of verbal demands made by the adult to the child.
Demanding
The proportion of the adult's utterances to the child that were demands.
Offering Choice
The number of times the adult offered the child a choice (of an activity, object, etc.).

A third important quality of the adult's interaction with the child was the adult's responsiveness to the child's needs and signals. This aspect of the adult's behavior was assessed with two variables:

Making Appropriate Responses
The number of times the adult made an appropriate response, including helping, to the child's request, demand, or offer.
Verbal Responsiveness
The proportion of the adult's utterances to the child that were responses to something the child had said or done.

Yet another dimension of the adult's interaction with the child was her physical behavior to him or her. Several aspects of physical contact were observed in the following variables:

Touching
The number of times the adult initiated physical contact with the child (touching, holding).
Touching, Proportion
The proportion of the adult's social interaction with the child that involved physical contact.
Affection
The number of physically affectionate gestures made by the adult to the child: hugs, kisses, cuddles, caresses, comforts.
Helping Child
The number of times the adult helped the child, not in response to a direct request by the child.
Play
The number of 10-second periods in which the adult played with the child (play may be physical, social, cooperative, dramatic, or a game).

In addition to the interactions the child has with the adult, one of the most salient aspects of the child's experience in day care is likely to be the interactions that the child has with other children. These interactions may be verbal or physical, friendly or hostile, playful or verbal. To assess these interactions we created the following variables:

Peer Interaction
The number of 10-second periods in which the child interacted with another child or children (including touching, playing, talking, helping, responding).
Peer Talk
The number of utterances by a peer directed toward the child.
Peer Play
The number of 10-second periods in which one or more peers played with the child (play may be physical, social, cooperative, dramatic, or a game).
Parallel Play
The amount of parallel play with peers, focused on the object. (This is a common form of peer "interaction" among 2-year-olds, less so in older children.)

Pretend Play
The amount of dramatic play, make believe, pretend. (This variable was used to index a relatively high level of peer interaction.)
Peer Aggression
The proportion of 10-second periods of interaction with another child or children in which aggression toward the target child was observed: hitting, kicking, threatening, grabbing toy away.

The next kind of observation involved the expression of positive or negative affect by the child or by another person directed to the child. This measure reflected the general emotional ambiance in the child's immediate environment.

Negative Affect
The number of expressions of negative affect observed: insults, scolding, criticism, refusals, reprimands, whining, fretting, crying.
Positive Affect
The number of expressions of positive affect observed: praise, smile, laugh, kiss, hug, use positive tone of voice.

Finally, the child's own activity was used as a reflection of his or her experiences in the setting. The following kinds of activity were assessed:

Child Alone
The number of 10-second periods in which the child was alone, out of another person's sight.
Child Watching Interactions
The number of 10-second periods in which the child watched and listened to interactions between other people but did not participate.
Child Watching Peers
The number of 10-second periods in with the child watched another child or children intently and noninteractively.
Child Watching Adult
The number of 10-second periods in which the child watched an adult or adults intently and noninteractively.
Child Playing with Object
The number of 10-second periods in which the child played alone with an object in a focused, concentrated manner.
Child Watching TV
The number of 10-second periods in which the child watched television and was not interacting with anyone.

In addition to making a running record of the child's experiences over the 2-hour period, at 15-minute intervals, the observer stopped the continuous recording and filled out a "snapshot" checklist of the people who were present and had interacted with the child during the preceding period. Two variables were created based on these checklists:

Number of Adults Interacting
Number of different adults interacting with the child during the observation (range = 1–10).
Number of Children Interacting
Number of different children interacting with child during the observation (range = 0–29).

Then, at the end of the observation (after eight 15-minute periods) the observer completed a checklist assessing the physical environment—its decor, equipment, messiness, and so on. The variables documenting variation in the physical environment were the following:

Decoration
The presence or absence of 20 different types of decorative element—rugs, ornaments, books, plants, pictures, lamps, piano, curtains, TV, fireplace, and so on—was observed in the home or center. For each of these decorative elements the observer indicated whether the setting had "any" (coded as 1) or "several" (coded as 2) of the item. The Decoration score for each setting was the sum of these checklist ratings (total possible = 40).
Toys
The presence or absence of 34 different types of toys and educational equipment—such as stuffed animals, trucks and cars, story books, puzzles, instructive games, wheel toys, dress-up clothes, animals, math activities, record player, sandbox, jungle gym—was observed in the home or center and the total number of these was tallied.
Mess
Dirty and disorganized aspects of the environment were inventoried on a checklist consisting of 40 items such as scattered toys, food, strewn clothes, dead plants, pet food, ashtrays, stained carpet, dirty floor, and peeling paint.
Hazards
The presence of 12 physical hazards in the setting, including unprotected heights, sharp objects, cleaning supplies, medicines, was checked and tallied.
Structure
Eight indicators of "structure" in the environment were observed. These included the following: clearly defined activity areas in the home or center; specific routines for each area; children assigned to areas; planned activities for the class, for groups of children, for individual children; by-the-clock schedule.

INTERVIEWS

To find out more about the child's experiences beyond what could be observed in these observations, and also to find out about the backgrounds of the adults who cared for the child, detailed in-person interviews were conducted each year with the child's mother, father, and nonparental caregiver(s). The caregivers interviewed in center day care were the center directors or the head teachers of the classes in which children were enrolled. For children who were in two different day-care arrangements (home and center), interviews were conducted with the two caregivers. The interviews with parents included questions about the parents' education, income, occupation, attitudes toward the child and childrearing, and about the child's social activities outside of day care. The interviews with caregivers included questions about the home caregiver's or head teacher's education, work history, attitudes toward the child and childrearing, and about aspects of the day-care program that could not be easily observed. The interviews were then coded into the variables that follow.

Most of these variables were coded on the basis of simple and straightforward interview questions ("What is your highest level of education?" "What is your occupation?" "Are you currently employed?" and so on). Several variables were based on more complex coding, consisting of scales created specially for this study. For these scales, measures of internal consistency (Cronbach's alpha) were computed. At this initial level of analysis, where variables are in a relatively raw and uncombined form, Cronbach's alpha of .50 may be considered acceptable and coefficients greater than .70 are good.

One set of interview variables consisted of the background demographics of the adults (parents and caregivers). These variables were the following:

Age
The age of the child's primary caregiver (mother, head teacher, sitter).
Education
The level of education of the mother, father, or caregiver, on a scale from 1 = junior high school to 6 = postgraduate degree.
Experience in Child Care
The level of experience with children or in child care that the mother or caregiver had, coded on the following scale:
1 = none,
2 = informal,
3 = professional child-care experience.
Training in Child Care
The number of courses in child care or child development taken by the mother or the caregiver, on the following scale:
1 = none,

2 = 1–3 courses,
3 = 4–6 courses,
4 = more than 6 courses.
Stability
The length of time the caregiver has been in the day-care setting.
Socioeconomic Status
A composite measure of the family's SES consisting of
(a) the sum of the father's occupation, the mother's occupation, and the
mother's father's occupation, coded on the following scale:
1 = unskilled,
2 = skilled,
3 = blue collar,
4 = white collar (sales),
5 = white collar (management),
6 = professional/executive;
(b) the mother's education and the father's education (weighted X 2),
coded on a scale from 1 = junior high school to 6 = postgraduate degree;
and (c) the mother's highest wage and the family's income, coded on a
scale from 1 = < \$400/month to 10 = > \$2,000/month.

In addition to these demographic indices, several interview variables
assessed family finances in more detail. These variables were the following:

Household Help
The amount of help the mother has for doing housework: a cleaning person,
a housekeeper, a dishwasher, a washer/dryer, the frequency with which the
family eats out or eats convenience meals, the frequency with which the
husband does chores without nagging (maximum possible = 25).
Money for Day Care (Monthly)
The amount of money spent by parents on day care per month (range = 0–\$700).
Money for Day Care (Hourly)
The amount paid by parents for day care on an hourly basis, calculated
by dividing the monthly amount for child care by full-time/part-time
day-care status.

To explore the issue of the adults' "childrearing expertise" we devised
some questions and a questionnaire to probe the adults' knowledge of child
development. This was a more detailed follow-up to our questions about
the extent to which the adult had received training in child development,
child care, or early childhood education. We expected it to distinguish
between professional and nonprofessional child-care providers.

Knowledge of Child Development
The scale consisted of the following components:
1. number of books and articles about child care or child development
the adult had read (5-point scale);

2. the degree to which it was important for the adult that a daytime care arrangement offer children educational stimulation (5-point rating);

3. the extent to which the adult believed that children have individual differences in behavior and needs (5-point scale); and

4. the degree to which the adult agreed with experts' solutions to child care problems. This last item was based on a multiple choice questionnaire consisting of 16 hypothetical situations requiring parental discipline. For example, "Suppose a mother was just finishing folding the clean laundry and her 2-year-old came in and messed it up. What should she do?

(a) Tell the child 'No,' and give her a slap.

(b) Ignore her behavior—just re-fold the clothes.

(c) Laugh—make re-folding the laundry into a game; play with her.

(d) Give her a couple of towels to play with—but that's all. Put the rest of the clothes out of reach.

(e) Teach her how to fold clothes."

"What if a 3-year-old child had not stopped sucking her thumb. What should parent do?

(a) Do nothing—accept and ignore it.

(b) Every time she puts her thumb in her mouth give her a slap on the hand, or else put some bad-tasting liquid on her thumb.

(c) Try to find out whether there is an emotional reason for the behavior.

(d) Think of some special treats and activities that will keep her busy so she won't have a chance to suck her thumb.

(e) Tie a string around her thumb so that she'll remember, and praise her when she doesn't suck it."

This questionnaire was sent to 20 child development experts around the country (including Bettye Caldwell, Burton White, William Kessen, Jerome Kagan, Ross Parke, and others) for their responses. Each of the multiple choice responses was weighted according to the number of experts who chose it, and the subject's score was the match with these weighted scores. The responses to the hypothetical questions were designed to reflect authoritarian, authoritative, and permissive discipline. "Correct" responses from the experts generally tended to be either permissive or authoritative. The internal consistency (Cronbach's alpha) for this knowledge of child development scale was .70 (maximum possible score = 60).

Another set of interview variables tapped the composition and history of the family. These variables were as follows:

Siblings
The number of brothers and sisters the child has, and whether they were older or younger than the child.

Extended Family
The number of people in the household and in the child's extended family, the frequency of the family's activities together, and level of participation of family members in the child's care (maximum possible = 100).
Geographic Stability
The length of time the parents had lived in the midwest, in Chicago, in the same neighborhood, in their present home, and the length of time they had been married (maximum possible = 58).
Family Changes
The number of changes in the family over the course of the year of the study: moving, a change in the father's or mother's job, work status, an increase or decrease in number of people in the household, a marital separation, a financial change, a significant parent-child separation, etc. (maximum possible = 16).

Related to the family's composition was an attitudinal measure of the adults' pro-family values. It was expected that this variable would distinguish between parents who were and who were not using day care for their children:

Traditional Values
The scale consisted of 20 statements reflecting either a traditional or a nontraditional ("liberated") view of the family. Mothers, fathers, and caregivers completed the questionnaire, indicating which statements described their "ideal family." Traditional statements included:
"The whole family eats dinner together almost every night."
"The family goes on vacations together."
"The family goes to grandmother's for Thanksgiving dinner."
"Father takes the boys to football games on Saturdays."
"Mother and daughters do the cooking."
"Father makes the important decisions for the family."
"The family goes to church together."
Nontraditional statements included:
"Mother has a job."
"The parents sometimes vacation without the children."
"Father and mother sometimes take separate vacations."
"People who are not related to the family live with them."
In addition the adults indicated (on 7-point scales) the extent to which they agreed or disagreed with the following statements:
"Day care is responsible for the disintegration of families."
"Parents should have the greatest influence on their children."
"The home offers children better care than day care."
"Women should not work outside the home while their children are young (under 6 years)."
The internal consistency of this scale was .76 (Cronbach's alpha; maximum possible score = 44).

It was also thought that perhaps the parent's attitude toward nontraditional family roles and toward day care, more specifically, would be reflected in whether the parent had spent time in day care as a child. Therefore, we inquired about the parent's history in day care and early education programs. The variable summarizing this information was the following:

Parent in Day Care as Child
The length and amount of time the parent spent in day care, nursery school, kindergarten as a child (maximum possible = 50).

Because this was a study of children in day care, the mother's employment was an important issue. Several variables were created to assess aspects of the mother's work status and commitment. These variables were as follows:

Mother's Work Status
The mother's employment status:
1 = not employed
2 = employed part time
3 = employed full time
Mother's Work Hours
Amount of time mother had worked in the past year: weeks x hours/week.
Mother's Career Orientation
An index of the degree to which the mother wishes she were working or is glad she is working; liked or likes working because of the type of work, career, job; prefers work activities; thinks work activities are important, enjoyable; chose child-care arrangement in order to work. This scale consisted of responses to the following questions:
(a) "How much do (or did) you enjoy working?" (7-point rating)
(b) "How happy are you that you are working now?" or "How much do you wish you were working now?" (7-point rating)
(c) "If money were not a consideration, how likely is it that you would still work?" (7-point rating)
How important are each of the following: (5-point ratings)
(d) "Getting a promotion at work."
(e) "Having your husband praise you for being competent in your work."
(f) "Having your boss praise you."
(g) "Having the esteem of colleagues."
(h) "Having a chance to accomplish something worthwhile in a job."
(i) Disagreement with statement "I feel no need to do my best at work." (7-point scale; Cronbach's alpha = .73; maximum possible score = 47).

Following up on the mother's commitment to work was a set of measures focused on the mother's satisfaction with her roles—as mother and as worker. These measures were the following:

Mother's Satisfaction with Maternal Role
The mother's satisfaction with her role as mother was assessed by means of fifteen 5-point ratings, on which the mother indicated her level of enjoyment in specific activities involving child care, teaching and playing with child, and sharing child care with her husband (Cronbach's alpha = .69).

Mother's Overall Role Satisfaction
Twenty 5-point ratings were used to assess the mother's satisfaction with her overall role. These ratings included how much she enjoyed her current role; how satisfied she was with her current role; how much she enjoyed juggling a job and motherhood (or coordinating her schedule); how satisfied she was with the time she had for herself; how satisfied she was with the time she had with her husband; how satisfied she was with her current accomplishments; how satisfied she was with the opportunities she had to meet and socialize with other adults; how satisfied she was with the opportunities she had to further develop her skills and abilities (Cronbach's alpha = .80).

Mother's Feeling of Alienation
This measure was derived from two questionnaires. One was a 78-item questionnaire developed by Maddi (1971). It consisted of questions like the following: "Most of my life is spent doing meaningless things." "I feel no need to try my best for it makes no difference anyhow." "Everyone is out to manipulate you toward his own ends." Mothers indicated on 7-point scales how much they agreed with each statement. The second questionnaire was a 56-item questionnaire, in which mothers selected preferred activities from a series of binary choices reflecting work, child care, spousal, recreational domains. The number of items that indicated that the mother preferred to spend her time alone, in self-centered pursuits rather than with the family or on work, was the score used in forming this variable. The scores from the two questionnaires were significantly correlated (r = .65), supporting their combination into a single, even more stable variable for subsequent analyses.

Two variables probed the adults' attitudes toward the child:

Expectations for the Child
This was a 20-item scale reflecting the parent's or caregiver's expectations of what the child would know before he or she started school. Each item represented a specific skill, such as knowing his or her own name and address, knowing the name of the president, knowing the name of the attorney-general, knowing what a pomegranate is, knowing how to answer the phone and take a message, knowing what to

wear to school, knowing how to count to 20, knowing how to read a few words, knowing to apologize when he or she hurts someone, knowing how to go downtown on the bus alone, and so on. The score was the total number of items on the scale that the adult agreed the child would know (Cronbach's alpha = .76).

Positive Attitude Toward Child
The adult's ratings of the child as bright, loving, lively, fun (combination of four 9-point rating scales; maximum possible score = 36; Cronbach's alpha = .94).

Another important area assessed in the interviews with the caregivers was the characteristics of the day-care program or setting. Several indexes of the social environment were collected in these interviews. Some of them were conventional indices such as class size and child-adult ratio; others involved more specific measures of the composition of the adults and children in the setting. These variables were as follows:

Children in Class
The number of children in the child's class, core group, or home-care arrangement.

Children in Center
The number of children in the nursery school or day-care center.

Number of Caregivers
The number of different caregivers in the child's class or home day-care arrangement who are in regular contact with the child.

Child–Adult Ratio
The number of children enrolled in the child's class divided by the number of adults who are regularly there.

Older Children Present
The number of children in the class or group who are more than 1 year older than the child.

Younger Children Present
The number of children in child's care arrangement who are more than 1 year younger than the child.

Middle-Class Peers
The proportion of children in the day-care group who are of middle or professional SES (scale 1–4).

Diversity
This variable indicated the child's exposure to a variety of other people in the day-care setting. It consisted of the sum of nine 4-point rating scales made by the interviewer on the basis of the caregiver's responses to specific questions concerning: (a) the number of different people in the day-care setting, (b) the number of different ages of children in the setting, (c) the variety of socioeconomic levels of the children in the setting, (d) the number of different ethnic groups represented by the

children in the setting, (e) the number of adult visitors to the day-care setting, (f) the instability of the staff in the day-care setting, (g) whether the other children in the setting included both boys and girls (0 = all one sex; 4 = both boys and girls), and (h) the caregiver's evaluation of how well the setting provided the child with experience with people from other backgrounds (maximum possible score = 36).

Caregivers were also interviewed about the structure in the day-care setting or program, in order to create the following variable:

Program
The extent to which the caregiver describes the day-care program as being high in structure, schedule, group activities, individual activities, teacher direction (maximum possible = 24).

Information about the degree of the child's involvement in day care was collected from the mother. This information was summarized in the following variables:

Hours in Day Care
The number of hours the child is in day care per week:
1 = none,
2 = less than 30 hours,
3 = 30–40 hours,
4 = more than 40 hours.
Months in Day Care
The number of months the child has been in day care.
Parent's Involvement in Child Care
Father's Involvement: The amount of time the child spends with the father (including dinner, outings, physical care, playing, learning, bedtime), when the father is responsible for the child's care, the degree to which the father participated in making decisions about the child's care (maximum possible = 50).
Mother's Involvement: The amount of time the mother spends in the day-care arrangement, has contact with the day-care staff, and says she knows what goes on in the day-care setting (maximum possible = 40).

Because not all children in the study were in day care, we thought it was important to try to assess the social experiences of children at home, as well, by asking the mother about their exposure to other people outside of the family. This information was also collected for children in day care, because their social experiences do not end at the door of the day-care center. The variable reflecting children's social experience outside of day care was the following:

Child's Social Activities (with Adults, with Children)
The child's social activities with nonrelated adults and children, not
including experiences in a regular day-care arrangement (frequency and
number of different people; maximum possible = 20).

An effort to assess the parents' and children's feelings about the experiences the child was having in day care was made by asking the parents to
complete some rating scales. These yielded the following variables:

Parent's Satisfaction with Child Care
The mother's and the father's satisfaction with the child-care arrangement:
overall rating of satisfaction, positive evaluation of features in the child-care
arrangement that the parent thinks are most important, number of features
parent would change (reverse coded; maximum possible = 30).
Child's Satisfaction with Day Care
Ratings by the parent and the caregiver of how much the child likes the
care arrangement and the frequency of distress upon separation from
parent (maximum = 35).

Finally, because of our interest in how children's development is affected
not just by day care or by family care alone, but by their combined effects, we
sought to devise a measure of the compatibility between the child's experiences at home and in day care. This led to a complex measure reflecting the
"mesh" between the child's home and day-care environments.

Mesh Between Home and Day Care
The "mesh" or compatibility between the child's home and day-care
environments was estimated by combining the following indices of
similarities or dissimilarities between the two environments: (a) the
number of hypothetical problems on the parental discipline questionnaire (see scale on knowledge of child development) on which the
caregiver and either one of the parents gave the same answer (out of 16);
(b) the difference between the caregiver and the parents on four 5-point
ratings concerning the importance of discipline, teaching, affection, and
opportunities for the child to learn in the day-care environment (each
score inverse coded by subtracting it from 5); (c) the difference between
the caregiver and parents in socioeconomic level (inverse coded by
subtracting from 12); (d) a rating of the difference between the caregiver
and parents in ethnic background (1 = different race from both parents;
7 = same ethnic group as both parents); (e) the difference between the
caregiver and parents in their level of expectations for the child (inverse
coded by subtracting from 20). Then, added to this score was a 6-point
rating of the degree to which the parents were involved in the day-care
arrangement (maximum possible = 94).

SAMPLE CHARACTERISTICS

Based on the information gathered in these interviews, we can paint a picture of the families who made up our sample. The ethnicity of the majority (85%) of families was Anglo-Saxon, European, or "American"; 12% were African American, 2% Asian, and 1% Hispanic. More than 50% of the fathers were native Chicagoans. Their education ranged from high school (15%) to postgraduate degrees (46%); 64% were college graduates. Most mothers (80%) were between 25 and 35 years old; 60% of them also were college graduates (15% had only high school education; 34% had postgraduate training). Slightly more than one third of the mothers worked full time, another third did not work, and the rest worked part time. Although we had not deliberately restricted subject recruitment according to SES, except to rule out families at the two extremes, nearly half (47%) of the families in the sample were of professional-class status, the fathers having professional or executive positions and graduate training. One fifth of the sample were of middle-class status, and 35% of the families were working class or lower. The most common occupations of the fathers in the sample were lawyer ($n = 13$), teacher ($n = 12$), professor ($n = 9$), and manager ($n = 8$). Most households consisted of the mother and father and one (44%) or two (44%) children.

The fathers all claimed to spend some time in child care, actively involved with their children or responsible for them; half of them reported that this was at least 4 hours a day. One quarter of the mothers in the sample had worked or were working with young children.[1] During the year-long investigation, 30 families moved (half of them out of town); six couples got divorced or separated; five had new babies. Nine mothers who had not been working took up employment; none stopped work.

There were 84 boys and 66 girls in the sample; their ages at the beginning of the study ranged from 24 to 48 months. The children in day care had been in their day-care arrangements for periods from 2 to 12 months ($M = 8$ months) at the time of the first observation.

The day-care arrangements observed ran the gamut from live-in housekeepers to large institutional centers. More than 60 different day-care settings were included in the study. Among the centers, the smallest had only 10 children enrolled, the largest, 500; 10 children were in centers with over 100 children; the average center size was 70 children. The average number of children in a center class was 17; the average adult–child ratio was 1:5. Of the head teachers in the sample, 38% had bachelor's degrees and an additional 42% had some graduate education; 94% had received some formal training in child development or child care; 53% had taken

---

[1]This high proportion of mothers who worked with children probably reflects two facts: (a) in this society working with children is considered women's work, and (b) mothers who would agree to participate in a study of children's development are likely to be biased toward caring about—and for—children.

more than six courses. Their ages ranged from 20 to 55 years ($M = 34$). In the home day-care arrangements, the average number of children in in-home care was two, in day-care homes, six. Only 15% of the home-care providers had college degrees; more than one third had not graduated from high school; only 14% of the in-home sitters and 55% of the day-care home providers had any formal training in child development or child care; only 9% had extensive training. The ages of the home caregivers ranged from 12 to 76 years. The average age of an in-home sitter was 47; of a day-care home provider, 36. Four of the home-care providers were relatives of the child (primarily in-home sitters), seven were friends of the family and five, neighbors; the rest were "professional" child-care providers.

These demographic characteristics of the day care used by families in the present study can be viewed within the context of statistics collected in the Profile of Child Care Settings (Kisker et al., 1991), a survey of a nationally representative sample of more than 2,000 center directors and 500 licensed day-care home providers throughout the United States. Similarities between our sample and this national sample were observed for most dimensions: the average number of children enrolled in centers ($M = 62$ in the national survey vs. $M = 70$ in our study) and day-care homes ($M = 6$ vs. $M = 6$); the ages of center teachers ($M = 36$ years vs. $M = 34$ years) and day-care home providers ($M = 40$ years vs. $M = 36$ years); the size of day-care center classes ($M = 17$ vs. $M = 17$); the likelihood that center teachers had received some training in child development or child care (93% vs. 94%); and the proportion of home-care providers who had graduated from college (12% vs. 15%). The home-care providers in our sample were less likely to have had formal training in child development than the national sample (64% in the survey vs. 55% in our study)—probably because the national sample, unlike our sample, did not include unlicensed providers. The teachers in our sample were somewhat better educated than those in the national survey (80% of our teachers had college degrees, whereas only 50% in the national survey did). This may be because our index of teacher education was based on the education of head teachers only, whereas the national survey included all teachers (although not assistant teachers or aides). In addition, the classes in which we observed had better adult–child ratios (1:5 vs. 1:7). It is likely, therefore, that our sample of day-care settings was of somewhat higher than average quality—not surprising, given the above-average socioeconomic backgrounds of the parents in the study.

4

Describing Children's Experiences

This chapter sets the stage for the main agenda of the study, which was to find out how variation in children's experiences is related to differences in their development. Here we discuss the variation in children's experiences, describing the kinds of experiences the children had and comparing their experiences in different settings. Because this was not a study of day care, per se, we did not focus on contrasting different types of day-care programs—nursery schools versus day-care centers, Head Start programs versus Montessori schools. Our focus was the more general one of contrasting children's experiences in different kinds of settings—at home with their families and outside their homes, in home settings or centers.

ENVIRONMENTS AND EXPERIENCES IN THE FAMILY

Our first treatment of the data was to examine the characteristics of the families in the study and to describe the children's experiences at home.[1] (The means, standard deviations, and maximum values for the variables representing these characteristics and experiences are presented in Table A.2 in the appendix.) This examination was useful for providing a glimpse into what is certainly a central aspect of the daily lives of young children—what happens to them at home at the end of the day when they are together with their families.

---

[1]Before we began our statistical analysis of variables representing children's experiences, we examined the distributions of all the relevant variables, and, when necessary, performed manipulations to normalize these distributions. Where there were outlying cases, these were pulled in to the extremes of the distributions, and when the shapes of the distributions were not bell-shaped we transformed the data using log, square root, inverse, or cubic transformations as needed. These manipulations were required for only a small number of the observation variables.

During the 2-hour observation at dinnertime, our analyses revealed,[2] although they were with their families, most children spent a significant amount of time by themselves; on the average, the children spent about 15 minutes alone (out of sight of other people) and another 15 minutes playing alone with toys. Some children spent much more time alone—several spent over an hour alone in the room or playing by themselves. The children also spent a considerable amount of time playing with brothers and sisters. More than half (80) of the children in the study had a sibling, with whom they interacted (for about 20 minutes, on average) during the dinnertime observation. A third common activity for these children was watching television. A substantial number (about 60%) of the children watched TV (for 25 minutes, on average). This is not surprising, given a recent national survey (National Center for Education Statistics, 1992) showing that nursery school children watch 2 1/2 hours of television at home every day. Thus, we see that even though these children were only 2 to 4 years old, they spent a significant amount of time at the end of the day in activities that did not involve their parents.

When they were interacting with their parents, children heard an average of 82 utterances from their fathers and 255 from their mothers during the 2-hour observation. These utterances were often demands for the children to do something. Both fathers and mothers gave twice as many demands as instructions or explanations (fathers on the average made 27 demanding and 11 didactic utterances; mothers made 40 demanding and 20 didactic utterances). Eighty fathers played with their children during the observation (for about 7 minutes, on average) and 40 read to them (for 4 minutes on average). About the same number of children (75) played with their mothers during the dinnertime observation as played with their fathers (for about the same length of time—6 minutes). A somewhat larger number (65, or 45%) heard the mother read a story, but the story was usually shorter (less than 2 minutes). This frequency of parents reading to the children fits well with the results of the recent national survey of children's activities at home (National Center for Education Statistics, 1992); 45% of the 3,500 3- to 4-year-old children in preschool programs in that survey were read to by their parents at home every day. The frequencies with which the parents touched, hugged, helped, physically controlled, gave lessons or objects to the children were low in most families (taking up less than 3 minutes, on average), although extremes in a few families were quite high (e.g., nearly 30 minutes was spent on lessons in one family).

This picture of children's experiences at the end of the day during dinner and the period before bed suggests that, although there is great variation in what children experience, most parents do not offer their children a

---

[2]For these descriptive analyses, Year 1 and Year 2 observations were combined.

steady stream of positive or stimulating interaction. Even though these were young children and even though their parents were not burdened by poverty or single parenthood, these mothers and fathers directed conversation or attention to their children during less than one third of the observation intervals, and that attention frequently consisted of giving directions or demands. When they were not interacting with their parents, the children spent their time alone, playing with toys, watching TV, or playing with a sibling.

Relations With Child's Age and Sex

Older and Younger Children. But how did children's experiences change with age? Did children get more attention from their parents as they got older? We followed our sample for 1 year's time, thus we were able to answer this question.[3] Analyses of differences over time revealed that parental attention decreased as children got older. Older children compared to younger children received less attention of all kinds from their parents (touching, playing, affection from their fathers and touching, playing, affection, talking, making demands, controlling, and teaching from their mothers). They spent more time alone, were more likely to have siblings and to interact with them. When they did receive attention from their parents it was less likely to involve physical contact or maternal teaching and more likely to include verbal responses and paternal teaching.

These findings extend the results of earlier studies with 9- to 18-month-olds (Clarke-Stewart, 1973) and 1- to 2 1/2-year-olds (Clarke-Stewart & Hevey, 1981), in which parents initiated less interaction with their children as the children got older and as the children initiated more. They also fit with popular wisdom and previous writing about the father's role in the family as a source of information and an introduction to the world beyond the home (see Lamb, 1975; Parke, 1979)—a role that is likely to increase as children get older.

Boys and Girls. It is not surprising to find differences in the experiences of older and younger children. But what about the experiences of boys and girls? Were these also distinct at this age? Analyses of variance comparing the experiences and environments of boys and girls revealed few differences related to the child's sex. Overall MANOVAs in Years 1 and 2 were nonsignificant, and significant univariate analyses of variance were infrequent. The latter revealed only that fathers of girls had more traditional family-oriented values [$F(1, 142) = 1.9$ ($p < .05$)] and that fathers of boys spent more time teaching them [$F(1, 142) = 2.4$ ($p < .05$)].

---

[3] Correlations between children's age and the variables reflecting their experiences in the family are presented in Table A.2 in the appendix.

Observed Patterns of Maternal and Paternal Behavior

To further explore the patterns in children's experiences at home, factor analyses of the observation variables in the dinnertime observations were performed. These analyses were done separately for Year 1 and Year 2, but as Table 4.1 shows, the factor structure was remarkably consistent from year to year. Seven (unrotated) factors were identified, accounting for approximately 65% of the variance in the observations. The first factor was the child's interaction with the father (the frequency of the father's talking to the child, touching, teaching, reading, playing, and making demands). A parallel factor was found for the frequency of these kinds of behavior from the mother. A second pair of factors consisted of physical contact with each parent (the amount of physical contact, the relative proportion of physical contact compared with other kinds of behavior, and the frequency of physical affection from each parent). The final three factors combined the contributions of mother and father in three distinct clusters reflecting different types of interaction: teaching, discipline, and responsiveness.

As the results of these factor analyses suggest, parents in a couple tend to be like each other in the style of their interaction with their children but different in the quantity of their interaction. Their rates of teaching and disciplining the child (as a proportion of the amount of time they interacted) were similar [correlations between mothers' and fathers' behavior for teaching $= .67$ $(p < .001)$, demanding $= .49$ $(p < .001)$, physical control $= .32$ $(p < .001)$], but the frequencies of their interaction with the child were different. In fact, the frequencies with which the two parents talked to the child were negatively correlated [r in Year 1 $= -.22$ $(p < .01)$]. That is, the more one parent talked to the child, the less the other one did, whereas the kind of talk, when they did interact—teaching, responding, demanding—was likely to be the same. These findings also replicate those of previous research, showing that mothers and fathers are similar in the quality, though not the quantity, of their interactions with their children (Clarke-Stewart, 1980; Pettit, 1991).

Although these analyses show that there are similarities between pairs of mothers and fathers in interactional style, it is worth noting that, overall, mothers do more of all these kinds of behavior than fathers. Mothers spoke to the children three times more than fathers, for example (255 vs. 82 utterances). Mothers, in fact, interacted with the children significantly more frequently than fathers in almost every way—touching, talking, teaching, giving lessons, making demands, exerting control [$Fs(1, 142) = 6.7$ $(p < .05)$ to 36.7 $(p < .001)$]. In only two ways did fathers interact with the children as much as mothers during the dinnertime observations—showing affection and reading stories. When parents read stories, however, there were more families in which only the mother read to the child than in which only the father read to the child (in 69% of the families in which the mother read,

TABLE 4.1
Factor Analyses of Family Variables

Factor[a]	Variables[b]	Loadings	
		Year 1	Year 2
Observation Variables			
Mother physical contact	Mother touching	.72	.85
(8.4%, 7.4%)[c]	Mother touching, proportion	.90	.86
	Mother affection	.68	.63
Father physical contact	Father touching	.34	.38
(6.1%, 6.2%)	Father touching, proportion	.80	.67
	Father affection	.63	.65
Parent discipline	Mother demands	.74	.79
(10.7%, 8.6%)	Mother demanding	.67	.73
	Mother control	.53	.55
	Father demands	.75	.70
	Father demanding	.72	.76
	Father control	.42	.51
	Parents' offering choice	− .57	− .41
Parent teaching	Mother teaching	.73	.87
(12.6%, 11.7%)	Mother teaching, proportion	.89	.82
	Father teaching	.63	.37
	Father teaching, proportion	.84	.50
	Parents giving lesson	.25	.64
Father interaction	Father talking	.90	.88
(11.6%, 15.5%)	Father playing	.65	.53
	Father teaching	.84	.85
	Father teaching, proportion[†]	.72	.73
	Father touching[†]	.84	.64
	Father demands[†]	.95	.90
	Father reading[†]	.67	.61
	Father affection[†]	.56	.21
Mother interaction	Mother talking	.87	.72
(8.5% 8.5%)	Mother playing	.40	.40
	Mother reading[†]	.65	.48
	Mother demands[†]	.53	.32
	Mother teaching[†]	.72	.72
	Mother touching[†]	.76	.69
Parent responsiveness	Parents' appropriate response	.70	.77
(7.3%, 6.6%)	Parents' responsiveness	.67	.74
	Parents giving object	.68	•
	Positive affect	•	.61
Interview Variables			
Working mother	Mother's career orientation	.59	
(13.4%)	Mother's education	.60	
	Mother's work hours	.79	
	Household help	.43	
	Father's involvement	.30	
	Money for day care/month	.78	
	Mother traditional values	− .59	
	Father traditional values	− .67	

(continued)

TABLE 4.1 (continued)

Factor[a]	Variables[b]	Loadings Year 1	Loadings Year 2
Interview Variables (continued)			
Mother expertise	Mother's training	.82	
(8.9%)	Mother's experience	.69	
	Mother's knowledge	.50	
Mother satisfaction	Overall role satisfaction	.77	.45
(7.9%, 9.4%)	Satisfaction with maternal role	.48	.41
	Satisfaction with child care	.57	.23
	Alienation		−.57
Stimulating home	Toys at home	.72	
(6.1%)	Home decoration	.63	
Hazardous home	Mess	.67	
(5.1%)	Hazards	.77	

[a]This table contains the results of two separate factor analyses: one for the observation variables, the other for the interview variables. These are unrotated factors.

[b]The complete set of variables included in the analyses is listed in this column.

[c]Percent variance accounted for.

[†]Variables that were not included in the factor-guided composite variables.

she was the only parent to do so; in only 51% of the families in which the father read, was he the only parent to do so). In only one way did fathers interact with the children more than mothers did—playing physical games [$F(1, 142) = 19.8$ ($p < .001$)]. These results both confirm and extend previous research. Research on younger infants has shown that mothers interact more with their infants and toddlers, that fathers adopt a more physically playful style (Clarke-Stewart, 1978, 1980; Pedersen, 1980; Yogman, 1981). In this study we see that the same trends continue throughout the preschool years.

Family Backgrounds

Factor analyses were also done to search for patterns in the parents' backgrounds, as reflected in the interview variables. Five factors were identified in the family interview variables, accounting for 43% of the variance. The first cluster of variables constituted a factor that might be labeled a *working mother* factor. In families high on this factor, the mother was more educated and more career oriented; she worked more hours and had more household help; the father was more involved in the child's care; the family spent more money on child care; and both the mother and the father expressed less traditional family values. We did not include the family's overall SES and the father's education in the factor analysis because they overlapped substantially with mother's education [correlation between mother's and father's education = .83 ($p < .001$)]; these variables, too, were highly related to the working mother factor [$rs = .65$ ($p < .001$), .49 ($p < .001$)]. "Working mother" families were also less geographically stable [$r = -.25$ ($p < .01$)], more likely to experience changes (like moving or switching jobs) over the course of the study [$r = .16$ ($p < .05$)], and engaged in fewer activities with their extended families [$r = -.17$ ($p < .05$)].

A second factor appearing in the interview data was the mother's childrearing expertise. This factor consisted of the mother's training, experience, and knowledge of child development. It was related to the working mother factor because of the strong correlation between the mother's overall level of education and her more specific training in child development [$r = .52$ ($p < .001$)]. A third factor reflected the mother's satisfaction—with her roles as mother and worker (or nonworker), with her life and relationships, and with the child's care arrangement. The final two factors identified the positive and negative aspects of the physical environment of the home: A *stimulating home* factor reflected homes that contained more decorations and toys; a *hazardous home* factor grouped homes that were messier, dirtier, and presented more physical safety hazards for the child.

These factors and the ones described for the observational variables are used in later chapters in the book as a way of organizing the variables reflecting children's environments and experiences. They were also used to guide some further analyses of family environments, which are described next.

Links Between Parents' Backgrounds and Behavior

One of the issues of interest in our study and in the literature on children's early experiences is the question of what makes adults—parents and other caregivers—act the way they do with children. For example, there has been a notable and longstanding interest in how adults' levels of education and training in child-related fields are related to their childrearing or caregiving behavior. The data collected in this study afforded an opportunity to examine this issue with respect to both mothers and fathers, both parents and caregivers, using identical scales to represent the adults' backgrounds.

To explore links between parents' backgrounds and their behavior, variables were created based on the factors we have just described[4] and then correlations among these and other family variables were calculated. These analyses revealed clear links between the parents' SES and their behavior. Parents with higher SES—both mothers and fathers—were less authoritarian, offering their children more choices [$r = .23$ ($p < .01$)] and less discipline [$r = -.39$ ($p < .001$)]. The fathers read and talked to their children

---

[4]This was done by transforming the original variables that were significantly loaded on the factor to standard scores, and then adding or subtracting them according to the sign of each variable's loading on the factor. Variables that appeared in more than one factor were included only once in the factor-guided variables.

more [rs = .34 (p < .001), .21 (p < .01)] and the children spent less time simply watching their parents [r = −.25 (p < .01)] or the TV [r = −.21 (p < .01)] during the dinnertime period. (These relations were entirely consistent in the two dinnertime observations 1 year apart.)

These findings are congruent with previous research linking SES with parental responsiveness, acceptance, and stimulation (Bradley et al., 1989). In previous research, however, this has been the extent to which links between parents' backgrounds and behavior were explored. Because of the wealth of information about both backgrounds and behavior, the present study afforded a more detailed examination of background–behavior links.

The mother's specific knowledge about child development, her childrearing expertise, has not been studied extensively before, but it has been widely assumed to be linked to maternal behavior in the literature on parent education (see criticism of this assumption in Clarke-Stewart & Apfel, 1979). In this study, the mother's expertise was not related to her own behavior. When mothers and fathers were more knowledgeable about childrearing, however, the fathers were less demanding and controlling [rs = −.16 (p < .05), −.18 (p < .05), −.23 (p < .01)]. This result demonstrates the complexity of processes within the family, in which the attitudes and behaviors of all participants—in this case husbands and wives—are linked.

The mother's satisfaction was related to her behavior. Mothers who were generally more satisfied about their roles talked, taught, and read to the children more [rs = .17 (p < .05), .20 (p < .05), .20 (p < .05)]; they also had higher expectations for the children [r = .25 (p < .01)] and held more positive attitudes toward them [r = .21 (p < .01)]. In addition, these women were married to men who were more affectionate to their children [r = .22 (p < .01)] and read to them more [r = .25 (p < .01)]. In these families, it seems, the pattern of parenting was active and enjoyable. This pattern demonstrates another set of links between the behavior and attitudes of husbands and wives.

In families with working mothers, the distinctive characteristic was that during the dinnertime observations children interacted more with their fathers [r = .24 (p < .01)]. This relation remained quite high (p < .08) even when the family SES was partialled out, indicating that the link was not accounted for solely by the educational levels of the parents. This finding is consistent with previous research showing that fathers with employed wives are more involved in child care (Ackerman-Ross & Khanna, 1989; A. E. Gottfried, Gottfried, & Bathurst, 1988; Hoffman, 1984, 1986, 1989; Larsen & Robinson, 1987; Winnett et al., 1977). (Recall that in this study, too, the link between fathers' involvement in child care and wives' employment was demonstrated by finding both these variables included in the working mother factor.) The finding differs, however, from observations made of actual family interactions at the end of the day when the children are younger. Researchers have found that, with infants, fathers whose wives worked were less likely to interact with their infants, not more, at the end of the day (Pedersen, Cain, Zaslow, & Anderson, 1982; Zaslow et al., 1985). These last researchers (and Hoffman, 1984) also observed that working mothers interacted more with their infants at the end of the day than did nonworking mothers (whether father was present or not). We did not find this pattern. Perhaps the novelty for working mothers of having a special time to interact with the baby after work, or to show off the baby to an observer, has worn off by the time the children are 2 or 3 years old. Our finding that the quality of parental interaction was comparable in families with working and nonworking mothers is consistent with the results of studies showing no differences in maternal behavior on HOME scales or their equivalent related to maternal employment (A. E. Gottfried et al., 1988; Mackinnon, Brody, & Stoneman, 1982; Owen & Cox, 1988; Winnett et al., 1977; but see Vandell & Ramanan, 1992).

Children's Interactions With Siblings

But as we have already mentioned, parents were not the only social contacts the children had in these families; over half of the children in the sample (56%) had at least one sibling (63 children had one sibling; 13 children had two siblings; 4 children had three siblings). In these families, compared to families with only one child, fathers expressed more traditional family values and were less involved in child care [$Fs(1, 142) = 2.0$ ($p < .05$), 2.3 ($p < .05$)]. This conventional picture of parents with more traditional family values having larger families is surprisingly distinct considering that it is based on a difference of having one child versus two or three! During the evening observation, children in these "larger" families spent less time interacting with their parents than children with no siblings. All types of parental interaction with the child were less frequent: teaching, responding, touching, talking, playing, making demands, helping, showing affection, reading, giving objects, giving lessons [$Fs(1, 142) = 2.0$ ($p < .05$) to 5.2 ($p < .01$)]. The more the children interacted with their siblings, moreover, the less they interacted with their fathers and mothers and the less time they spent alone in the room or alone playing with objects [$rs = -.39$ ($p < .001$), $-.18$ ($p < .05$), $-.22$ ($p < .01$)]. When the siblings were older than the child, their interactions were more likely to be verbal and positive [$r = .26$ ($p < .01$)]; when they were younger, their interactions were more likely to include physical aggression and negative affect [$r = .33$ ($p < .001$)]. These findings are consistent with common sense and the results of other research, for example, Woollett's (1986) research showing that, in the presence of older siblings, 2-year-olds receive less language and responsiveness from their mothers. They do serve the purpose of illustrating clearly what a difference a sibling makes—a difference which, as we shall see later, is reflected in the child's development.

The Physical Environment

The quality of the physical environment was also related to the family's characteristics and behavior patterns. In messier and potentially more hazardous homes, parents were of lower SES; mothers worked longer hours and had less household help; there were more children in the family and more negative affect was expressed during the dinnertime observation [rs = −.17 ($p < .05$) to −.23 ($p < .01$); $Fs(1, 142)$ = 2.0 ($p < .05$), 2.7 ($p < .05$)]. Homes containing more decorations and toys belonged to families of higher SES, in which mothers worked less and had more household help, and fathers interacted more with the children [rs = −.24 ($p < .01$) to .29 ($p < .001$)]. The parents in these more stimulating homes were more responsive to the children and less demanding; they were more likely to offer the child choices and toys; the children were more likely to play alone with the toys and to express positive affect [rs = .35 ($p < .01$) to .45 ($p < .001$)]. Clearly, in the worlds of preschool children, the physical and the social aspects of the home environment are linked. A physically optimal environment is backed up by available and responsive parents and appreciated by the children who play there.

ENVIRONMENTS AND EXPERIENCES IN THE DAYTIME

To explore the experiences of preschool children in their daytime environments, analyses identical to those for their dinnertime environments were performed. (The means, standard deviations, and maximum values for these variables reflecting children's daytime experiences and environments are presented in Table A.3 in the appendix.) Most interesting in the examination of these variables were the ranges of variation observed in children's daily experiences—ranges that exceeded those observed in the dinnertime observations, ranges that clearly demonstrated our success in achieving broad variation in our sample. During the 2-hour observations, utterances from the caregiver to the child ranged from nearly none to nearly 900. Some children were never alone and several spent over 1 1/2 hours of the 2-hour observation on their own. Sixty children never watched TV and a few spent more than an hour glued to the set. The amount of time children spent playing alone with a toy ranged from none to more than an hour and a half. Similarly, the time the children spent in "lessons" ranged from none to 1 1/2 hours. These lessons were most often quite intellectual: More than half of the lessons observed were "academic" (about letters, colors, counting, science); about one quarter were about arts, crafts, music, sports, toys; the remainder focused on everyday knowledge or socialization rules. Play with other children was an important activity for most of these children; only 10 children in the first year and 6 children in the second year did not have another child present during the daytime observations. How much the children interacted with one another, however, varied sharply. At the extremes, children interacted either not at all or nearly all the time.

As these figures indicate, the clearest picture that emerges from the observations of children's daytime experiences is one of variability. Different children were exposed to vastly different environments during the day. It makes no sense to describe a "typical" daytime environment for today's preschool children. There were only a couple of commonalities in the children's experiences. For one thing, it was quite common for the caregiver to read or sing to the child or give a "lesson." Only 30 children heard no reading or singing; only 40 received no "lessons." But usually these activities took up very little time during the observation. On average, children heard only 6 minutes of reading or singing and 3 minutes of "lessons," and the most reading or singing any child heard was only 30 minutes. Caregivers also rarely expressed affection to the child; on average, children were hugged or kissed or patted affectionately only twice during the 2-hour observation. The picture that emerges from these latter observations, then, is like the one drawn from the observations at home with parents: For most young children, positive and stimulating interaction with adults was quite limited in frequency.

In fact, it was even more limited than the stimulation at home at dinner. In the daytime observation children received less of all kinds of individual attention from their caregivers (teaching, talking, touching, hugging, helping, getting objects) than they did at home at dinnertime. They were more likely to be involved in activities with other children than they were at night (interacting with peers, listening to the caregiver talking to a group, teaching a group, reading, and giving lessons). These differences were highly significant [$Fs(1, 142)$ ranged from 22.0 ($p < .001$) for affection, to 520.7 ($p < .001$) for group education); substantial (e.g., there were twice as many utterances directed to the child individually in the evening observation as in the daytime observation), pervasive (they involved all aspects of behavior), and consistent (they were replicated in Year 1 and Year 2 observations).

There are a number of possible reasons for the differences between day and night, including different settings, different times of day, different ratios of children to adults, and different relationships between the adults and the children. All of these factors apparently contributed to the observed differences.

The contribution of the setting was evident in the finding that differences in experiences at night and during the day were greater for children in day-care centers than for children in home day care. But the setting was not the whole story, because although differences between children's experiences at night and in the daytime were not as large if the child was in home care during the day, they were still significant. Children received less physical contact, affection, one-to-one talk, appropriate responses, and choices; they spent more time alone, watching TV, playing alone with objects, and interacting with other children when they were with home day-care providers than with their parents at night [$Fs(1, 142) = 4.4$ ($p < .05$) to 62.2 ($p < .001$)].

These differences were undoubtedly related to there being more children in the daytime settings. But this, also, was not the only reason for the differences. Analyses of covariance, covarying out the number of children present, showed that the differences between night and day were still significant, although somewhat less so [$Fs(1,141) = 4.2$ ($p < .05$) to 9.6 ($p < .01$)].

It might be reasoned, therefore, that the observed differences were related to the time of day of the observation. The contribution of time of day was explored by comparing the daytime and dinnertime experiences of children who were in the same setting for both observations. Children who were with their mother at dinnertime and during the day did not interact more with her during the evening observations than they did during the day. In fact, differences were in the opposite direction. At night, mothers played, talked, taught, made demands, and expressed affection to the children less than they did during a comparable period of observation during the day [$Fs(1, 82) = 5.0$ ($p < .05$) to 14.8 ($p < .001$)]. The last remaining difference between day and night observations, then, was the presence of the child's father. At night, although mothers interacted with the children less, the combined frequency of the parents' talking, giving, helping, demanding, showing affection, and responding appropriately was greater than for the mother during the daytime observation [$Fs(1, 82) = 6.8$ ($p < .01$) to 17.1 ($p < .001$)]—because the father also was interacting with the child. The significance and salience of the father's interaction with the child is an issue that is considered in later chapters.

Relations With Child's Age and Sex

Older and Younger Children.   As we have already seen, in the dinnertime observations, the older the children were, the less interaction they had with adults. The same was true in the daytime.[5] In the daytime, as at night, as children got older they received less attention from their caregivers (touching, playing, talking, demanding, teaching, helping, controlling, responding appropriately, giving objects, offering choices, and showing physical affection), and the attention they received was relatively less likely to be teaching or demanding. As at home with their siblings, older children were observed to spend more time than younger children talking together. Regardless of setting, the evidence is clear: As children get older they are cut loose from interaction with adults and turn more to peers (the beginning of a lifelong trend!)

---

[5]Table A.3 in the appendix presents the correlations between children's age and their experiences during the daytime.

In the daytime observations, as well as spending more time talking with other children, older children were observed to be in settings with larger groups of children and to interact with more different children than younger children did. The reason? Older children were more likely to be in day-care centers or nursery schools. As a consequence of being in these centers, older children also spent more time in structured activities, with more toys and more professionally experienced caregivers than younger children did. Within the group of children who were in centers, however, the programs the older children attended were not relatively more structured than the programs younger children attended; quite the reverse. Older children in centers were in less structured programs [$r = -.32$ ($p < .01$)] and received less teaching and talking by the caregiver when they were in groups [$rs = -.25$ ($p < .05$), $-.28$ ($p < .01$)] than did younger children in centers.

Boys and Girls. Parallel analyses were done to compare the environments and experiences of boys and girls in the daytime as had been done for dinnertime—with similar results. There were few differences related to the child's sex. Overall MANOVAs in years 1 and 2 were nonsignificant and significant univariate analyses of variance were infrequent. The latter revealed only that daytime caregivers disciplined and played with boys more [$Fs(1, 142) = 2.0$ ($p < .05$), 2.2 ($p < .05$)]; boys' interactions with peers were more aggressive [$F(1, 142) = 2.2$ ($p < .05$)]; and boys spent more time playing alone with toys [$F(1, 142) = 2.2$ ($p < .05$)]. These differences between boys and girls, although few in number, are consistent with the literature in developmental psychology, as well as gender-role stereotypes, and demonstrate yet again the familiar sex differences in children's aggression and play and adults' differential styles of interacting with boys and girls (e.g., disciplining boys more; Barnard et al., 1984).

Patterns of Daytime Experience

To summarize the patterns in children's experiences in different daytime environments, factor analyses were performed on the variables from the daytime observations and interviews (see Table 4.2). Analyses of the interview variables revealed a factor structure that was consistent in Year 1 and Year 2 interviews, with a single factor in both years accounting for about 30% of the variance. This factor reflected the distinctive qualities of a *center environment*: a more structured program and physical setting, a larger group of children, and more professional caregivers. Two factors based on the observation variables also reflected center environments. One was a factor comprising *school-like activities*. The children receiving high scores on this factor were in settings in which the caregivers read, sang, recited, talked to or taught a group of children, and the children imitated the adult; the children spent less time alone or watching television. The second was a factor focused on *peer interaction*, reflecting settings in which children

TABLE 4.2
Factor Analyses of Daytime Variables

Factor[a]	Variables[b]	Loadings	
		Year 1	Year 2
Interview Variables			
Day-care center	Children in care arrangement	.92	.85
(32.5%, 27.3%)[c]	Children in class	.92	.84
	Number of children interacting	.86	.75
	Diversity	.88	.76
	Structure	.80	.68
	Program	.85	.52
	Toys	.67	.67
	Adult's education	.51	.71
	Adult's training	.60	.59
	Adult's experience	.72	.50
Observation Variables			
School activities	Adult reading or singing	.59	.78
(11.0%, 9.2%)	Adult teaching group	.60	.65
	Adult talking to group	.80	.63
	Child imitating adult	.47	.63
	Child watching TV	−.41	−.69
	Child alone	−.41	−.51
Peer activities	Peer interaction	.78	.75
(14.1%, 8.6%)	Child imitating peers	.66	.67
	Child watching interactions	.79	.27
	Child watching peers	.73	.23
	Positive affect	.15	.72
Adult responsiveness	Adult appropriate response	.63	.80
(9.8%, 8.1%)	Adult offering choice	.72	.67
	Adult giving object	.72	.29
	Showing object	.52	•
	Adult responsiveness	•	.58
Adult discipline	Adult control	.69	.55
(6.1%, 5.9%)	Adult demanding	.64	.33
	Negative affect	.25	.56
	Adult responsiveness	.72	.27
	Peer aggression	•	.72
Adult teaching	Adult teaching child 1:1	.81	.89
(6.9%, 8.9%)	Adult teaching, proportion	.89	.84
	Adult giving lesson	.50	.53
Adult play	Adult touching	.62	.22
(6.7%, 5.1%)	Adult affection	.58	.41
	Adult playing	.51	.71
	Positive affect	.49	.21
	Adult helping child	.47	•
	Child plays with object	−.53	.16

[a]This table contains the results of two separate factor analyses: one for the daytime interview variables, the other for the daytime observation variables. These are unrotated factors.

[b]The complete set of variables included in the analyses is listed in this column.

[c]Percent variance accounted for.

watched, imitated, interacted, and had fun with peers. All three of these factors were indeed demonstrably higher in center settings than in home settings [$Fs(1, 142) = >200$ ($p < .001$), 24.2 ($p < .001$), 7.9 ($p < .001$)].

The other four factors in the observation data reflected four different kinds of adult caregiving behavior, which were similar to the factors found for the parents' behavior: responsiveness, discipline, teaching, and physical interaction and play. Only the responsiveness factor was significantly different for centers and home environments: more of the behavior of caregivers in homes was responsive to the child's behavior than was the behavior of caregivers in centers [$F(1,142) = 5.3$ ($p < .01$)].

Homes Versus Centers

As these factor analyses suggest, there were significant and pervasive differences between two kinds of environments: homes and centers. To probe these differences in more detail, analyses of variance were performed for each of the daytime variables comparing children's experiences in the more institutional setting of centers and the more informal setting of homes (with mother or another caregiver). The results of these analyses (presented in Table 4.3) allow us to describe more specifically the two kinds of setting and children's experiences there. The results are not surprising, but they do document the extent of the differences between these two kinds of environment.

In centers, on the average, there were three caregivers; in homes, there was one. The caregivers in centers were likely to be college graduates with professional experience and training in child care; in homes, only 10% of the caregivers had these qualifications. In centers, children listened to stories or songs for 7 minutes on average; in homes the average length of time they heard songs or stories was less than 2 minutes. Children in centers spent twice as much time as children in homes having "lessons" (4.5 vs. 2.4 minutes). On the other hand, children in home settings were offered more choices (17 vs. 5), received appropriate responses more often (23 vs. 10), and heard more utterances by the caregiver that were directed to them alone (319 vs. 115). As the analyses of the factor scores had indicated, the home caregiver's utterances were relatively more likely to be responses (52% vs. 43%) and less likely to be demands (19% vs. 24%).

As one would expect, the activities of children in centers were more structured; their physical environments, more organized. The environment was more child-oriented—containing a greater array of toys, objects, and materials (19 vs. 12 categories on our checklist), less mess (2 vs. 5 items), fewer hazards (1 vs. 2 items), and fewer adult decorations (12 vs. 20). Children in centers never watched TV; children in home settings spent an average of 11 minutes of the 2-hour observation doing so. Children in homes were as likely as children in centers to spend their time playing alone with toys or objects (about 20 minutes, on the average), but the toys and materials they played with were less likely to include art supplies and

TABLE 4.3
Differences Between Home and Day-Care Center Settings

	Setting				
	Home[a]		Day-Care Center[b]		
Variables	Mean	SD	Mean	SD	F[c]
Caregiver Variables[d]					
Age	38.0	(8.9)	33.5	(5.6)	ns
Training in child care	2.5	(1.8)	3.2[e]	(1.0)	41.9***
Education	3.6	(2.6)	5.1	(1.7)	32.5***
Experience in child care	1.6	(0.6)	2.9	(0.4)	173.3***
Knowledge of child development	47.2	(5.5)	49.4	(5.1)	ns
Traditional values	21.6	(6.9)	10.0	(5.1)	3.5+
Positive attitude	30.1	(6.6)	24.0	(5.1)	ns
Expectations for child	11.3	(2.2)	14.3	(2.2)	6.6**
Number of caregivers[f]	1.5	(1.8)	3.3	(1.9)	48.3***
Touching child	54.2	(35.6)	34.3	(9.4)	4.1*
Playing	30.2	(38.5)	5.3	(17.6)	24.4***
Affection	1.9	(3.4)	0.9	(2.5)	8.7**
Talking to child	336.9	(105.5)	217.8	(95.0)	36.6***
One-to-one talk	318.8	(107.8)	115.5	(74.3)	130.2***
Talk to group	9.1	(18.0)	60.6	(42.1)	468.9***
Demands	52.1	(23.6)	28.4	(25.5)	13.9***
Demanding	.19	(.10)	.24	(.13)	23.5***
Teaching child	28.7	(25.3)	15.8	(13.5)	12.9***
Teaching one-to-one	27.2	(28.4)	9.5	(9.8)	21.4***
Teaching group	0.8	(5.7)	6.3	(7.7)	181.7***
Teaching, proportion	.08	(.07)	.08	(.06)	ns
Reading or singing	9.1	(28.3)	42.1	(17.9)	156.0***
Giving lesson to child	14.3	(32.8)	27.3	(39.2)	12.1***
Giving object to child	12.8	(12.1)	10.9	(10.6)	ns
Offering choice to child	16.7	(10.0)	5.5	(6.0)	58.2***
Helping child	15.8	(14.3)	8.8	(12.1)	8.7**
Appropriate response	23.4	(22.6)	10.2	(11.8)	17.4***
Verbal responsiveness	.52	(.19)	.43	(.16)	31.9***
Control of child	.60	(.83)	.50	(.70)	ns
Peer Variables					
Children in class	3.0	(2.0)	17.2	(7.0)	322.0***
Child-adult ratio	2.5	(1.9)	5.0	(4.0)	134.0***
Number of children interacting	2.0	(2.0)	9.5	(3.6)	112.3***
Older children present	1.7	(3.3)	1.9	(3.5)	ns
Younger children present	.77	(2.0)	.12	(2.5)	10.3***
Child watching peers	3.5	(6.5)	8.2	(9.5)	56.3***
Peer interaction	90.0	(59.9)	133.5	(66.7)	16.3***
Peer talk	76.5	(79.5)	96.9	(58.7)	8.9**
Child imitating peer	1.3	(2.7)	3.0	(4.6)	38.7***
Peer aggression	.07	(.20)	.03	.25	ns

(continued)

TABLE 4.3 *(continued)*

| Variables | Setting | | | | |
| | Home[a] | | Day-Care Center[b] | | |
	Mean	SD	Mean	SD	F[c]
Setting Variables					
Decoration	20.0	(5.0)	12.0	(4.7)	117.0***
Toys	12.0	(5.1)	18.7	(6.3)	62.3***
Mess	4.5	(2.2)	2.0	(1.6)	18.7***
Hazards	1.8	(1.7)	1.0	(1.0)	5.7*
Program Variables					
Program	8.0	(2.3)	14.0	(2.7)	100.5***
Structure	.40	(1.0)	3.3	(1.8)	89.7***
Diversity	5.8	(3.0)	14.8	(6.5)	66.5***
Child watching adult	4.7	(9.4)	5.6	(10.6)	2.7+
Child imitating adult	0.5	(8.1)	6.5	(12.4)	107.7***
Child watching interactions	10.8	(16.9)	33.8	(30.5)	142.6***
Child alone	105.2	(104.0)	5.2	(9.9)	146.6***
Child playing with object	132.6	(91.5)	122.8	(75.5)	ns
Child watching TV	66.6	(76.2)	0.0	(0.0)	74.3***
Showing object	4.1	(10.0)	5.3	(10.4)	ns
Negative affect	22.7	(23.2)	14.8	(17.0)	5.8*
Positive affect	88.3	(52.6)	77.1	(42.4)	3.1+
Pretend play	15.6	(38.9)	12.9	(29.2)	ns
Parallel play	6.1	(24.0)	13.9	(32.7)	18.3***

[a] $n = 125$ in Year 1 (73 with mother, 30 with caregiver in child's home, 22 in day-care home); 102 in Year 2 (62 with mother, 20 with caregiver in child's home, 15 in day-care home).

[b] $n = 65$ in Year 1 (40 part time, 25 full time); 92 in Year 2 (61 part time, 31 full time).

[c] These are F values for analyses of variance combining across subjects and the 2 years' assessments after partialling out the child's age at each of the assessments. Results of repeated measures analyses of variance were comparable.

[d] For children who were at home with mother during the day, these caregiver variables refer to the mother.

[e] Median = 4.

[f] Not including parents.

$+p < .10.$ $*p < .05.$ $**p < .01.$ $***p < .001.$

academic materials (18% vs. 61%) and more likely to include outdoor equipment and vehicles (45% vs. 28%).

In centers, on the average, there were 17 children in the child's class, and the child was observed to interact with 10 of them. In homes, the average number of children was three and the child usually interacted with both of the other children. When other children were present in the home setting, children spent as much time interacting with them as did children in centers (20 minutes). Yet, in centers, children were as likely to interact with other children as with an adult; in homes, they interacted with adults four times as much as with other children.

All these differences were highly significant in both between-group analyses of variance and repeated measures analyses of variance for children who spent some part of each day in a home setting and some part in a center.

Most of these differences are consistent with the research literature summarized in the introduction describing differences between home and day-care center environments. This literature corroborates the structural differences we found between the two kinds of setting (differences in numbers of caregivers and children, caregivers' education and training, structured activities and spaces) and the finding that children in day-care centers interact more with other children and less with adults.

Previous studies comparing center and home day care have shown that, on the average, physical conditions (space, ventilation, light, toilets, cleanliness, toys, safety, nutrition, and immunization) are better in day-care centers, whereas day-care homes rank higher in social-personal conditions (fewer children per adult, more interaction with the caregiver, more conversation, more socialization attempts, more emotional input, and more sensitive approaches to the child by the caregiver; Cochran, 1977a, 1977b; Golden et al., 1978; Prescott, 1973; Tyler & Dittman, 1980).

Even more striking, perhaps, are the differences in educational style observed in the two kinds of setting. In centers, researchers have observed, children spend more of their time in structured, teacher-directed, educational activities (38% in the national Profile of Child Care study; Kisker et al., 1991). They hear more questions from the caregiver and have more rules to follow. Their activities are punctuated by formal lessons. A comment about food, for example, might lead to a "mini-lesson" consisting of questions posed by the teacher like "Are peas a vegetable?" "How many vegetables can you name?" and "What colors are they?"

In day-care homes, in contrast, children spend less of their time in formal teacher directed education (29% in the Kisker et al. study) and more time in free exploration, "messing around," casual learning in real-life tasks with real role models. A question from the caregiver, "What would you like for lunch?" might lead to a long discussion about finding something everyone likes, which foods are more nutritious, what ingredients are necessary, how long it takes to prepare, and so on. In one interview study of day-care home providers (Bryant, Harris, & Newton, 1980), most providers saw their role as providing for children's physical needs, not as offering them education, play, or enrichment. They thought it was important for caregivers to be warm-hearted and accepting, but few mentioned the importance of any outgoing qualities. Less than one fifth, for example, suggested that the care provider should be prepared to play with or talk to children on their own level, and less than one tenth suggested that they should be imaginative or have ideas for doing things with children. Most thought that a caregiver should know about first aid, have common sense or experience bringing up her own children, and know something about children's play. Only 30%

of the care providers in this study reported that they had carried out specific educational or entertaining activities with the children, such as painting, reading, cutting out, playing with blocks or tiddlywinks, on the previous day. Instead, the children watched TV, played outside, and went shopping. Three quarters of the home providers in the national Profile of Child Care study (Kisker et al., 1991) reported that their main goal was to provide a warm loving environment for children; only 7% said that their goal was to foster children's development and 6% said it was to prepare children for school. In the National Day Care Home Study (Fosburg et al., 1980; Stallings, 1980), which included 350 day-care homes in 25 cities, caregivers on the average spent only about half their time involved with the children. They fed, washed, and dressed them, chatted, labeled objects, explained and demonstrated how things work, read stories, and played games. They did not give formal lessons. The children spent about half their time playing alone with sand, water, clay, and toys. The biggest difference between centers and home day care observed in the Profile study was that in most centers children did not watch TV, whereas in almost all day-care homes they did.

One way in which our findings differ from previous results is that we did not find that caregivers in day-care centers were less directive and "authoritarian" than caregivers in homes; we found that the setting did not determine the level of this kind of behavior. Caregivers, in homes or centers, exerted more discipline when children were more involved with other children [r with the peer factor = .35 ($p < .001$)].

Experiences in Home Settings in the Daytime

To further examine the patterns of children's experiences within each of the two kinds of environment—homes and centers—the next set of analyses performed were factor analyses of the data collected in each kind of setting. The results of these analyses for home settings are presented in Table 4.4.

In the data describing the home environments, we found six factors:

1. number of children in the home;
2. degree to which the child spent time watching, interacting with, and imitating these other children;
3. qualifications of the caregiver (education, training, experience, knowledge, and youth);
4. frequency of the caregiver's attention to the child (talking, helping, touching, teaching, playing, giving objects, or responding appropriately);
5. positive quality of the caregiver's behavior (specifically, reading, offering choices, and interacting responsively rather than being demanding and controlling); and

TABLE 4.4
Factor Analyses of Home-Care Variables

Factor[a]	Variables[b]	Loadings	
		Year 1	Year 2
Observation Variables			
Peer orientation	Peer interaction	.77	.66
(14.3%, 9.5%)	Caregiver talk to group	.84	.67
	Child watches peers	.78	.56
	Child watches interactions	.78	.58
	Caregiver teaching group	.73	.69
	Child imitating peer	.68	.59
	Child alone	−.52	−.57
	Positive affect	•	.65
Caregiver attention	Caregiver one-to-one talk	.76	.80
(14.9%, 13.6%)	Caregiver giving object	.68	.62
	Caregiver helping child	.25	.56
	Caregiver touching	.45	.82
	Caregiver giving lesson	.72	.38
	Caregiver offering choice[†]	.68	.47
	Caregiver teaching	.66	.31
	Caregiver playing	.64	.49
	Caregiver appropriate response	.63	.46
Positive caregiving	Caregiver reading or singing	.50	.70
(7.7%, 6.2%)	Caregiver responsiveness	.72	.47
	Caregiver offering choice	.37	.24
	Caregiver demanding	−.59	−.45
	Caregiver control	−.17	−.35
	Positive affect	.39	•
	Child imitating caregiver	.52	•
	Child watching TV	•	−.67
Interview variables			
Child oriented	Structure	.65	.78
(12.9%, 15.3%)	Decoration	−.56	−.80
	Toys	.61	•
	Program	•	.86
Number of children	Number of children in care	.93	.91
(16.2%, 14.4%)	Diversity	.76	.76
	Number of children interacting	.72	.42
	Child–adult ratio[†]	.76	.62
Caregiver qualifications	Caregiver's training	.61	.62
(12.0%, 7.6%)	Caregiver's education	.70	.33
	Child care experience	.68	
	Knowledge of child development	.50	.23
	Age[†]	−.26	−.87

[a]This table contains the results of two separate factor analyses: one for the daytime interview variables for the subjects in home settings, the other for the daytime observation variables for the subjects in home settings. These are unrotated factors.

[b]The complete set of variables included in the analyses is listed in this column.

[†]Variables not included in the factor-guided variables.

6. degree to which the home was physically organized around the child's activities.

Correlational analyses to examine the links among these factors revealed predictable associations. More qualified caregivers gave children more attention [$r = .20$ ($p < .05$)] and positive caregiving [$r = .35$ ($p < .001$)]. This finding parallels those from the National Day Care Home Study (Stallings, 1980), in which it also was observed that caregivers with more education were less directive with the children, and a more recent study by Kontos (1993), in which a marginally significant association was observed between the caregiver's specialized training and the overall quality of care in the day-care home. In the National Day Care Home Study, there was also great variation in caregiver's behavior related to whether they were licensed or part of a training network and to how much they viewed themselves as professional caregivers. Day-care home providers who were licensed, or, even better, part of a network, and who considered themselves child-care professionals, who read child-care books, went to meetings, took classes in child development, and kept records on the children they were looking after were more likely to talk, help, teach, and play with the children and to provide a physical environment with more music, dancing, books, educational TV, and nutritious food. Day-care home providers who were doing it only because no better job was available, or as an informal agreement with friends, neighbors, or relatives were less interactive and stimulating and spent more time on housework.

In neither the National Day Care Home Study nor this one, however, were the caregiver's qualifications related to the nature of the physical environment or to the likelihood that the child would be involved with peers. It was the number of children present that determined the child's involvement with peers [$r = .57$ ($p < .001$)]. This factor also affected the caregiver's availability. Even with only one other child present, the child received less attention from the caregiver [$F(1, 117) = 3.9$ ($p < .001$)], and when there were more children and they were more involved with each other, the child received both less caregiver attention [$r = -.39$ ($p < .001$)] and less positive caregiving [$r = -.54$ ($p < .001$)], and the physical environment, although more child oriented [$r = .54$ ($p < .001$)] was also more hazardous [$r = .25$ ($p < .01$)]. This finding of differences in caregivers' behavior related to the number of children present also echoes the results of the National Day Care Home Study (Fosburg et al., 1980; Stallings, 1980). When more young children were present in day-care homes in that study, they were more unruly and the caregivers were more directive; the children experienced less one-to-one interaction with the caregiver and spent more time alone or with the other children. Similarly, Howes (1983) found that in day-care homes with more children caregivers offered less facilitative social stimulation, positive affect, and responsiveness and were more restrictive and negative. It is clear that day-care environments, even when they are in home settings, vary markedly depending on how many children are present. This is probably the single most important determinant of what happens to the child in the care setting, predicting as it does the nature of the physical environment and the interactions the child has with both peers and adults. It even predicts the caregiver's own behavior (attention and positive caregiving to the child) at higher levels than the caregiver's qualifications [$rs = .20$ ($p < .05$) vs. $-.39$ ($p < .001$); $.35$ ($p < .001$) vs. $-.54$ ($p < .001$)]. In the next section we look further at differences in children's experiences related to differences in their home caregivers.

At Home With Mother Versus a Sitter

The major comparison of interest here was what the differences in children's experiences are when they are in a home setting with their own mother versus a home setting with another caregiver. To examine this issue, we first analyzed the differences between mothers and caregivers in the child's own home. Compared to caregivers in the family's home, the mothers in the study who were at home with their children were younger and more highly educated; they had received more training in child development and even had more professional experience in child care [$Fs(1,182) = 14.1$ ($p < .001$) to 17.9 ($p < .001$)]. There were, however, no significant differences between mothers and these caregivers in their behavior toward the child (either in specific types of behavior or on overall factors of attention and positive caregiving). The only observed difference in children's daily experiences when they were with mother or a sitter in their own home was that when another child (usually a sibling) was present in the home, children interacted with that child more when they were with their mother than when they were with a babysitter [$F(1,182) = 10.1$ ($p < .001$)]. This may be because mothers have a "family agenda" that other caregivers do not, and, therefore, are more likely to promote interaction between siblings.

We next examined the differences between mothers and caregivers in family day-care homes. Here we found that even though mothers and family day-care providers were comparable in age, education, and experience, mothers interacted more with the child in every way [$Fs(1,167) = 9.6$ ($p < .01$) for caregiver attention, 16.4 ($p < .001$) for positive caregiving]. One reason for this difference was that there were more children in day-care homes ($M = 4.5$) than in children's own homes [$M = 2$; $F(1,167) = 31.3$ ($p < .001$)]. But this was not the only reason. Analysis of covariance covarying out the presence of other children reduced the differences in the adults' behavior, but did not eliminate them. Mothers were still more attentive and offered their children better care than did child-care providers [$Fs(1,80) = 4.9$ ($p < .05$), 5.8 ($p < .05$)]. These findings are consistent with previous research showing that children's interactions with their mothers are more emotional, responsive, and social than their interactions with home-care providers (Rubenstein, Pedersen, & Yarrow, 1977; Siegel-Gorelick et al., 1981a; Stith & Davis, 1984).

Research on day-care homes (Bryant et al., 1980; Fosburg et al., 1980; Stallings, 1980) hints at some reasons for these differences. It seems that children in day-care homes are incorporated into the provider's family, not given special attention. The day-care child may play second fiddle to the caregiver's own children, because in nearly half of the day-care homes observed, the children in the day-care home included one of the day-care home provider's own. Day-care home providers usually spend about half of their time on housework or personal activities. Most do not see their role as being sensitive to the child's feelings and problems or feel that special knowledge about children's feelings or problems is necessary.

It is interesting that the differences between mothers' and caregivers' behavior were not found in the present study when the caregiver was in the child's own home (without her own children). Perhaps the reason for this similarity was that mothers had selected these in-home caregivers because they were warm and responsive; perhaps it was because the mothers kept a closer eye on these caregivers' behavior with the child; perhaps these caregivers were influenced by the mother's behavior with the child and tried to follow her example; perhaps they had formed a closer relationship with the mother and were more emotionally invested in the child. The similarity between mothers and caregivers would have made sense if the in-home sitters were related to the mother and the out-of-home caregivers were not, but this was not true in the present study. (Only three in-home caregivers were relatives, and so was one family day-care provider.) Perhaps it is simply that caregivers in the child's home are not encumbered by their own families and household needs during the hours they are providing care. This study does not answer the question of just what makes a caregiver act like mom, but it suggests that the particular setting—child's own home or caregiver's home—makes a difference.

Spending the Daytime in a Center

The next analyses provided an opportunity to examine the patterns of children's experience in center settings. Among the observation variables, six factors were identified (see Table 4.5). Two factors focused on traditional school-like activities. One of these consisted of the teacher's teaching, talking, reading, singing, and giving lessons to a group of children; we labeled this factor *group education*. The other factor consisted of the child's imitating the teacher and looking at objects shown by the teacher while in a group; this factor we labeled *see-and-do*. These two factors were correlated with each other [$r = .66$ ($p < .001$)]. There were also two factors reflecting two kinds of peer interaction: *negative peer interaction* and *lively peer fun*. These factors were also correlated [$r = .29$ ($p < .01$)]. Finally, there were two factors reflecting the teacher's interaction with individual children; one was the teacher's one-to-one attention to the child (talking, teaching, touching, helping, responding, and expressing affection); the second was the teacher's discipline (demanding and controlling). The teacher's discipline was related to group education and see-and-do [rs = .40 ($p < .001$), .27 ($p < .01$)], whereas the teacher's attention was related to more peer fun and less negative peer interaction [rs = .39 ($p < .001$), −.29 ($p < .01$)].

TABLE 4.5
Factor Analyses of Day-Care Center Variables

Factor	Variables[a]	Loadings	
		Year 1	Year 2
Observation variables			
Teacher attention	Teacher appropriate response	.75	.58
(14.0%, 11.6%)	Teacher one-to-one talk	.63	.63
	Teacher touching	.56	.77
	Child plays with object	−.27	−.44
	Teacher teaching	.81	.54
	Teacher teaching, proportion	.63	.70
	Teacher helping child	.24	.70
	Teacher affection	•	.49
Group education	Teacher talk to group	.83	.87
(10.5%, 11.1%)	Teacher giving lesson	.59	.58
	Teacher teaching group	.58	.75
	Teacher reading or singing	.82	.74
	Teacher giving object	.46	.57
	Teacher responsiveness	−.64	•
	Teacher offering choice	•	.53
Negative peer interaction	Peer aggression	.53	.21
(9.2%, 5.6%)	Negative affect	.56	.46
	Child watching interactions	.41	.30
	Child watching teacher	−.80	−.23
	Teacher responsiveness	−.50	•
	Teacher helping child	•	−.49
	Teacher talking to child[†]	•	−.29
Peer fun	Peer interaction	.68	.82
(7.8%, 6.3%)	Positive affect	.69	.43
	Child imitating peer	.58	.21
"See and do"	Showing object	.33	.35
(4.1%, 7.8%)	Child imitating teacher	.26	.51
	Teacher talking to group	•	.60
Discipline	Teacher demanding	.83	.48
(7.5%, 9.3%)	Teacher control	.26	.32
	Teacher responsiveness	−.78	−.49
	Teacher appropriate response	−.46	−.34
	Teacher one-to-one teaching	•	.53
	Teacher teaching, proportion	•	.70

[a]This table contains the results of the unrotated factor analysis of the daytime observation variables for the subjects in center settings.
[†]Variables not included in the factor-guided variables.

Factor analysis of the interview variables collected in the day-care centers produced no consistent overall factors, although there were some predictable correlations between specific pairs of variables. Specifically, replicating the finding in the National Child Care Staffing Study (Whitebook et al., 1990), teachers' education was found to be related to specific training in child development [$r = .56$ ($p < .001$)]. Also, paralleling the association observed in the national Profile of Child Care Settings (Kisker et al., 1991) between center size and child–adult ratio, in the present study the number of children in the class was found to be related to the number of children in the center, the number of teachers, and the child–adult ratio [$rs = .46$ ($p < .001$), $.31$ ($p < .01$), $.50$ ($p < .001$)].

In addition, in the present study, features of a higher quality physical environment were intercorrelated: More toys were found in classrooms with more decorations, fewer hazards, and better organization [$rs = .45$ ($p < .001$), $-.19$ ($p < .10$), $.38$ ($p < .001$)].

Correlations between interview variables and observation factors were examined next. We expected to find links between the caregivers' professional qualifications and behavior. In other research, caregivers with more training in child development have been observed to behave in ways that are more positive and less authoritarian, to interact more with the children, talking, teaching, and helping, and to provide more group activities (Arnett, 1989; Berk, 1985; W. Hayes et al., 1983; Howes, 1983; Kinney, 1988; Ruopp et al., 1979; Whitebook et al., 1990). There were, however, surprisingly few significant correlations between teachers' qualifications and observed behavior in the present study. Neither training in child development nor general educational level was significantly related to teachers' observed behavior, in either year.

There are several possible reasons that we did not find significant links between teachers' qualifications and behavior in this study. One possible reason was the restricted range of variation in education and training among the teachers interviewed in our study. Only 20% of our teachers had less than a college degree; only 6% had no formal training in child development. Another possible reason was that in our study the level of training assessed was that of the lead teachers only rather than of all the adults in the center who were observed interacting with the child. But in the National Day Care Study (Ruopp et al., 1979), also, the index of training was the lead teacher's level of training. Because our focus was on the child's experience rather than on the behavior of individual teachers, we cannot establish in this study the extent of the link between teachers' qualifications and behavior. But our results do suggest that one should be cautious in assuming that the two are closely and inevitably tied, at least within the "normal" range of variation that occurs in day-care centers available to most parents.

We also expected to find links between the number of children present and the teachers' behavior. In previous research, children in large classes or in classes with lower adult–child ratios have been found to experience less interaction with the teacher and more interaction with peers (Asher & Erickson, 1979; Ruopp et al., 1979); their interactions have been observed to be more emotional (Asher & Erickson, 1979), less responsive and facilitative of social development (Howes, 1983); their behavior, less cooperative and reflective, more hostile, aimless, and uninvolved (Ruopp et al., 1979). What we found was that, in the Year 2 observations only, the more children there were, the less time they spent in formal group activities [group education and see-and-do, $rs = -.37$ ($p < .001$), $-.32$ ($p < .01$)] and the more time they spent interacting with their peers—that is, in free play [$r = .32$ ($p < .01$)]. Although consistent with the previous findings, the differences we observed were not as pervasive as those previously reported. Possibly this was because in our sample the effect of large class size was compensated for by the higher levels of education and training that the teachers of large classes had [$Fs(1,90) = 2.9$ ($p < .01$), 2.0 ($p < .05$)].

PATTERNS OF EXPERIENCE REVIEWED

The analyses that we have described paint a picture of the contemporary "lifestyles" of today's preschool children. These lifestyles are distinctly different depending on the setting—home or day-care center—where the child spends his or her time; depending on the cast of characters who are present in the setting—parents or caregivers, siblings or peers; and depending on the circumstances of the family—richer or poorer, with working or stay-at-home mom. They also change markedly as children get older. Even in this truncated sample, children were found to have widely differing experiences depending on these four conditions.

Settings

Differences between children's experiences in different settings were most marked. In centers, children interacted with more other children, more toys, and more professionally trained caregivers; their activities were more structured, academic, and educational. In homes, children watched more TV and played outside on slides and tricycles; they were given more choices, and their caregivers were more likely to speak to them individually and responsively. In day-care homes, children were less likely to experience positive, affectionate interaction with the caregiver than they were in their own homes (with mother or sitter).

Still, there were similarities in children's daily experiences across settings, too. Even children in home settings usually had at least one other child to play with, and when the presence of other children was taken into account, the time the child spent playing with other children was comparable in the two kinds of setting. Home and center settings were also similar in the degree to which caregivers' interactions included teaching and discipline.

People Present

Within the same kind of setting, children's experiences were affected by who was present and who interacted with the child.

At home at night, children had different experiences with their mothers and their fathers. Mothers interacted with the children more frequently than fathers in every way except reading and hugging (which mothers and fathers did equally often). The amounts mothers and fathers in any particular family interacted with children were complementary; that is, if mother was busy making dinner, father took up the slack; if father played more with the child, mother interacted less.

Still, as in different settings, there were similarities in children's experiences with these different people. The interactional styles of mothers and fathers in any particular family were correlated: If the mother was relatively positive and responsive or strict and demanding, compared to other mothers in the study, the dad was relatively positive and responsive or strict and demanding compared to other fathers.

The most striking difference in children's experiences was due to the presence or absence of other children. When other children were present during the home observation at night or during the daytime observation in day care, children spent less time interacting with adult caregivers or by themselves, and the more other children who were present, the less attention, stimulation, and positive care from the caregiver they received.

The age of the other children in the setting also made a difference. Whether at home with a sibling or in a day-care environment with unrelated peers, children's experiences in settings with older children were more positive and verbal; their experiences with younger children, more negative and aggressive.

Family Circumstances

Children's experiences also differed depending on family circumstances. In yet another demonstration that the "rich get richer," children from families of higher SES had more varied toys, spent less time watching TV, and interacted more with their fathers. Both their parents behaved more responsively, read to them more, offered them more choices, and were less demanding. Interactions at dinnertime were characterized by more positive affect. If their mothers worked, they worked fewer hours and had more household help. In families of lower SES, children had messier and more hazardous physical environments at home; their interactions at dinnertime were characterized by more negative affect and less teaching. If their mothers worked, they worked more hours and received less help running the house.

Another family circumstance that affected children's experiences was the mother's work status. Children whose mothers were working were more likely to be in child care; their fathers were more involved in looking after them. However, their interactions with their mothers were not different in quantity or quality from those of children whose mothers were not employed.

Age Differences

Not only did children's experiences differ depending on where they were and with whom, they also changed as the children grew older (from 2 to 5 years of age). Older children demonstrated their advanced development and increased opportunities for growth in a number of ways. At home at night and in their daytime settings as well, older children expressed less negative affect and received less adult attention, teaching, and discipline than younger children. They showed their independence by spending more time alone at home. They exhibited their social maturity by interacting more with other children, both at home with their siblings and with peers in day care. They were more involved in educational activities—both more teaching by their fathers at home and more time in school-like activities in day care. Clearly, life and lifestyles change during the brief years of early childhood.

In Brief...

In this chapter we have seen that children's experiences vary dramatically depending on time and place. Today's young children, moving from setting to setting and hour to hour, sample that variety every day. A single snapshot observation of a child's experience does not do justice to the complexity of the ecology of contemporary childhood or the richness of the child's individual experience. We have described a little of the complex lifestyles of today's young children as they vary with casts of characters, changes from morning to night, diverse playmates. But not all children experience the same complexity. Some are exposed to an abundance of settings and situations, whereas others experience a more "traditional" lifestyle limited to home, parents, and siblings. Our primary question in this study is what difference it makes if children have such enriched and varied experiences or more limited ones. In the following chapters we explore the effects of these different patterns of experience on children's development.

5

Links Between Family and Day Care

Before we explore the effects of different patterns of experience on children's development, it is important to find out whether and how children's experiences in different contexts are related. What are the links between the child's experiences in the two worlds of family and day care? It is obvious that such links must exist. We did not randomly assign children to day-care arrangements or randomly assign their mothers to work in order to eliminate such associations and investigate "pure" day-care effects. We studied children in the child-care arrangements that parents had freely chosen on the basis of their own needs, goals, and opportunities. In previous research on day care such parental "self-selection" has often been considered a nuisance, limiting the interpretation of day-care "effects." In the present study, we confronted the issue of parental self-selection and exploited that issue by exploring the nature of parents' selections. We do that in this chapter by analyzing the links between the characteristics of families and the day care they selected.

LINKS BETWEEN DAYTIME ENVIRONMENTS
AND FAMILY CHARACTERISTICS

Analyses of the empirical associations between family and day-care characteristics revealed, first, that there were links between parents' demographic characteristics and their use of day care. According to analyses of variance, the parents of children who were in day care were better educated [$F(1,142) = 10.8$ ($p < .001$); Ms for father's + mother's education = 9.3 vs. 8.4; maximum = 12] and of higher SES [$F(1, 142) = 37.1$ ($p < .001$); Ms = 48 vs. 38; maximum = 65]; the mothers worked more and were more career-minded [$Fs(1, 142) = 58.3$ ($p < .001$), 20.6 ($p < .001$)]; the fathers were more involved in child care [$F(1, 142) = 13.8$ ($p < .001$)]. Findings like these are not new or surprising; they have been reported in previous research (Larsen &

Robinson, 1987; Melhuish et al., 1991). In addition, in the present study, children who were home with their mothers all day came from more extended, stable, and larger families, in which, not surprisingly, fathers expressed more traditional family values [$Fs(1, 142) = 6.3$ ($p < .01$) to 52.1 ($p < .001$)].

What was perhaps more interesting was the fact that there were no demographic differences between the families who selected home day care versus center day care, or who selected part-time day care versus full-time day care. Nor were there any differences in parents' behavior related to whether or not their children were in day care. In Year 1, the only difference between families that were and were not using day care was that the fathers of children in day care read more to their children [$F(1, 142) = 3.4$ ($p < .05$)], and even this difference was not significant when SES was covaried out. In Year 2, mothers of children in day care gave more explanations, demands, and help to their children during the dinnertime observation [$Fs(1,126) = 4.8$ ($p < .05$) to 6.9 ($p < .01$)], but these differences were the result of having fewer children in the family and disappeared when the number of children was covaried out. There was no difference in the physical environment of the home or the amount of interaction with siblings if the child had a sibling. In brief, the only significant differences between the families of day-care and nonday-care children were the completely predictable demographic ones.

Links With the Quality of Center Care

But previous research has suggested that there may be associations between family characteristics and the quality of day care that parents select (e.g., Whitebook et al., 1990). In the next analyses we searched for these associations in the sample of the parents who had selected center care for their children. The overall MANOVA for families of higher versus lower SES was nonsignificant and there were only a few correlations with SES that were statistically significant. These links were, however, sensible ones and consistent with previous research. Parents of higher SES—having more money—spent more on day care [$r = .48$ ($p < .001$)]. The other children in the day-care class—like their own children—were of higher SES [$r = .37$ ($p < .001$)]. The day-care centers they chose—like their own homes—had more toys [$r = .31$ ($p < .01$)]. The teachers they selected—like themselves—were less demanding [$r = -.35$ ($p < .001$)]. Separating out the educational component from overall SES revealed more specific links related to the parents' educational orientation: More educated mothers and fathers chose day care in which teachers were better educated [$r = .25$ ($p < .05$)] and more knowledgeable about child development [$r = .30$ ($p < .01$)]; these teachers read and sang more to the children [$r = .29$ ($p < .01$)] and did more teaching [$r = .25$ ($p < .05$)].[1]

---

[1]These correlations were the same for mother and father; one parent's education was not more predictive than the other's.

These links with SES and parents' education paralleled those observed in previous research for the variety of toys and materials (Holloway & Reichhart-Erickson, 1988) and the educational content of the teacher's behavior—teaching, reading (Holloway & Reichhart-Erickson, 1988; Tizard et al., 1976). It seems, then, that to the extent they can afford it, parents select day care that is similar to their own home environment, their own behavior, and their own characteristics.

This suggestion is further supported by the findings linking parents' observed behavior with the day care they had selected for their children. Parents who spent more time at home at dinnertime teaching their children had chosen day-care centers with more structured programs [rs with structure and see-and-do activities = .33 ($p < .01$), .23 ($p < .05$)]. Children whose mothers were more demanding had more demanding teachers [$r = .22$ ($p < .10$)]. Children whose parents gave them more individual attention at home received more teacher attention at the day-care center [$r = .28$ ($p < .05$)].

Clearly, selectivity is a factor in parents' choice of a day-care center program for their child. This does not mean, however, that these associations are entirely the result of a conscious selection process on the parents' part. These parents had not done a lot of comparison shopping. Their choice of a day-care setting was influenced by what care was available to them and what information they had about it. Some of the links between the parents' behavior and the teacher's behavior, also, might have been influenced by the contribution of the child to both sets of interactions; some children may simply need more attention or teaching or disciplining wherever they are. When the child's behavior (compliance and competence) was partialled out of the associations between parents' and caregiver's behavior, however, the relations remained strong and significant. So it seems that these links do represent self-selection and are not just a by-product of the child's behavior.

Links With the Quality of Home Day Care

To look for evidence of selectivity in making home day-care arrangements, similar analyses were carried out correlating parents' characteristics with the home-care variables. In selecting a home caregiver, parents of higher SES chose caregivers whose behavior was higher on the positive caregiving factor [more responsive, less demanding; $r = .28$ ($p < .05$)]. Among those who chose to use day-care homes, parents of higher SES selected day-care homes in which there were fewer physical hazards in the setting [$r = -.62$ ($p < .01$)]. Parents using day-care homes, in fact, selected homes in which the quality of the physical setting was similar to that of their own home [(a stimulating home environment was correlated with more toys, fewer hazards, and less mess in the day-care home, $rs = .58$ ($p < .01$), $-.62$ ($p < .01$), $-.45$ ($p < .05$)]. Parents with more child development expertise (training in child development, knowledge of childrearing) selected caregivers who were older [r = .49 (p < .001)] and more knowledgeable about childrearing[2] [r = .55 (p < .001)], and selected settings with fewer children [r = −.35 (p < .05)]. As we observed for children in day-care centers, there were links, as well, between the kinds of behavior exhibited by parents and by home caregivers. Children whose parents behaved in a less authoritarian way and spent more time teaching them had caregivers who were less demanding [rs with positive caregiving factor = −.30 (p < .05) for parent demanding, .42 (p < .01) for parent teaching].[3] Mothers' and caregivers' attitudes toward the child were also correlated [rs for attitudes and expectations = .35 (p < .01), .55 (p < .001)].[4] Thus, the results of these analyses suggest that parents use home-care providers with childrearing values, attitudes, and behaviors that are compatible with their own.

One way in which the selection of home care differed from the selection of center care was that more highly educated parents chose less educated home caregivers rather than more educated ones [r = −.40 (p < .01)]. The reason for this was that these (more affluent) parents were able to afford and had selected in-home caregivers (who had low levels of education) rather than day-care home providers (who had higher levels of education) [$F(1, 57)$ for SES of parents using in-home care vs. those using day-care homes = 5.3 (p < .05), Ms = 53 vs. 43; $F(1, 57)$ for educational level of in-home caregivers vs. day-care home providers = 6.3 (p < .05), Ms = 1.5 vs. 3.4].

It is interesting that highly educated parents apparently do not "select" home day-care arrangements according to characteristics that psychologists have been concerned with—like caregivers' education and training—but according to more functional criteria—like physical safety, in-home convenience, and shared attitudes toward discipline. This finding is not surprising—we know that there is a gulf between parents and professionals—but it does lead to the question of whether parents or professionals know best about what kind of day care is good for children. We see how all these variables are related to how well the children in day care do in later chapters.

PARENTS' SATISFACTION WITH CHILD CARE

But are parents themselves sensitive to differences between day-care arrangements and satisfied with the care arrangements they have selected for their children? The links we observed between parents' qualities and the

---

[2]This association was not found by Kontos (1993), but the day-care home providers in her sample were all licensed; ours were not.

[3]These correlations were not reduced when the child's behavior (competence and compliance) was partialled out.

[4]These correlations were not reduced when the child's behavior (competence and compliance) was partialled out.

qualities of the day care they were using suggest that parents may have been deliberately choosing day care about which they felt comfortable. Here we discuss the parents' satisfaction with the child-care arrangements they had selected.

Rates of Satisfaction

In general, parents claimed to be quite satisfied with their children's day-care arrangement: 87% said they would not change to another type of care for the child; almost three quarters claimed they would use the same arrangement for another child. This high rate of satisfaction is typical in studies of day-care users. In the Detroit Child Care Survey (Mason & Duberstein, 1992), for instance, 86% of the mothers surveyed were "extremely" or "very satisfied" with their child's day-care arrangement. Even when parents are asked whether they would like to switch arrangements, few appear to be dissatisfied (Sonenstein, 1990). In the Detroit Survey, only 17% said they would prefer an alternative arrangement if they could afford to spend any amount on child care. In a recent survey of 1,762 readers of *Working Mother* magazine (Cadden, 1993), a sample of mothers similar in education and age to the sample in our study were asked "Would you change your arrangement if another affordable option were available?" Only about one quarter of the mothers said that they would change.

Reasons for Satisfaction

What are the reasons that parents are satisfied with their child's particular day-care arrangement? This study allowed us to explore this question by correlating the level of the parents' satisfaction with qualities of the day-care arrangement and measures of the child's development.

Congenial Values. Among parents whose children were in centers, both mothers and fathers were more satisfied if the "mesh" between home and center (agreement with the teacher's opinions about childrearing, similarity with the teacher's ethnic and SES characteristics, etc.) was greater [$rs = .48$ ($p < .01$), $.56$ ($p < .01$)]. Among parents whose children were in home day care, both parents were more satisfied if the caregiver was more demanding and controlling [$rs = .42$ ($p < .01$)], and these more satisfied parents were more demanding and controlling themselves [$rs = .46$ ($p < .01$) for mothers, $.34$ ($p < .05$) for fathers]. Thus, congenial values and views of childrearing do seem to be a relevant factor in determining parents' satisfaction with care.

Thriving Children? Another possible basis for parents' satisfaction might be the progress their child is making in the day-care arrangement. As it turns out, this was not a major source of satisfaction. Parents' satisfaction was not related to how satisfied they thought their child was with the care arrangement. In a study of low-income mothers, Sonenstein and Wolf (1991) found that the child's happiness with the arrangement was one of the things the mothers of older preschoolers mentioned as being important in a child-care arrangement. But in our study, the only link of this sort with parent's actual (reported) satisfaction was that mothers using center care were more satisfied if, in our observations, the child experienced more positive affect—was happier—there [$r = .25$ ($p < .05$)].

Parents' satisfaction was also not strikingly affected by how well their children were developing overall. Contrary to expectations, parents were not more satisfied with the child's care arrangement if the child was developmentally advanced in cognitive abilities or social competence or was easier to get along with at home. Satisfaction with child care was not related to children's general competence at home and, in fact, the parents who expressed more satisfaction with their child's care arrangement were those whose children scored lower on tests of cognitive development[5] [$rs = -.15$ for mothers; $-.34$ ($p < .01$) for fathers] and who were less compliant with requests by researchers or parents [$rs = -.19$ ($p < .05$), $-.29$ ($p < .01$) for mothers]. Mothers were, however, more satisfied with the child-care arrangement if the child had a better relationship with her [more sociable; $r = .26$ ($p < .05$) yet less physically dependent on her in our laboratory assessment; $r = -.17$ ($p < .05$)] and was more sociable with a friend who came to the house to play [$r = .24$ ($p < .05$)]. These relations make sense. These factors are probably more salient and significant to parents than how well children perform on tests of cognitive abilities. Mothers can see and care about the child's relations with them and with playmates at home.

Cost and Convenience.   Mothers were more satisfied with the day-care arrangement if they were working more hours [$r = .24$ ($p < .01$)] and were less involved in the arrangement [$r = -.20$ ($p < .05$)]. There are several possible interpretations of this finding: Mothers might have preferred a day-care arrangement that did not make demands on their time. They may have valued the arrangement because it allowed them to work longer hours at a full-time job. Or, possibly, the mothers who worked more hours and used more day care simply had a vested interest in thinking that they had a more satisfactory care arrangement (thus reducing their cognitive dissonance). One has to question the meaning (validity?) of mothers' reports of their own satisfaction with care rather than simply taking these "at face value." More than once in the study, a mother who reported a high level of satisfaction with her child's day care in the first year of the study was using a different arrangement for the child in the second year and only then admitted that she had had serious reservations about the first care arrangement.

---

[5]Details of all these measures of child development are discussed in the next chapter.

Cost-conscious mothers were also more satisfied if they paid less for child care [$r = -.24$ ($p < .05$)]; they apparently preferred an arrangement that was economical. Fathers, in contrast, were more satisfied if they paid more for care [$r = .19$ ($p < .05$)]. Perhaps they thought that if they paid more for it the care must be better (you get what you pay for), or perhaps fathers simply were more satisfied with the kind of care that comes with a high price tag; namely, an in-home caregiver.

Center Care Best?   Fathers with children in "nanny care" were, in fact, more satisfied with the care arrangement than fathers with children in centers [r with center care = $-.18$ ($p < .05$)]. This may reflect a more traditional family-oriented preference for fathers: Children (if not their mothers) should be at home. Mothers, on the other hand, were more satisfied with the child-care arrangement if the child was in a center [r with center care = $.26$ ($p < .01$)]. Only 5% of mothers using centers (vs. 22% of mothers using home day care) said they would change to another type of care. The mothers' preference for centers may have been influenced by what they thought was best for children. In the *Working Mother* survey (Cadden, 1993), 56% of the respondents preferred center-based care as a learning environment and believed that one-on-one care, whether by a nanny, a relative, or the mother herself, is of lesser educational value. Only 12% of center users believed the child would learn more if the mother stayed home, whereas 37% of nanny users did. On the other hand, this preference for centers also fits well with the convenience factor for mothers: using in-home or home day care places additional burdens on the mother, who is likely to find that this kind of day care is less stable and reliable than a center (a center does not close down when the caregiver doesn't feel well or gets married) and requires more continued personal involvement on her part. These findings point to a gender difference in mothers' and fathers' preferences and priorities regarding child care: For fathers, priority is apparently given to approximating the ideal of children at home; for mothers, priority goes to practical benefits for the mother herself (the freedom to work) and educational benefits for the child.

High Quality?   When asked what specifically they were satisfied with in their child's care arrangement, mothers whose children were in centers were most likely to mention the qualifications of the staff (mentioned by 50%) and the materials and planned activities (56%). These were also the reasons mothers gave for choosing center care over a home-care arrangement (75% mentioned staff training; 70% mentioned the curriculum). So were these mothers more satisfied with day care that would merit a Good Housekeeping seal of approval from the National Association for the Education of Young Children or score highest on a popular checklist of how to choose a day-care center? Probably not. The satisfaction expressed by these mothers was not related to the general level of education or specific training in child development of the teacher they selected, the variety of materials, tidiness, and safety in the classroom, or the number of children in the class. Thus, three major indexes of high quality day care—a professionally qualified caregiver, a stimulating physical setting, and a small class size and low child–adult ratio—were not predictive of the mothers' satisfaction with the day-care centers they had selected.

By what aspects of the day-care center environment were they influenced, then? Mothers using center care for their children were more satisfied if the teacher was more experienced [$r = .31$ ($p < .01$)], if the program included more structured and educational activities [teaching, reading, lessons, imitating the teacher, planned activities, $rs = .21$ ($p < .05$) to .25 ($p < .05$)], and if the child spent less time playing alone with toys [$r = -.29$ ($p < .05$)]. Thus, it seems that mothers have bypassed the regulable standards of training and numbers recommended by professionals to favor programs with more educational curricula (bypassed "structure" for "process," some would say.)

Users of home day care also were not more satisfied if the home setting for their child met the professional criteria that might be set by day-care "experts": Mothers were not impressed by the variety of materials and tidiness of the day-care home, the caregiver's level of education or training, the number of children in the home. Mothers using home care were unlikely to mention the caregiver's qualifications (10%) or materials and planned activities (7%) as sources of satisfaction and they did not often mention staff training (20%) or curriculum (30%) as reasons they chose a home-care arrangement. Mothers using home day care were more satisfied with loving, "grandmotherly" caregivers—older women [$r = .35$ ($p < .05$)] who were more physically helpful and affectionate with the child [$r = .33$ ($p < .05$)]. There does seem to be a logic in these sources of satisfaction, even if they are not the ones that experts might prescribe.

The situation was, again, different for fathers. Not only were their reported levels of satisfaction not dependent on what experts might recommend, but in some instances they were in the opposite direction. Fathers of children in day-care centers were more satisfied if the teacher was older [$r = .21$ ($p < .05$)] and had been in the center longer [$r = .24$ ($p < .05$)] and if the child was in a messy classroom [$r = .33$ ($p < .01$)]. Fathers of children in home day care were more satisfied with what might be considered more custodial care: They were more satisfied when the home caregiver was less "qualified" [had less training and education, $rs = -.32$ ($p < .01$), $-.27$ ($p < .05$)]—presumably because they prefer in-home nannies.

These findings again point to a gender differences in mothers' and fathers' views of desirable child care. They also reveal a lack of concordance between what parents are most satisfied with and what professionals might prescribe as being "high-quality" care. Clearly, parents' satisfaction with child care is no gauge of "good" care.

LOOKING FORWARD

In the following chapters we examine the links between children's development and their experiences in different care environments—at home and in day care; we will weigh the relative contributions of these different experiences to different aspects of development. As the analyses discussed in this chapter have revealed, children's experiences at home and in day care are not independent. Parents have arranged for them both, and although being in day care broadens children's horizons and enriches their experiences, there are similarities in the two environments. Parents selected (or were fortunate enough to find) day care that was compatible with their own characteristics: Parents with high incomes selected day-care centers that cost more and had more things in them (toys and educational materials). Parents with high levels of education chose teachers who were more educated and educating. Mothers chose day-care centers with caregivers whose characteristics and values meshed with their own and home day-care providers whose attitudes toward the child and toward childrearing and behavior (especially discipline) were like their own. They even chose day-care homes that were relatively like their own residences in terms of the variety of toys and decorations.

In addition to choosing care that fit with their own quirks and characteristics, parents were more satisfied with the care the greater was this match. Beyond this point, mothers' and fathers' satisfaction with child care diverged. Mothers were more satisfied if their children were in full-time centers, with experienced teachers and a structured program. Father preferred care by in-home caregivers (nannies or housekeepers). Neither mothers' nor fathers' satisfaction was related to the criteria day-care experts have identified as indicating high-quality care: more staff training, a higher adult–child ratio, a safe and stimulating physical environment. We see in the following chapters whether the day-care qualities apparently valued by mothers, fathers, or professional experts are better at predicting children's development.

6

Assessing Children's Development

In this chapter we describe the methods and instruments used in the study for assessing the children's behavior and development. We used a wide variety of measures and then combined them into a relatively small number of "outcome" variables. We followed this strategy because there were no standardized measures for most of the areas of development in which we were interested. Our goal was to study outcomes quite broadly and to include all the areas of psychological development in which there was the strongest reason to expect that day care would have an effect. To have restricted ourselves to single measures would have reduced the reliability of our assessments; to have restricted ourselves to a single domain of development would have produced a very limited view of the contributions of experience to children's overall development.

KINDS OF MEASURES

Structured Assessments

To assess children's social and intellectual abilities, an elaborate battery of structured and semi-structured tasks was administered each year in a laboratory playroom, and, between the two assessments, at home. These tasks included both standard and original tests of the child's cognitive development and staged encounters with unfamiliar adults and peers and with a familiar playmate. The assessments were integrated into two complex but smooth-flowing scenarios for each child.

For the laboratory assessments children came with their mothers individually to a room at the university. Despite its one-way window, the room gave the appearance of a comfortable living room, with an oriental rug on the floor, pictures on the walls, comfortable chairs for the mother, and a child-sized table and chairs for the children. Each child and mother first went through an hour-long series of assessments that included episodes of free play with toys and brief separations from the mother; interactions with two researchers, a man and a woman; tests of the child's knowledge of gender roles, emotional labels, and perspective-taking; and simulated affective incidents in which the mother or researcher acted distressed or in need of help.

At the completion of these assessments, another mother and child from the study, of the same age, sex, and type of care as the first child, arrived. During the next hour, the two children were given opportunities to interact, play, converse, and cooperate with each other. This part of the session also took approximately 1 hour. Episodes of peer interaction included semi-structured probes of the children's ability to cooperate and to play together with a variety of toys or with no toys.

Similar assessments were conducted in the child's home during the first year of the study, but in these assessments the child played with a familiar playmate who had been invited to the child's home by the mother. At this visit the researcher also administered a series of tests of the child's cognitive ability. Some of these tests were standard measures of intelligence; others were original.

To reduce the information collected in these structured assessments and to create relatively robust indexes of development involved a combination of conceptual clustering and empirical correlating. Variables were conceptualized as comprising various related components, and if the components were found to be empirically as well as conceptually related, they were combined into a single variable. When measures were not correlated with the clusters they were dropped from further analysis.

Unstructured Assessments

Although these structured and semi-structured assessments were considered the best ways of measuring children's abilities because they were equivalent for all the children regardless of their home and daytime environments, a number of additional measures of children's behavior were collected in the natural observations that we have described in chapter 3. Parents and caregivers were also used as a source of information about the child and we used a number of their ratings of the child's behavior. These were collected in interviews also described earlier in chapter 3.

The variables of children's behavior and development that were derived from all these methods of assessment are described next.

MEASURES OF CHILDREN'S DEVELOPMENT

Cognitive Development

Of central interest in the study were two variables created to capture the child's cognitive level and abilities—intellectual ability and social cognitive ability. These variables were based on both standard intelligence measures and other facets of cognitive development gleaned from the research literature. Each consisted of a number of separate tests, which were combined when it was confirmed that they were significantly interrelated. Most of the tests were designed specifically for children of this age and were considerably more detailed than any omnibus intelligence test.

Intellectual Ability

1. *Memory.* One standardized measure of intelligence that we used was the digit-span scale from the WISC-R. This scale is simply the number of digits the child can repeat back to the examiner.

2. *Language Comprehension.* The measure of language comprehension we used was devised by Huttenlocher and Levine (1990). It assessed the child's ability to understand grammatical constructions, by having the child pick out correct pictures from pairs of pictures. For example, to pick out the picture in which "the lady is following the boy" (vs. "the lady is followed by the boy"); "the man is washed by the girl" (vs. "the man is washing the girl"); "the car is pushing the truck" (vs. "the car is pushed by the truck"); "the monkey is knocked over by the bear" (vs. "the monkey is knocking over the bear").

3. *Verbal Fluency.* Verbal fluency was measured by recording the number of words given when the child was asked to name all the colors, foods, and animals he could think of.

4. *Object Recognition.* A measure of the child's ability to recognize objects pictured in unusual perspectives (Huttenlocher & Levine, 1990) was also included in the intellectual competence variable. The speed with which children could correctly match the unusual photographs—of a tire, a hat, a coffee pot, a radiator, a hammer, and so on—with photographs of these objects taken from a conventional perspective was recorded. The child's score was the average speed across items.

5. *Knowledge of Concepts.* The final measure of intellectual competence was an assessment of the child's knowledge of concepts (Huttenlocher & Levine, 1990). Children were shown pictures illustrating action concepts like kicking, pushing, squeezing, cutting, peeling, and spatial concepts like under, outside, inside, face to face, and side by side. They were asked to "put the picture with the one that's like it," that is, to match it with another picture illustrating the same concept.

These measures were collected during the structured assessments in the home. The intercorrelations among the measures ranged from .47 to .55 (Cronbach's alpha = .79). To create the variable, we converted the five measures to standard scores and summed them.

Social Cognitive Ability

To create this variable, four different kinds of social cognition were assessed in tests administered during the laboratory session.

1. *Visual and Conceptual Perspective-Taking.* The first kind of social cognition assessed was the child's ability to take the perspective of another person (the mother or the researcher). Two perspective-taking tasks were taken from Flavell (1968): (a) spatial perspective-taking (the child was asked to show a picture to the mother and then to the researcher, and was given credit for showing the picture in the appropriate orientations), and (b) perceptual perspective-taking (the child was shown a poster with identical pictures on both the front and the back. The researcher then covered one of the pictures on the side of the poster facing her, and the child was asked what pictures the researcher could then see). A third perspective-taking task, assessing conceptual perspective taking, was taken from Marvin, Greenberg, and Mossler (1976). The researcher, the mother, and the child sat around a small table on which were three toys. The mother was asked to cover her eyes while the researcher and the child picked one of the toys to be their "secret." The child was then asked whether he or she knew the "secret," whether the researcher knew the "secret," and whether the mother knew the "secret." This procedure was repeated several times with different people taking turns covering their eyes.

2. *Communication Ability.* The procedure used by Krauss and Glucksberg (1969) to assess nonegocentric communication ability in adults and older children was simplified to be appropriate for 2- to 4-year-olds. Six simple geometric forms were pasted on two sets of blocks. One set of blocks was placed in front of the child, the other in front of the mother. A screen was set up on the table between them. In the guise of a "spy game," the researcher asked the child to pick out a block showing the same pattern as the block the mother was holding. Then she asked the child to pick out one of his or her blocks and to describe it so that the mother could find it. This was repeated six times. The child's ability to describe the patterns accurately and nonegocentrically so that mother could pick out the patterns from her set of identical figures was coded.

3. *Knowledge of Gender Roles.* The third aspect of social cognition assessed in the laboratory session was the child's knowledge of gender roles. The child was shown pairs of pictures with stereotyped boys' toys and girls' toys and asked "What do boys like to play with? What do girls like to play with? What do you like to play with?" (train vs. doll, plane vs. pram, airport vs. dollhouse, etc.) The child's score was the number of gender-stereotyped choices.

4. *Emotional Labeling and Problem Solving.* A set of stimulus materials, based on work by Borke (1971), Urberg and Docherty (1976), and others, was created to assess the fourth aspect of social cognition—the child's

knowledge of emotion labels and actions. The materials consisted of cartoons, in which the main character's face was a blank, accompanied by brief "stories." The researcher showed the picture to the child and read the story and then asked the child to pick out the face showing the appropriate emotion (happy, sad, or afraid) to go with the story. For example:

"Here is a mommy and a daddy. They love each other very much. The daddy is giving the mommy a nice big kiss. How does the mommy feel?"

For some of the stories, the researcher also asked the child to tell how he or she would act if he or she were there.

"See, all these children are outside playing and having fun—except this child. She has to stay in bed all day long because she has a broken leg and a broken arm. How does she feel? If you were there, what would you do or say? How could you help the child?"

"This child was outside playing and a big, mean dog started chasing her and growling at her. How does she feel? If you were there, what would you do or say? How could you help the child?"

The child's score was the number of correct emotion labels and the number of appropriate helpful responses given.

Correlations among all these measures ranged from .24 to .72 (Cronbach's alpha = .82). To create the variable social cognition, standard scores for these four measures were calculated and combined.

Social Competence

A second facet of development that has appeared in the research literature to distinguish children with day care experience from those who are at home with their mothers is social competence—how the child deals with new social situations and unfamiliar people. For this reason, we constructed the variables that follow from our observations of the children's interactions with strangers.

Social Competence With Strangers

Six measures were combined to create a variable reflecting the child's overall social competence with strangers. The measures were all based on semi-structured activities with the researchers in the laboratory playroom. The six measures were as follows:

1. *Friendliness.* Procedures based on those used by Clarke-Stewart, Umeh, Snow, and Pederson (1980) were followed to give the child repeated opportunities to engage in interaction with the researchers. The child's behavior in these interactions was coded as (a) antisocial—avoids the researcher; (b) asocial—ignores the researcher; (c) watches the researcher with interest but does not approach or participate; (d) approaches the researcher hesitantly, participates minimally; (e) approaches the researcher

willingly, participates actively; and (f) approaches the researcher eagerly, participates enthusiastically. The coding was made for each of the following 12 separate episodes during the laboratory session: the female researcher (a) entered the room, (b) ignored the child and worked on a puzzle alone, (c) invited the child to come over, (d) invited the child to work on the puzzle, (e) invited the child to sit on her lap, (f) worked on the puzzle with the child, (g) asked the child to go with her to another room, and (h) offered the child her hand; the male researcher (a) entered the room, (b) played with blocks by himself, (c) said "Who wants to play with me?", and (d) played with the child with blocks.

2. *Cooperation in Joint Tasks.* This measure reflected the degree to which the child cooperated with the researchers in the following structured activities: putting together a puzzle, coloring a picture, building with blocks, looking at a book, playing a game. For each of these activities, the child's behavior was coded as (a) takes turns, (b) follows suggestions, and (c) contributes to the goal of the task. The frequency of any of these behaviors was counted to create the cooperation score.

3. *Comforting and Helping.* Five simulated affective incidents (Zahn-Waxler, Radke-Yarrow, & Brady-Smith, 1977; Zahn-Waxler, Radke-Yarrow, & King, 1979) were staged by the researcher, as by the mother, and coded similarly. The researcher dropped a puzzle on the floor, had trouble getting out toys and putting them away, dropped a heavy board on her toe, and hurt her hand getting out a game. The degree to which the child expressed concern and offered help or comfort was coded.

4. *Trust in "Dangerous" Situations.* A measure suggested by Gordon, Lally, Yarrow, and Beller (1973) was used to assess another element in children's social competence with a stranger—trust. This measure involved setting up situations in which children's participation demonstrated that they trusted the researcher. In the laboratory session we set up two situations in which children had to trust that the researcher would not let them fall. Children's behavior was coded when the researcher asked them to jump off a chair (first frontward, then backward, then with their eyes closed), and to walk along a balance beam (first normally, then blindfolded, then blindfolded stepping over obstacles). At each request the child was coded as (a) refuses to participate, (b) participates partially or hesitantly, or (c) participates completely and willingly. To be sure that this measure was not differentially assessing bold and timid children, the situations were repeated with the mothers rather than the researchers guiding the children. The measure of trust was the child's behavior with the researcher, controlling for behavior with the mother.

5. *Ratings of Social Competence.* At the end of the laboratory session, the researchers completed ratings of the child's behavior during the laboratory assessment on the following 5-point scales: (a) friendly, but not "promiscuous"; (b) sensitive and responsive to other's behavior; (c) may be shy, but anxiety, if any, is moderate, does not cry, fret, whine, cower, cling; (d)

self-reliant, makes decisions and exerts will when appropriate, in an appropriate manner, not blindly compliant, not dependent on others for suggestions or contact; (e) cooperative in joint activities; (f) aware of social norms and conventions, polite; (g) not hostile. The measure of social competence was the average of these ratings across researchers and scales.

6. *Rating of Child's Likeability*. Finally, at the end of the laboratory session, after 2 hours of observing, and interacting with, and assessing the child, the researchers completed a simple 5-point likeability rating, which ranged from *never want to see this child again* to *want to adopt this child*. This measure was the average of the ratings made by the two researchers.

To create the social competence with strangers variable, these six measures were converted to standard scores and combined. Correlations among the measures ranged from .29 to .65 (Cronbach's alpha = .84).

Social Competence With Visitor

Our intention with this variable was to separate the child's discomfort about being in an unfamiliar place (as was reflected in the preceding variable) from his or her ability to interact with an unfamiliar adult. To get the measure we adapted the semi-structured procedures with the stranger in the laboratory playroom to fit the home environment and conducted the assessment in the comfort of the child's own home.

1. *Friendliness*. As in the laboratory, the child was given repeated opportunities to interact with the researcher who came to visit him or her at home. The specific activities where this was possible in the home were: (a) the researcher's arrival at the child's home, (b) introductions to the mother and child, (c) giving mother and child drawing materials, (d) asking the child to show her his toys and room, (e) playing games with the child, and (f) bidding the child and mother farewell. The scoring categories were the same as in the laboratory assessment.

2. *Cooperation in Joint Tasks*. The particular tasks used for assessing cooperation in the home were the following: taking out the toys and materials for the tests, looking at a picture book, carrying a large box together, playing with a stacking toy, and building a road with blocks. The coding was the same as in the laboratory assessment.

3. *Comforting and Helping*. In the home assessment, the simulated affective incidents were the researcher's hurting her hand while she was putting away the toys and dropping a box on her toe. Coding was the same as in the laboratory.

4. *Trust in "Dangerous" Situation*. The dangerous situations used in the home assessment for assessing trust were jumping off a box backward with eyes closed and leaving the house with the researcher.

5. *Social Competence*. Social competence was measured in the home assessment by making a number of specific requests of the child and

observing his or her willingness and capability to carry them out. These requests were the following: (a) to get the researcher a Band-aid, (b) to show the researcher to his or her room and point out his or her toys, (c) to get the researcher a drink of water, (d) to deliver a message to the mother, (e) to teach the mother how to play a game, and (f) to deliver a message to the friend who was visiting.

The intercorrelations among these measures ranged from .19 to .44 (Cronbach's alpha = .63). Standard scores were summed to form the composite measure.

Relationship With Mother

A third dimension of interest in the child's development was the child's relationship with his or her mother. In recent years, much concern has focused on the question of how being in day care affects the development of infants' attachments to their mothers (Belsky, 1988; Clarke-Stewart, 1989). This debate has not been discussed here because it concerns only children who begin full-time day care in the first year or so of life. The children in the present study did not enter day care before the age of 2 years. Nevertheless, even after children have formed an attachment, there is interest in whether being in day care, especially full time, affects the quality of the mother–child relationship. For this reason we created two variables to index the child's relation with mother.

Independence From Mother

This variable reflected the child's willingness to leave the mother's side and either play alone or interact with other people. It was based on the following three measures:

1. *The Child's Proximity to the Mother*, coded on a 5-point scale as (a) on mother's lap, (b) touching mother but not in her lap, (c) within arm's reach (2 1/2 feet) of mother but not touching, (d) moderately close to mother (within 6 feet), (e) far apart from mother (more than 6 feet). These codings were made during three play periods; (a) a 7-minute free-play period at the beginning of the laboratory session, when mother and child were alone in the room; (b) a 3-minute period in which the mother and child were alone and the mother was asked not to initiate any play with the child; and (c) a 7-minute period at the beginning of the part of the laboratory session when the mother and child were with the other mother and child. These observation periods were divided into alternating 10-second periods of observing and recording the mother's and child's behavior.

2. *The Child's Physical Contact and Proximity to Mother When the Researcher Was Present.* This was coded as follows: (a) child holds on to or clings to mother, (b) child gets into or stays in chair with mother, (c) child goes to or

stays near mother, (d) child does not approach mother. The coding was made five times: when the researcher entered the laboratory playroom, invited the child to leave the room with her, and engaged the child in three different tasks.

3. *Physical Contact and Proximity to Mother After Brief Separations From the Mother.* The same coding as in the preceding measure was used after four staged separations of mother and child (when mother left the room for a phone call, when she left the room because she was coughing, when the two mothers left the room so that the two children could play alone, and when the researcher and child left the room to go look at pictures in the next room).

To form the variable of independence from mother, standard scores for the three measures were calculated and combined. Intercorrelations among the three measures ranged from .30 to .38 (Cronbach's alpha = .65).

Sociability With Mother

This variable reflected cooperative, reciprocal interaction between mother and child. It consisted of the four measures that follow.

1. *Social Interaction With Mother During the Three Mother–Child Play Periods.* The play periods were free play with mother and child alone; free play with the other mother and child present; play when mother was instructed not to initiate any play with the child. In each 10-second observation interval, the interaction between mother and child was coded as (a) social or informational conversation; (b) reciprocal interchange, not mother-dominated or child-dominated; and (c) positive affect (smiling, laughing).

2. *Positive Interaction and Greeting After Mother–Child Separations.* After each of the four separations of mother and child, the child's behavior was coded as (a) smiles or speaks in greeting, (b) avoids or turns away from, (c) acts angry toward mother. The first of these was coded positively; the second two, negatively.

3. *Cooperation With the Mother in a Structured Task.* During the laboratory session, the mother and child were asked to draw a face together on an easel, with magic markers. The child's participation was coded as (a) cooperates with mother, (b) takes turns drawing, (c) follows the mother's suggestions, (d) draws complementary parts of the face. The frequency of these codes was the score.

4. *Helping and Comforting Mother When She Needed It.* Three "simulated affective incidents" with the mother were staged during the laboratory session. The mother was instructed to knock over a stack of magazines, bump her elbow, and act out a "coughing fit." For each of these incidents, the child's behavior was coded as (a) no response, (b) approaches only, (c) expresses concern verbally, (d) comforts or helps physically.

To create the variable sociability with mother, standard scores for each of these measures were calculated and combined. The correlations among the measures ranged from .29 to .41, Cronbach's alpha = .55).

Compliance

A fourth domain in the child's behavior that has been found in previous research to be related to participation in day care is the child's willingness to comply with an adult authority. Research has suggested that children in day care are not as obedient with adults as are children who are at home with their parents. Because there is no standard assessment of compliance, we included several measures of this kind of behavior in our study.

Child's General Competence at Home

One measure of the child's compliance was collected by means of a checklist filled out at the end of the dinnertime observation. This variable consisted of the sum of eight scales on this checklist, which reflected the child's obedience, self-confidence, sociability, autonomy, assertiveness, playfulness, cheerfulness, and nonaggression. Each of these scales (from Baumrind, 1967) was based on a 7-point behavioral checklist with +, −, and 0 ratings for each item. For example, the autonomy scale consisted of the following items:

1. willing to pursue tasks alone versus needs support of others
2. has a mind of his own versus is suggestible
3. argues with people to get point across versus backs down whenever opposed
4. questions adult authority—says "no"—when has a good reason versus does not question adult authority
5. expresses preferences for certain activities over others versus does not express preference
6. self-reliant in dealing with adults versus dependent on adults
7. spends time alone, working or playing versus always wants to be with people.

The ratings for each scale were summed to form this variable. A measure of internal consistency, Cronbach's alpha, was calculated and found to be = .81.

Compliance With Parents

A second measure of compliance was taken from the unstructured observations made at home at dinnertime. The measure consisted of the proportion of the parents' demands during the dinnertime observation with which the child complied ($r = .50$).

Compliance With Requests

A third variable indexing the child's compliance was focused on the child's compliance with requests. It consisted of the following measures:

1. To assess the child's willingness to comply with specific requests, we incorporated into the assessment sessions in the laboratory and semi-structured home visits a number of requests by the mother and the researcher for the child to put away the toys or research materials after playing with them. The measure coded from these probes was the proportion of these requests with which the child complied without urging.

2. The second measure that was included in this variable was the sum of the following 9-point ratings, made by mothers and by fathers about their child:

- obedient, cooperative, always does what he or she is told;
- quiet, peaceful, no trouble;
- likes doing things by himself or herself, assertive, has a mind of his or her own, stands up for his or her rights (scored in negative direction);
- adventurous, outgoing (scored in negative direction);
- disobedient to parents (scored in negative direction).

This information was collected by means of questionnaires given to the parents.

The range of intercorrelations among the component measures forming this variable was from .38 to .49; mean $r = .42$ (Cronbach's alpha = .74).

Peer Relations

Finally, the last area of the child's development on which we focused was the child's interactions with other children. We divided this into positive and negative interaction, with familiar and unfamiliar peers.

Social Competence With Unfamiliar Peer

The assessment of the child's social competence with an unfamiliar peer was based on observations of the child's interactions with the unfamiliar child who came to the laboratory playroom, during both free play and structured activities. The variable of social competence with the unfamiliar peer consisted of the following:

1. *Positive Interaction With Unfamiliar Peer.* This measure was taken during four 5-minute free-play episodes: with an assortment of toys, a set of blocks, a jack-in-the-box, and without toys. For the first two episodes, the mothers were present; for the second two, they were absent. Coding was done in 10-second intervals (10 seconds of observation, 10 seconds of

recording). In each 10-second interval the incidence of the following kinds of positive social behavior (which were taken from the ethological literature on peer interaction; e.g., Blurton Jones, 1972; Eckerman, Whatley, & Kutz, 1975; Garvey, 1974; Smith & Connolly, 1972) were coded: talk, play, affection, imitation, cooperation, giving, sharing, positive affect. The child's score was the total frequency of these kinds of behavior which he or she initiated toward the unfamiliar peer.

2. *Cooperation in Joint Tasks.* The two children were also given several opportunities to interact together in more structured activities: building a tower and a road with blocks, coloring a picture, playing "train." This last activity was a cooperative task based loosely on procedures suggested by S. Kagan and Madsen (1971). It was necessary in the task for the children to take turns being the "train driver" or the "bridgekeeper," and only the train driver got to keep the marbles that the train was delivering. The children's willingness and ability to participate cooperatively and to join efforts with the other child in these tasks was coded.

The intercorrelations among the measures of cooperation and the measure of positive peer interaction ranged from .33 to .37 (Cronbach's alpha = .52).

Social Competence With Familiar Peer

As in the laboratory assessment of the child's social competence with an unfamiliar peer, the variable of social competence with a familiar peer was based on the observation of positive and cooperative interaction with the familiar child who was invited to come to the child's home to play. This variable consisted of the following two measures:

1. *Positive Social Interaction* (talk, play, affection, etc.) during free play (with a stacking toy and blocks).
2. *Cooperation in a More Structured Task* (building a road together with blocks).

The correlation between the two measures was .38.

Negative Behavior With Unfamiliar Peer

During the same episodes of free play and structured play in the laboratory procedure that were coded for positive interaction with the unfamiliar peer, we coded the child's negative behavior toward the peer. The measure then calculated to form the basis of this variable was the frequency of occurrence of the following kinds of negative behavior: taking away toys from the peer, physically controlling the peer's actions, saying negative things to the peer, refusing the peer's overtures or requests, withdrawing from or avoiding the peer. (Hitting was not observed in any laboratory session.)

Aggression Toward Peers

Because aggressive acts were not observed during our semi-structured observations, we also included a measure of the child's naturally occurring aggression in the daytime observations. This measure was the frequency of aggressive acts by the child directed toward peers during the observation: hitting, kicking, pinching, biting, threatening, grabbing toy away (inter-observer $r = .99$). The variable was calculated only for children who had a peer present during the observation.

VALIDITY OF MEASURES

To explore the validity of these variables several analyses were carried out. It was especially important to conduct such analyses because all the outcome variables and many of the measures on which they were based were original. The first such analysis was to see how the variables were related to age. (These correlations are presented in Table 6.1.) It would be expected that if the variables were indexing development, rather than simply indicating differences in children's behavior, they should be significantly correlated with age. The analyses showed that all the variables except the observational measures of compliance to parents and aggression to peers were related to the child's age, thus giving us some confidence that they did reflect development.

A second kind of analysis to explore the validity of the "outcome" variables was to look at how these variables were related to other measures of the child's behavior. In the daytime and dinnertime observations we had collected a number of measures of children's behavior that could be used in such analyses. These measures were the following:

Talking
The number of utterances by the child during the observation directed toward mother, father, etc. (interobserver $r = .79$).
Touching Adult
The amount of touching the child initiated toward an adult during the observation ($r = .80$).
Avoiding Adult
The number of times during the observation that the child actively avoided physical contact with an adult ($r = .66$).
Complying With Caregiver
The proportion of the caregivers' demands during the daytime observation with which the child complied ($r = .50$).
Demands
The number of verbal or nonverbal demands (for objects, food, help, attention, etc.) that the child directed to an adult during the observation ($r = .59$).

TABLE 6.1
Correlations[a] Among Child Variables

	Intellect. Ability	Social Cognition	Social/ Stranger	Social/ Visitor	Indepen- dence	Social/ Mother	General Competence	Comply/ Requests	Comply/ Parents	Social/ Peer	Social/ Friend	Negative/ Peer	Aggres- sive
Cognitive Ability													
Intellectual ability	.29***	.29***	.20*	.40***	•	.18*	•	•	.19*	.16*	•	−.20*	−.22**
Social cognitive ability	.29***	.36***b	.29***	.25**	.19*	.13+	.24**	•	•	•	•	•	−.27**
Social Competence													
Social competence with strangers	.20*	.29***	.28***	.36***	.50***	.37***	.16*	−.38***	•	.33***	•	•	•
Social competence with visitor	.40***	.40***	.36***	•	.18*	.17*	•	−.27**	•	.18*	.24**	•	−.24**
Independence from mother	•	.19*	.50***	.18*	.30***	.18*	.20*	−.25**	•	.27**	•	•	•
Relationship with Mother													
Sociability with mother	.18*	.18*	.37***	.17*	.18*	.24**	.15+	•	•	.17*	•	•	•
Compliance with Adults													
General competence at home	•	.13+	.16*	•	.20**	.15+	•	•	.22**	•	•	.15+	•
Compliance with requests	.24**	.24**	−.38***	−.27**	−.25**	•	•	.57***	.17*	•	•	−.22**	•
Compliance with parents	•	•	•	•	•	•	.22**	.17*	•	•	•	−.20*	•
Interaction with Peers													
Social competence with unfamiliar peer	.19*	.16*	.33***	.18*	.27**	.17*	•	•	•	•	•	•	−.20*
Social competence with friend	•	•	•	.24**	•	•	•	•	•	•	•	•	•

(continued)

TABLE 6.1 (continued)

	Intellect. Ability	Social Cognition	Social/ Stranger	Social/ Visitor	Indepen- dence	Social/ Mother	General Competence	Comply/ Requests	Comply/ Parents	Social/ Peer	Social/ Friend	Negative/ Peer	Aggres- sive
Interaction with Peers (continued)													
Negative behavior with unfamiliar peer	-.20*	•	•	•	•	•	•	-.22**	-.20*	•	•	—	•
Aggression toward peers	-.22**	-.27**	•	-.24*	•	•	•	•	•	•	•	•	.38***
Age	.69***	.70***	.38***	.52****	.40***	.27**	.26**	-.21**	•	.55***	•	-.29***	•
Observed Behavior with Parents													
Touches mother at dinnertime observation	-.13+	-.25**	-.19*	•	-.16*	•	•	•	•	•	•	•	•
Talks to mother	•	•	•	•	•	.16*	•	•	•	•	•	•	•
Avoids mother	•	•	•	•	.13+	•	•	•	•	•	•	•	•
Refuses mother's or father's request	-.13+	•	•	.13+	.14+	•	•	•	-.29***	•	•	.14*	•
Observed Behavior with Caregivers													
Touches caregiver in daytime observation	-.24**	•	•	•	-.19*	•	-.23**	•	•	•	•	-.22**	•
Talks to caregiver	•	.19*	•	•	•	•	•	•	•	•	•	-.19*	•
Refuses caregiver's requests	•	•	•	•	•	.27**	•	•	•	•	•	•	•
Complies with caregiver's requests	•	.19*	.18*	.18*	-.21**	•	.18*	.15+	.23**	•	.18*	-.23**	•

(continued)

TABLE 6.1 (continued)

	Intellect. Ability	Social Cognition	Social/ Stranger	Social/ Visitor	Indepen-dence	Social/ Mother	General Competence	Comply/ Requests	Comply/ Parents	Social/ Peer	Social/ Friend	Negative/ Peer	Aggres-sive
Demandingness													
Demanding during daytime or dinnertime observations													
	−.12+	−.33***	.13+	•	•	•	−.30***	•	−.22**	.15+	•	.14+	.23**
Negativity during daytime or dinnertime observations													
	−.21**	−.30***	•	−.17*	.16*	•	−.14+	•	•	•	•	•	.30***
Difficult temperament													
	−.17	−.23**	−.14+	−.38***	.27***	•	−.24**	.15+	•	•	•	•	•
Observed Behavior with Peers													
Touches peer in daytime observation													
	•	•	−.33***	•	•	−.24**	•	•	•	−.21**	•	•	•
Talks to peer													
	.40***	.20*	.16*	.32***	•	.22**	•	•	•	.52***	•	.31***	•

[a]All correlations except for those with age have age partialled out.

[b]Underlined correlations are of the child variable in Year 1 × the same child variable in Year 2.

•$p > .10$. $+ p < .10$. *$p < .05$. **$p < .01$. ***$p < .001$. (two-tailed tests)

Demanding
The proportion of the child's utterances during the observation that were demanding ($r = .90$).
Negativity
The amount of negative behavior from the child during the observation: fretting, crying, whining, complaining ($r = .73$).
Refusing
The proportion of requests with which the child refused to comply during the observation ($r = .79$).

In addition to these observation variables, we collected another measure from the mothers that could be used to validate our outcome variables. The measure was the following:

Child's Difficult Temperament
This variable was derived from the Carey Temperament Questionnaire (Carey & McDevitt, 1978), which mothers completed at the conclusion of the study. Mothers indicated on 44 7-point scales, from 1 = *hardly ever* to 7 = *almost always*, how often their child acted in the ways described. For example: "When upset or annoyed with a task, my child may throw it down, cry, yell, or slam the door." "When playing with other children my child often argues with them." "When my child gets angry about something it is difficult to sidetrack him or her." "My child has difficulty in adjusting to the rules of another household if they are different from those at home." A high score indicated that the child had a difficult temperament. (Cronbach's alpha = .84.)

The outcome variables were then correlated with these measures of the child's observed behavior (as can be seen in Table 6.1). These analyses, too, supported the validity of our indexes of children's development. Children who scored high on cognitive abilities (intellectual ability and social cognition) were more verbal (talked more to caregivers and peers). Children who were socially competent with strangers in the structured assessments were less negative, difficult, and physically dependent (less likely to initiate physical contact with their mothers or caregivers), and more compliant with their caregivers' requests. Children who maintained more distance from their mothers in the laboratory initiated less physical contact with them at home and also refused more of their requests. Children who were high in social reciprocity with their mothers in the laboratory talked to them more at home. Children who were assessed as being more compliant in the laboratory or at home at dinnertime were less difficult, negative, and demanding and more compliant in their daytime observations as well. Children who interacted more with the unfamiliar peer in the laboratory (both positively and negatively) talked more to other children during their naturally occurring daytime observations.

These analyses, then, suggest that the outcome variables are valid and support their use. It is not possible to prove that all of these variables reflect good or "optimal" development, and no such claims are made here. They are, however, comparable to the usual indices of child development used in psychological research.

STABILITY OF MEASURES

Finally, to explore the reliability of the outcome variables, we analyzed their stability across time by calculating the cross-time correlations for those variables that were measured twice, 1 year apart. (The results of these analyses are also found in Table 6.1; these are the underlined coefficients on the diagonal.) Of the 10 repeated variables, 6 were significantly correlated at the two assessments: social cognitive ability, social competence with strangers, independence from mother, sociability with mother, compliance with requests, and aggression toward peers [rs = .24 ($p < .01$) to .57 ($p < .001$)]. Two kinds of behavior were not correlated from one year to the next. One was compliant behavior with parents (compliance with parents and general competence at home). The reason that these two measures of compliance were not significantly correlated from one year to the next may be that they were based on unstructured observations; the more structured measure of compliance was indeed highly correlated from Year 1 to Year 2. The second kind of behavior that was not highly correlated across annual assessments was social behavior with an unfamiliar peer (social competence with unfamiliar peer and negative behavior with unfamiliar peer). The reason that these variables were not related probably reflects the substantial shifts in social competence with peers over these preschool years.

In brief, then, as far as we could determine, the measures we had collected and the variables we had created to reflect children's behavior and development did seem to be robust, valid, and reliable. In the next chapters we investigate just how each of these variables was related to the child's experiences at home and in day care.

7

Cognitive Development: Family Predictors

This chapter examines the relations between children's experiences at home and their cognitive development. There were two variables identified in the study that reflected children's cognitive development—intellectual ability (digit-span memory, language comprehension, verbal fluency, object recognition, and knowledge of concepts) and social cognitive ability (visual and conceptual perspective taking, nonegocentric communication, knowledge of gender roles, and ability to label emotions and solve hypothetical emotional problems). As we saw in chapter 6 (Table 6.1), these two variables were significantly correlated with each other.

A variety of analyses were performed to relate these two "outcome" variables to the variables reflecting children's experiences: simple correlations, curvilinear analyses, regression analyses, and path analyses. These analyses were conducted both contemporaneously and across time.

We begin our presentation of the results of these analyses at the most elementary level by examining correlations between children's experiences and their cognitive abilities, and then build up to the results of more complex multivariate analyses. The reason for presenting the details of these simple analyses is that sometimes, in the rush to combine variables and run the most powerful possible statistical analyses, researchers lose the trees in the forest. We thought that it was helpful to look at relations first at the level of actual observations, before combining them into complex statistical models. Our intention in presenting these results was not to dwell on any single statistically significant correlation coefficients, but to look for patterns among the correlations—patterns that were similar for the two measures of cognitive development, for related aspects of the environment, and for identical assessments made 1 year apart. We used this strategy of looking for patterns of correlations rather than simply applying a conservative statistical procedure for multiple comparison (e.g., Bonferroni) because it made sense conceptually to do so and because, as it turned out, the size of most of the correlation coefficients we obtained was quite modest.

EXPERIENCES AT HOME

The correlations between the cognitive variables and the set of variables reflecting children's experiences at home are presented in Table 7.1, organized according to the family factors described in chapter 4. Because the dependent variables reflecting cognitive development were strongly correlated with the child's age at the time of the assessment, for these and all other analyses, the child's age was partialled out.

Interaction With Father

One clear pattern appearing in these correlations was the significant association between the children's cognitive development and the amount of interaction they had with their fathers. At home with their families at dinnertime, children who were more cognitively advanced interacted with their fathers more than children who were less advanced. Their fathers played, talked, taught, and read to them more and reported that they were more involved in child care. Their interactions with the children were less likely to be physical (and more likely to be verbal).

We cannot tell from these correlations whether fathers were, in these ways, fostering their children's development, or merely responding to their advanced abilities. However, there were some suggestions in the data that the former was true. For one thing, if fathers were merely responding to their children's advanced development by talking and teaching them more, we would have expected these paternal behaviors to be positively correlated with the child's age. That is, fathers would have talked, played, read to older children more than to younger ones. This was not the case, however, as we discussed in chapter 4 (see Table A.2 in the appendix). This is one hint that the frequency of father's talking, playing, and reading is more likely to be a source of children's cognitive advance than a reflection of their developmental maturity. A second hint was found when we examined the correlation between these paternal behaviors observed in the first year of the study and the child's cognitive performance in the second year (with the child's cognitive performance in the first year partialled out). Higher scores in social cognition in Year 2 were predicted by more interaction with the father in Year 1 [$r = .33$ ($p < .05$)]. These two pieces of evidence, then, support the view that fathers' stimulating behavior fosters children's cognitive development.

The fact that fathers of less advanced children were more likely to interact with them physically rather then verbally was probably a reflection of these children's immaturity, not a cause of delayed development. Fathers were observed to be more physical in their interactions with younger children (Table A.2, appendix), and there were no significant cross-time correlations between physical interaction and cognition.

The link between children's cognitive ability and more frequent interaction with the father is reminiscent of the literature on absent fathers (see Biller, 1974). Children without fathers at home, this literature revealed, did more poorly on tests of intelligence and school performance. In more recent research, specific associations with fathers' behavior have been obtained by Ackerman-Ross and Khanna (1989) for father's language activity time, by A. E. Gottfried et al. (1987), Radin (1976), Reis and Gold (1977), and Ruopp et al. (1979) for interaction with father, and by Epstein and Radin (1975), Jordan et al. (1975), and Radin (1973, 1976) for father's warmth and nurturance.

Interaction With Mother

At the same time as they interacted more with their fathers, the children whose cognitive development was most advanced interacted less with their mothers. Their mothers touched, hugged, played, taught, and helped them less, talked to them less, made fewer demands of them, and gave them objects less often during the dinnertime observations than did the mothers of less advanced children. At first glance, this result is somewhat surprising. In previous studies it has been common to find a positive linear relation between children's intellectual ability and interaction with the mother, particularly verbal interaction[1] (e.g., Clarke-Stewart, 1973; Huttenlocher et al., 1991; Olson, Bates, & Kaskie, 1992). Perhaps the time of day and context for the family interactions in the present study accounts for this difference. Mothers are busiest at dinnertime and may therefore be "neglecting" more cognitively advanced children who can get along on their own. At night mothers played, talked, taught, made demands, and expressed affection to the children less than they did during a comparable period of observation during the day [$Fs(1, 82) = 5.0$ ($p < .05$) to 14.8 ($p < .001$)]. In other studies, researchers have collected data on mother–child interaction at less hectic, more "convenient" times at which it may be more reasonable to expect mothers to chat with their youngsters. This difference should be taken into account in trying to understand why we found that mothers of more cognitively advanced children interacted less with them, in general, during this family-time observation.

---

[1] Adding together the frequency of maternal and paternal talk to the child and correlating this with children's cognitive scores did not produce a positive relation with "parental" talk, because fathers talked to the children so much less than mothers did that their contribution (although it had relative significance, i.e., was by itself positively correlated with children's intellectual ability) did not balance things out.

Another reason that these mothers were not interacting with cognitively advanced children was that these children were spending more time interacting with their fathers. Recall (from chapter 4) that the amount of interaction the child had with the two parents at night was complementary, so that if the father was interacting with the child a great deal the mother interacted less. It may not be, therefore, that interacting with mother had any negative effect but that interacting with father had distinct advantages. Research by Masur and Gleason (1980) suggests that interaction with the father is potentially more important than interaction with the mother for stimulating cognitive development. In their study, fathers, compared with mothers, were more cognitively and linguistically stimulating with their preschool children (used more different terms) and demanding (requested labels and functions) when observed in semistructured play. The children were observed to produce more different words in their interactions with their fathers.

But maybe we are dismissing the importance of the mother's behavior too quickly. Perhaps there are relations with children's cognitive development that do not show up in simple correlations. To examine further the nature of the associations between children's cognitive development and their mothers' behavior, we looked for curvilinear relations, using a standard regression approach with a squared independent term to test the curvilinear effect. The one significant curvilinear relation that was replicated in the first- and second-year assessments was with the mother's language to the child. How much the mother talked to the child was curvilinearly related to the child's cognitive ability ($ps < .03$ in Year 1, $< .01$ in Year 2): mothers spoke less to children who were most advanced in cognitive development and to children who were least advanced.

How is this curvilinear association to be interpreted? The fact that mothers interacted less with more cognitively advanced children probably reflects the greater maturity of these children; recall that all these kinds of maternal behavior became less frequent as children got older. Note also that except for physical interaction (help, affection, and contact), the negative relation with maternal interaction appeared only in the second year of the study, with older children. Examining correlations across time revealed that mothers of children who were advanced in Year 1 talked to them less in Year 2 [$r = -.29$ ($p < .05$)], further supporting this suggestion that the negative link between cognitive development and maternal talk was the result of mothers giving their children more independence as they mature. On the other hand, the fact that mothers of children who were least advanced spoke less to them may indicate that the development of these children was being hampered by the lack of verbal stimulation from the mother. Cross-time correlations showed that when mothers talked more to the child in Year 1 children's cognitive performance was advanced in Year 2 [$r = .24$ ($p < .05$)]. Thus, we see in this curvilinear relation evidence that how much mothers interact with their children is both a cause and a consequence of children's development.

Maternal Involvement

Our finding of negative and curvilinear links with maternal behavior is in apparent disagreement not only with the studies reporting positive associations with the frequency of maternal stimulation, but also with studies documenting a positive linear relation between cognitive development and mothers' "involvement" with their children. In these other studies, however, the measures of maternal involvement have been qualitative rather than quantitative. They have included whether or not the mother watches, plays, talks, teaches or encourages the child during an informal chat with an interviewer (Bradley, 1986; Bradley et al., 1989; A. W. Gottfried, 1984) and how positively affective her interaction with the child is (Barocas et al., 1991; Estrada et al., 1987; Jennings & Connors, 1989). We did not collect precisely equivalent measures of maternal involvement in our study. However, we did find that somewhat comparable variables reflecting the proportion of the mothers' interaction that was affectionate (affectionate tactual contact divided by total interaction) or physical (physical contact divided by total interaction) were negatively, not positively, related to children's intellectual ability.[2, 3] For this sample, observed at this time of day, then, children's cognitive performance was not predicted by more maternal involvement in the ways that we measured it.

There was a link between children's cognitive development and their mother's positive attitude toward them, another variable that reflects maternal involvement. But this link did not suggest that mothers were contributing to their children's development through more positive involvement. The link was with the gain in children's cognitive performance—but not in the direction of mothers influencing children. The children who made the greatest gains in cognition over the year of the study were found to have mothers who expressed more positive attitudes toward them in the second year [$r = .31$ ($p < .01$)]. Thus, the mother's positive and accepting attitude appears to be a consequence of the children's accelerated development rather than a cause.

---

[2]r with affectionate interaction $= -.18$ ($p < .05$)

[3]Analyses of covariance were used to explore differences in predictions from all the family variables for children in different socioeconomic levels. These analyses revealed few interactions with SES that were significant or consistent from Year 1 to Year 2. The only consistent difference was that parents'—both mothers' and fathers'—expressions of affection to the child were negatively related to cognitive development in lower SES families ($r = -.34$) and positively related in high SES families ($r = .30$; significance of interaction term $= .01$).

Parents Reading and Giving Lessons

There was only one kind of maternal behavior that was more frequent for children with higher cognitive levels and unequivocally related to accelerated development. This was the amount of time that the mother spent reading stories to the child during the 2-hour observation before the child's bedtime. In this way the mother's behavior paralleled that of the father. The amount both the mother and the father read to the child was associated with the child's advanced cognitive development.[4] The amount of time the parents spent actually giving a "lesson" to the child was also related to advanced cognitive development, although not as consistently as reading.

Reading to the child, by mother or by father, did not occur in every home, however. Only 37 fathers and 59 mothers in the first year, and 32 fathers and 48 mothers in the second year read to their children during the evening observation. A question of interest was whether children benefited by having their parents read to them at all—no matter how much—or whether the more the parents read to the children the more advanced was the children's development. Further analyses to explore these two possibilities were performed. Correlations calculated for just the sample of children whose parents did read to them showed that among these children, the more the parents read the higher were the children's cognitive scores [r for fathers = .27 ($p < .05$), r for mothers = .28 ($p < .01$)]. The same was true for lessons [$r = .30$ ($p < .01$)]. Thus, for these variables there was evidence that within the limits observed (the maximum being less than 30 minutes in the 2-hour observation), more reading or lessons may have had a beneficial effect on children's cognitive development. A link with reading has also been observed in other research, although perhaps not as pointedly. Reading was included in the HOME inventory scale that was most closely correlated with children's intelligence (Bradley et al., 1989; A. W. Gottfried & Gottfried, 1984) and showed up as a significant predictor of children's intellectual ability when studied separately by Laosa (1982) and Milner (1951).

A suggestion that reading actually contributes to children's cognitive development and is not just associated with it is found in cross-time correlations. Higher cognitive scores in Year 2 and a greater gain in cognition between Year 1 and Year 2 (both analyses with Year 1 cognition partialled out) were predicted by more reading by the mother in Year 1 [rs = .25, .28 ($p < .05$)]. (There was no correlation between children's cognitive performance in Year 1 and mother's reading in Year 2; $r = -.02$.)

---

[4]The correlation between children's intellectual performance and the sum of their mother's and father's reading was higher than the correlation with either parent's reading alone [$r = .28$ ($p < .001$)].

Discipline

Another pattern appearing in the correlations between cognitive development and parents' behavior, in which associations for mothers and fathers were parallel, involved discipline: controlling, punishing, demanding, requesting. More cognitively advanced youngsters consistently experienced less parental discipline in the evening observation. Their parents, particularly their mothers, made fewer demands, exerted less control, were less demanding relative to other kinds of behavior, and offered the children more choices. This was not a developmental phenomenon; younger children received both more choices and more control and neither mother's nor father's demanding style was related to the child's age. The link between cognitive ability and discipline was consistent in both years, for both measures of cognitive development, and remained significant even when the frequency of the child's demands was partialled out. It was also significantly related to the child's development over time. Higher cognition in Year 2 and the gain in cognition from Year 1 to Year 2 (with Year 1 social cognition partialled out) were predicted by less parental discipline in Year 1 [$rs = -.32, -.24$ ($p < .05$)]. (There was no correlation between cognition in Year 1 and discipline in Year 2; $r = -.03$.)

This link between parents' controlling discipline and children's cognitive development also has been observed before, for mothers (Barnard et al., 1984; Hess & McDevitt, 1984; Nelson, 1973; Olson et al., 1992; Scarr et al., 1989) and fathers (Epstein & Radin, 1975; Radin, 1976). In the present study there was no evidence that too little discipline was related to less advanced cognitive development, as there was in a study by Roberts (1986), however. We found no curvilinear relation with this variable. Perhaps this was because our sample did not include permissively neglectful parents; perhaps the time we sampled parents' behavior—the end of the day—did not permit parents to be excessively permissive.

A significant association with the style of parental behavior that might be considered complementary to discipline was also found in the present study. The parents of children with advanced cognitive development were more verbally responsive than the parents of children with less advanced development. Other studies confirm this relation between children's intellectual development and their mothers' verbal responsiveness (Barnard et al., 1984; Bradley et al., 1989; A. W. Gottfried, 1984; Levenstein, 1986; Olson et al., 1986).

FAMILY ENVIRONMENTS

Parents' Backgrounds

In addition to these correlations with parents' behavior, there were significant relations between children's cognitive development and parents' background characteristics. Children with higher levels of cognitive ability, measured in Year 1 or Year 2, came from families of higher SES, in which parents, especially mothers, had higher levels of education. Their mothers were more likely to work,[5] more career oriented, and had more household help, and the parents spent more money on day care. Many of these relations were predictable. Previous research has demonstrated that children's cognitive ability is related to the family's SES in general and to the mother's education in particular (e.g., Bradley et al., 1989; Desai et al., 1989; Scarr, 1993). They have found that children achieve more in school if their mothers have been employed during their preschool years (Vandell & Ramanan, 1992). In the present study, in addition, variables that have not been measured before, the mother's childrearing expertise and the father's knowledge of childrearing, were also related to advanced cognitive development, particularly with younger children (2- to 3-years-olds).

Associations with parents' backgrounds were found not only for the level of children's cognitive ability but also for the gains in cognitive development that the children made over the course of the year. Children who made the largest gains came from families of high SES, in which mothers had more training in child development and were more career oriented [rs for gain in social cognition with Year 1 cognition partialled out = .27 ($p < .01$), .25 ($p < .01$), .18 ($p < .05$), respectively]. Regression analyses predicting cognitive gains from family variables confirmed that these variables had an independent effect on children's gains in social cognition beyond the contributions of other family variables [$F = 3.6$ ($p < .01$)].

Because of these strong links between children's cognitive performance and parents' backgrounds, it is possible that the correlations with parents' behavior might be a mere by-product of the associations between the ability levels of parents and children. Perhaps it is parents' own intellectual level that accounts for the correlations observed between the child's intellectual performance and the parents' behaviors and attitudes. To examine this possibility, partial correlations, partialling out the family's SES, as a proxy for parents' intellectual abilities, were calculated for all the variables listed in Table 7.1. All the associations remained equally strong.[6]

Mother's Work

In fact, when the influence of SES was partialled out, this strengthened the association between children's cognitive performance and the mother's work schedule. The trend in Table 7.1 suggesting that the more hours the

---

[5]ANOVA for mother work status significant only for social cognition in Year 1[$F = 2.3$ ($p < .05$) $Ms = .28$ ($n = 43$), .58 ($n = 101$)].

[6]Correlation coefficients in the table were increased or decreased by .00 to .04.

TABLE 7.1
Correlations[a] Between Children's Cognitive Development and Family Variables

Family Variables	Cognitive Development			
	Intellectual Ability		Social Cognitive Ability	
	Year 1	Year 2	Year 1	Year 2
Family Background				
Socioeconomic status	.26**		.19*	.30**
Father's education	.14+		•	.26**
Father's knowledge of development	.29**		•	•
Father in day care as child	•		.17*	•
Mother in day care as child	•		.28*	.13+
Working Mother	•	•	.30***	.18*
Mother's education	.29**		.24**	.31**
Mother's work hours	•	−.20*	•	•
Mother's career orientation	•		.19*	.21*
Household help	•		•	.17*
Money for day care/month	.18*		.23**	
Mother's traditional values	•		−.17*	•
Father's traditional values	•		•	•
Father's involvement in child care	•	•	.17*	•
Mother's involvement in child care	•	•	•	•
Mother's Child-Rearing Expertise	.13+		.13+	.17*
Mother's child-care training	.14+		•	•
Mother's child-care experience	•		.16*	.19*
Mother's knowledge of development	•		•	•
Father's Physical Contact	•	•	•	•
Father touching	•	•	•	•
Father touching, proportion	•	−.16*	•	•
Father affection	.15+		•	•
Father's Interaction	.18*	.22*	•	.17
Father playing	.14+	.20*	•	.14
Father talking	.17*	.19*	•	•
Mother's Physical Contact	−.18*	−.14+	−.22**	•
Mother touching	−.18*	−.26*	−.17*	•
Mother touching, proportion	−.20**	•	−.22**	•
Mother affection	−.18*	•	−.20**	•
Mother helping child	−.21*	•	−.13+	•
Mother's Interaction	•	−.37***	•	•
Mother playing	•	−.19*	−.16*	•
Mother talking	•	−.40**	•	•
Parents' Reading				
Father reading	.24**	.22**	•	•
Mother reading	.20**	•	•	.14
Parents' Discipline	−.24**	−.27**	−.29***	•
Parent offering choice	.15+	.22*	.16*	.16*
Mother demands	−.20**	−.40**	−.20**	•
Mother demanding	−.20**	•	−.23**	•
Mother control	−.16*	−.21**	−.21**	•
Father demands	•	•	•	•
Father demanding	−.14+	−.22*	•	•
Father control	−.13+	•	−.17*	−.21**
Negative affect	−.24**	•	−.23**	•

(continued)

TABLE 7.1 *(continued)*

Family Variables	Cognitive Development			
	Intellectual Ability		Social Cognitive Ability	
	Year 1	Year 2	Year 1	Year 2
Parents' Teaching	•	•	•	•
Mother teaching	•	− .28**	•	•
Mother teaching, proportion	•	− .16*	•	.14
Father teaching	.16*	•	•	•
Father teaching, proportion	•	•	•	•
Parent giving lesson	.16*	•	•	•
Parents' Responsiveness	•	•	•	•
Parent appropriate responses	•	− .15$^+$	•	•
Parent verbal responsiveness	.19*	•	.17*	•
Parent giving object	•	− .22*	•	•
Positive affect	•	•	•	•
Parents' Attitudes				
Father's expectations for child	•		•	•
Father's positive attitude to child	− .21*		•	•
Mother's expectations for child	•		.16*	.16
Mother's positive attitude to child	•		•	•
Mother's overall role satisfaction	•		•	•
Mother's satisfaction as mother	•		•	•
Mother's alienation	•		•	− .15$^+$
Child Activities				
Child alone	•	•	•	•
Child playing with object	•	•	•	•
Child watching TV	•	•	•	•
Child watching parent	− .22**	− .25**	− .15$^+$	− .25*
Family Environment				
Number of people at home	•	•	•	•
Extended family	•		•	•
Geographic stability	•		•	•
Family changes	•		.19*	
Siblings	.20*		•	•
Brothers	.32*		•	.16
Sisters	•		•	•
Older siblings	•		•	•
Younger siblings	•		− .15$^+$	•
Sibling interaction (for total sample)	.14$^+$	•	•	•
Sibling interaction (for subsample with siblings)	.20*	.20*	•	.20*
Sibling aggression	•	•	•	•
Physical Environment				
Stimulating home	.29***	.21*	.15$^+$	•
Decoration	.20*	.17*	.18*	•
Toys	.28**	.18*	•	•
Hazardous home	•	•	•	•
Mess	•	•	− .13$^+$	•
Hazards	•	•	•	•
R [b]	.65***	.65***	.56***	.43$^+$

^{a}With child's age partialled out.

^{b}These regression coefficients are for the regression analyses described in the text. The selected set of variables they included is listed there.

•p > .10. ^+p < .10. *p < .05. **p < .01. ***p < .001. (Two-tailed tests) mother worked the worse her child did on our tests of intellectual abilities was supported when the contribution of SES was removed [$rs = -.17$ ($p < .05$) in Year 1; $-.25$ ($p < .01$) in Year 2].

But this seems inconsistent with the finding that more career-oriented mothers had children with advanced development. Working more hours and being career oriented were maternal variables that both appeared in the "working mother" factor (discussed in chapter 4), and correlational analyses confirmed that more career-oriented mothers worked more hours [$r = .37$ ($p < .01$)]. Curvilinear analyses shed more light on the negative association with mother's work hours. They revealed a significant inverted-U shaped relation between mother's work hours and children's cognitive development: Children whose mothers worked part time (10 to 30 hours per week) performed at higher levels ($M = .30$) than children whose mothers did not work ($M = -.02$) or who worked full time (more than 30 hours per week) [$M = -.19$; $F(2, 141) = 4.6$ ($p < .01$)]. The number of hours the mother worked was related to higher intellectual ability for children in part-time day care [$r = .28$ ($p < .05$)] and to lower intellectual ability for children in full-time day care [$r = -.24$ ($p < .10$)]. This analysis suggested that a work schedule of about 20 to 30 hours per week might be best for children's cognitive development. Other researchers (e.g., Desai et al., 1989; Scarr et al., 1989; Schachter, 1981) have not reported this association—but perhaps they have not looked for this curvilinear relation. A recent analysis of data from the National Longitudinal Survey of Youth by Baydar and Brooks-Gunn (1991) revealed that the cognitive scores of children whose mothers worked more than 20 hours per week during the child's infancy were higher than those of children whose mothers were employed only 10 to 20 hours per week, but unfortunately their analyses did not include a breakdown of the effects of hours of employment beyond 20 hours per week. A more recent analysis of this same data set by Rosenthal (1993) showed that among the children whose mothers scored in the top half of the sample on an intelligence test (as the mothers in our study would likely have done), cognitive performance (PPVT score) was higher if the mother worked part time than if she worked full time.

A Stimulating Home

The physical environment in the home was linked to children's cognitive development in the predicted direction: Advanced cognition was observed in children from more homes with more stimulating toys and materials and decorations. This association with the variety of toys available to the child has also been found in previous research (Bradley, 1986; Bradley et al., 1989; A. W. Gottfried, 1984). In the present study, as well, cross-time correlations supported the suggestion that the link was causal: more toys and decorations in Year 1 predicted higher cognitive scores in Year 2 [$r = .18$ ($p < .10$)]; more mess and possible hazards in Year 1 predicted lower cognitive scores in Year 2 [$r = -.21$ ($p < .05$) with Year 1 cognitive scores partialled out]. (The correlations between children's cognition in Year 1 and the home variables in Year 2 were nonsignificant; $rs = .08, .03$.)

Being Alone

There were no significant associations in the contemporaneous correlations between children's cognitive performance and the time they spent being or playing alone or watching television. But children who spent more time alone in Year 1 did worse on tests of cognitive abilities in Year 2 [with performance in Year 1 partialled out; $r = -.35$ ($p < .05$)] and those who spent more time playing alone with objects gained less in cognition between Year 1 and Year 2 [$r = -.26$ ($p < .05$)]. The effects of spending a lot of time simply watching their parents and not interacting with them were even more striking. The more children watched their parents during the dinnertime observation, the lower were their scores contemporaneously (see Table 7.1) and over time [r with gain in cognition = $-.33$ ($p < .05$); r of cognition in Year 2 with watching parents in Year 1 = $-.35$ ($p < .05$)]. Clearly, there is no support for the suggestion that simply playing alone (figuring out how objects work) or watching people from afar (role modeling) has the same benefits for children's cognitive development as actively interacting with these people.

Siblings

The last set of relations between children's development and their experiences at home documented in Table 7.1 concerns the other children in the family. These relations showed that children with younger siblings (as 32 children had) scored lower on the social cognitive assessment; but children with a brother (as 46 of the children had) scored higher on the tests of intellectual ability. In fact, however, this second relation held only for boys. For girls, the sex of the sibling was not related to cognitive development [$rs = .10$ ns for brothers, .07 ns for sisters), whereas for boys, having a brother was positively related to cognitive development [$r = .39$ ($p < .01$); mean level of intellectual ability for boys with brothers = .46 and for boys without brothers = $-.24$] and having a sister was negatively related to cognitive development [$r = -.25$ ($p < .05$)]. Analysis of covariance confirmed that the interaction of the sex of the child with the sex of the sibling in predicting cognitive development was significant (significance of interaction terms = .03 for brothers, .05 for sisters).

The associations we found between children's cognitive ability and having a brother have not been observed before. Cicirelli (1975) found that children in Grade 1 solved problems more quickly when they were helped by a sibling of the same sex than when they were helped by a sibling of the opposite sex. This may help explain our finding for boys. But even in that study, overall, sisters were more helpful than brothers. Perhaps the reason that, in our study, the development of boys with brothers was advanced was that with two boys in the family the father spent more time reading to the children [t = 2.0 (p < .05)]. Perhaps the reason was that children with brothers spent less time interacting with their mother than children without brothers [t = 3.2 (p < .01)]. But perhaps the most direct explanation is that children with brothers spent more time interacting with their siblings than children with sisters [t = 2.2 (p < .05)].

Among those children who had a sibling, more advanced children were found to spend more time in our evening observation interacting with the sibling. Previous research has suggested that spending more time with siblings is negatively related to children's early language development (Nelson, 1973). The time of day we sampled might account for the fact that, unlike Nelson, we found positive rather than negative relations with sibling interaction. It may be positive to interact with siblings at the dinner table but not necessarily to spend all morning playing with them rather than interacting with an adult language model. It has, however, been observed in other research that younger siblings direct more complex utterances to older siblings who are teaching them something than to their mothers in the same situation (DeHart, 1987), so one should not underestimate the possible benefits of more frequent conversations with siblings. It has also been observed that triadic conversations between mothers, their 2-year-olds, and their preschool children are longer and offer the younger child more turns than dyadic conversations between the mothers and 2-year-olds alone (Barton & Tomasello, 1991). Thus, siblings help create a language learning environment in the family, which may account for our finding a link between children's interacting with siblings and advanced intellectual development.

To further explore the importance of siblings in predicting children's cognitive development, we conducted analyses of covariance with the other family variables, looking for significant interactions with the presence or absence of a sibling. Significant interactions were found for a number of variables. Correlations with cognitive development were then calculated separately for the children with and without siblings. For all but one of the variables in the analysis, correlations were higher for the children who did not have siblings. Correlations were higher with father's education [average rs = .34 (p < .01) for only children vs. .07 for children with siblings] and interaction [average rs = .35 (p < .01) vs. .08]; with mother's career orientation [average rs = .40 (p < .001) vs. .05 and discipline (average rs = −.38 (p < .01) vs. −.06).[7] Recall from our previous discussion in chapter 4 that children with no siblings experienced more interaction with their parents and also had more career-oriented mothers. Perhaps it is not surprising then to find a closer link with these predictors for these children. In addition, for

---

[7]It is noteworthy that the only parental variable that was significantly correlated with cognitive development for both only children and children with siblings was the amount the parents (mothers and fathers) read to the child. This finding underscores the significance of this particular—educational—activity for children's cognitive development

children without siblings, watching TV was negatively related to cognitive development, whereas for children with siblings, watching TV was positively related to cognitive development [average rs in Year 1 = $-.32$ ($p < .01$) vs. .23 ($p < .05$)]. For children with siblings, interacting with siblings was positively related to cognitive development [average $r = .24$ ($p < .05$)], whereas for children without siblings, playing alone with toys was positively related to cognitive development [average $rs = .27$ ($p < .05$) vs. $-.11$].

The results of these analyses of sibling variables suggest that previous researchers—often restricting their samples to firstborn children—may have seriously underestimated the effects of siblings on children's cognitive development, both directly through their behavior and indirectly through the effect of their presence on parents' behavior.

COMPARING[8] AND COMBINING PREDICTIONS

Different Predictions for Girls and Boys

The finding that the benefits of having a brother occurred only for boys suggests that different patterns of prediction occurred for the two sexes. This was not the case for the vast majority of associations we have discussed. When analyses of covariance were performed on all the family variables only a few variables showed significant interactions with the child's sex. In addition to the significant interaction with the sex of the

---

[8]Because the correlations presented in Table 7.1 were not always consistent across the 2 years in which they were assessed, analyses were carried out to investigate whether these differences were related to either age or cohort effects. Analyses of covariance were performed to establish the significance of interactions with age for each of the family variables. For 16 variables, these interactions were significant. The sample was then divided by a median split for age in each of the 2 years, yielding four groups: (a) 2-year-olds in Year 1, (b) 3-year-olds in Year 1, (c) 3-year-olds in Year 2, and (d) 4-year-olds in Year 2. The patterns of correlations for these four groups were then calculated for those variables in which there was a significant interaction with age. For only one of these variables did the pattern suggest that there was difference related to age. For parental responsiveness, the correlation with intellectual development was positive for younger children (2-year-olds) and negative for older children [4-year-olds; rs for the four groups respectively were: .36 ($p < .01$), ,.11, .04, $-.25$ ($p < .05$)]. Perhaps this variable was less predictive of cognitive performance for older children because it was more commonplace for them—parental responsiveness was positively correlated with age (see Table A.2, appendix); perhaps it was less predictive because this kind of adult behavior becomes less significant with age (see Clarke-Stewart et al., 1980). In any case, all the other significant interactions with age were either uninterpretable (they were not consistent from Year 1 to Year 2) or related to cohort effects: correlations with being offered choices (.27, .24, .40, .37 vs. $-.07$, .07, .01, $-.16$), mother's training (.31, .14, .31, .34 vs. $-.06$, .12, $-.04$, $-.03$), mother's career orientation (.24, .29, .26, .35 vs. $-.15$, .11, $-.12$, .12), having an older sibling (.26, .16, .32, .18 vs. $-.17$, $-.15$, $-.15$, $-.31$), and interacting with the sibling (.25, .18, .31, .38 vs. .02, $-.02$, .05, $-.06$), were stronger for the cohort that began the study as 2-year-olds; the correlations with father interaction were stronger for the cohort that began the study as 3-year-olds (.29, .38, .28, .33 vs. $-.07$, .02, .14, .06).

sibling, these analyses suggested that the amount the mother read to the child and the number of toys in the home were more important positive predictors of cognitive development for boys than for girls [$ts = 2.0$ ($p < .05$), 1.9 ($p < .10$)] and that the time the child spent alone or playing alone with toys was more negatively associated with cognitive development for girls than for boys [$ts = 2.1$ ($p < .05$), 1.9 ($p < .10$)]. No other interactions with sex were found.

Combined Predictors

The next kind of analysis that was performed went one step beyond these correlations. Multiple regression analyses were conducted to explore the combined and independent contributions of the family variables to children's cognitive development. First, we identified conceptually distinct aspects of children's family environments and experiences; then, on the basis of the statistical relations with cognitive development that we have discussed, we selected a small number of variables to represent each of these aspects;[9] and finally, we carried out regression analyses to ascertain the separate, independent contribution of each of these aspects with the other aspects statistically controlled. The seven aspects we identified (and the representative variables we selected) were as follows:

1. mother's background (education and knowledge of childrearing);
2. father's background (education and knowledge of childrearing);
3. mother's behavior to the child (touching, teaching, talking, demanding);
4. fathers' behavior to the child (touching, teaching, talking, demanding);
5. parents' reading to the child;
6. presence of siblings; and
7. stimulation in the home environment.

The overall multiple Rs obtained in these regression analyses were all significant (see Table 7.1) and accounted for about 40% of the variance in children's cognitive performance.

Both mothers' and fathers' backgrounds contributed to the children's scores significantly. For example, for intellectual ability, the multiple R for the mother's background was .33 ($p < .001$), the multiple R for the father's background was .29 ($p < .001$). Parent's backgrounds also both contributed to the children's scores independently: Significant Fs for tests of independent contributions were 3.8 ($p < .01$) for mothers' background and 5.5 ($p < .01$) for fathers' backgrounds. In addition, mothers' and fathers' behavior

---

[9]We chose to use representative variables rather than combining variables into composite variables because this seemed truer to the data.

made significant contributions to children's cognitive development that were independent of the contributions of their backgrounds. For intellectual ability, multiple $Rs = .43$ ($p < .01$) for mothers' behavior, $.23$ ($p < .01$) for fathers' behavior; $Fs = 6.3$ ($p < .001$) for mothers' behavior, 4.4 ($p < .01$) for fathers' behavior.

Other studies have also demonstrated that both parents' backgrounds (SES) and their behavior have independent effects in regression analyses predicting children's intellectual ability (e.g., A. W. Gottfried, 1984). The present study extended these findings, however, by discovering that having a brother, living in a stimulating home, and hearing stories read by the mother each also made significant independent contributions to children's intellectual development [$Fs = 5.3, 5.1$ ($p < .05$), 10.2 ($p < .01$)].

Comparing Predictions for Children in Day Care or at Home With Mother

The next analyses were carried out to explore whether these predictions of children's cognitive development from variables reflecting their environments and experiences with their families were as strong for children who were in day care as for children who spent their days at home with mother. It was expected that predictability from family variables would be higher for children who were at home more and that children in day care would be more influenced by experiences in their non-home environments. Therefore, the sample was divided into children who were at home with mother full time ($n = 48$ in Year 1, $n = 22$ in Year 2), children who were in day care part time ($n = 36$ in Year 1, $n = 47$ in Year 2), and children who were in day care full time ($n = 57$ in Year 1, $n = 58$ in Year 2). Analyses of covariance were carried out to look for significant interactions of family variables with this day-care variable, and correlations were examined separately for the three groups.

The hypothesis that predictability of cognitive development from family variables would be greatest for children who spent most time at home received no support. Only a few of the interactions were significant and consistent for the 2 years assessed. Among these, correlations were stronger for children in full-time day care for the following variables: stimulation of the home environment [$r = -.19$[10] for children home with mother; $r = .26$ ($p < .05$) for children in day care part time; $r = .40$ ($p < .01$) for children in day care full time]; maternal discipline [r for mother demanding $= -.11$ for children at home with mother; $r = -.30$ ($p < .05$) for children in day care part time; $r = -.49$ ($p < .001$) for children in day care full time]; and father teaching

---

[10]For ease of presentation, the correlation coefficients reported for these analyses are the averages for the two measures of cognitive development across the Year 1 and Year 2 assessments.

[$r = -.05$ for children at home with mother; $r = -.15$ for children in day care part time; $r = .20$ ($p < .10$) for children in day care full time]. The results of these analyses should allay the concerns of those who fear that placing children in day care reduces the "influence" of the family on children's development.

Although this issue has not received much systematic study heretofore, some supporting evidence comes from Ramey et al.'s (1979) work showing that the intellectual ability of children enrolled full time in a model day-care program was still predicted by maternal talk, as it was for children who spent more time at home with their mothers. In the present study, only one variable—mother reading—was more closely linked to cognitive development for children who were at home all day [$r = .48$ ($p < .01$) for children at home with mother; $r = .27$ ($p < .10$) for children in day care part time; $r = -.10$ for children in day care full time]. This last finding may be a consequence of the facts (discussed in other parts of the book) that children in day care, compared to children at home, were exposed to significantly more reading in day care during the daytime and more reading by their fathers at home at night.

SUMMARY

Evidence in this study that children's cognitive development was directly influenced by their experiences at home was suggested by a variety of analyses—correlations within and across time, regression analyses, and analyses of gain scores. In these analyses the central theme around which the results can most parsimoniously be organized is the importance of education for promoting children's cognitive development.

Children's development in this area was linked, first, to their parents' education, and more specifically to their parents' education about childrearing. It was also linked to the children's own educational experiences. Children whose cognitive development was advanced had more stimulating home environments, with more varied toys and educational materials. They received more stimulation from their parents—more lessons and reading from both parents, more teaching by the father. They had more stimulating siblings—brothers rather than babies—and spent more time playing with them. They spent less time alone or passively watching their parents.

Supporting the suggestion that the central theme in this area is education was the fact that the measure of cognitive development that most clearly showed the effects of these stimulating educational experiences was the more purely cognitive measure, the measure of intellectual ability, which tapped children's memory recall and recognition, language comprehension and fluency, and knowledge of concepts. This variable was more strongly predicted than the measure of social cognition (which assessed children's perspective taking and knowledge about social roles and emotions) by all aspects of the child's stimulation at home (parents' lessons; father's teaching, talking, and reading; mother's reading; stimulating physical environment; interaction with a brother).

The significance of parents' reading and singing to the children as a source of cognitive stimulation was a particularly notable part of the pattern of prediction. This variable was predictive for both fathers and mothers—in fact it was the only maternal behavior observed at dinnertime that was positively related to children's cognitive development. It was predictive for children who had siblings and those who did not. More reading and singing was significantly correlated with development within the group of children who heard any reading or singing as well as distinguishing between the cognitive level of this group and that of children who heard no stories or songs at all. It was related to cognitive development even when the effects of all other sources of stimulation were removed statistically. It was related to cognitive development for both children who were at home with their mothers and children who were in day care.

The links with this and the other kinds of stimulation at home, it should be reiterated, were independent of the parents' education and of each other. It was not the case that the parents' education was the basis for predictions of children's cognitive development and the other sources of stimulation were merely associated with it. Independent effects were found for mothers' backgrounds and for fathers' backgrounds; for stimulating interactions with mothers and with fathers; for the presence of brothers. Each of these sources of education contributed separately to the child's cognitive development.

Along with these linear predictions of cognitive development, the data discussed in this chapter also revealed some more subtle and complex curvilinear relations. One of these was with the amount mothers talked to children. During the dinnertime observations, mothers talked less to the most advanced children then to the least advanced children. They talked less to the most advanced children, apparently, because these children, being more advanced, didn't need the attention. We believe this to be true because mothers in the study spoke less to 4-year-olds than to 2-year-olds, and spoke less in Year 2 to children whose cognitive abilities were more advanced in Year 1. But not talking to children also apparently delayed their cognitive development, because the mothers of the least advanced children were observed to speak less to them at the time, and also the children whose mothers talked less to them in Year 1 had less advanced cognition in Year 2.

Another curvilinear relation observed was with the number of hours the mother worked outside the home. Children's cognitive development was promoted when mothers worked a moderate amount—20 to 30 hours a week. There are several possible explanations for this finding. For one thing, compared to working full time or not at all, working part time may enhance the mother's frame of mind: Mothers' role satisfaction was significantly higher if they worked part time than if they worked full time or not at all [$F(2,142) = 6.1$ ($p < .01$)]. This improved frame of mind may allow these mothers to provide better care. On the other hand, it may be that when children spend more than 30 hours a week in day care their cognitive development suffers. Or perhaps, spending all their time at home with mother is less beneficial than receiving some outside stimulation that part-time day care would provide. This issue in considered in the next chapter, in which we take a look at the prediction of children's cognitive development based on their experiences outside the family and see how these predictions compare with the ones discussed in this chapter.

8

Cognitive Development: Day Care and Beyond

In chapter 7 we saw how children's cognitive abilities were predicted by their experiences at home at dinnertime. But the main thrust of this study was to find out whether what happened to the children in the daytime also contributed to children's development and to investigate how the influence of experiences children had in day care added to or subtracted from the influence of their experiences at home. In this chapter we examine a parallel set of analyses to those discussed in chapter 7, which focus on the prediction of children's cognitive abilities from their experiences during the daytime.

DAILY EXPERIENCES AND ENVIRONMENTS AS PREDICTORS OF COGNITIVE DEVELOPMENT

Table 8.1 presents the correlation coefficients for relations between children's cognitive abilities and their daytime experiences. To begin with, we discuss the results presented in the first column of the table—the results for the total sample, including children who were and were not in day care.

Being in Day Care

Clear and significant relations were found between children's cognitive development and being in day care. Children in day-care centers were advanced in cognitive development. Positive correlations were found between cognitive development and the factor reflecting center day care and, more specifically, with the independent variables representing caregiver's professional credentials (education, training in child development, and experience in child-care settings), the number and variety of children in the care arrangement (number of children in the center, in the class, per adult caregiver, and interacting with the study child, and diversity of children in

TABLE 8.1

Correlations[a] Between Children's Cognitive Development and Daytime Variables

	Cognitive ability											
	All children				Children in Centers				Children in Homes			
	Intellectual		Social Cognitive		Intellectual		Social Cognitive		Intellectual		Social Cognitive	
Year	1	2	1	2	1	2	1	2	1	2	1	2
n =	144	127	144	127	62	92	62	92	119	97	119	97
Daytime Variables												
Child-Care Arrangement												
Day-care center factor	.19*	.18*	.23*	.22*								
People in Care Arrangement												
Children in care arrangement	.19*	.14	.25**	.16	•	•	•	•	•	•	•	•
Children in class	.18*	.20*	.25**	.22*	•	•	•	•				
Child-caregiver ratio	.14	.20*	.22**	.12	•	•	•	•	•	•	•	•
Number of children interacting	.14	.14	.18*	.16	•	•	•	•	•	•	•	•
Diversity of people	.21**	.21*	.26**	.19*	.39**	.21*	•	•	•	•	.18	•
Older children present	•	.15	.14	.13	.14	.28**	.20	.24	•	.34*	•	.17
Younger children present	•	•	•	•	•	•	•	•	•	•	•	•
Middle-class peers	.25**	.23*	.21*	.23*	.32**	.19	.27	•	•	•	•	•
Number of caregivers	•	•	•	•	•	•	•	•	•	•	•	•
Amount of interaction with any nonparental caregiver	.26**	•	.26*	.17*								
Setting/Structure												
Structure	•	•	.21**	.22*	•	•	•	•	•	•	•	•
Decoration	•	•	−.18*	−.13	•	•	•	•	.15	•	•	•
Toys	.15	.16	.19*	.14	•	•	•	•	•	.17	•	•
Program	.21**	•	.24**	•	•	•	•	•	•	•	•	•
Mess	•	•	−.26**	−.19*	•	•	−.25	•	•	•	−.23*	−.45**
Hazards	•	•	•	•	•	•	•	•	−.19	•	•	•
Money for day care/hour	•	•	•	•	.41**		•		•		•	

(continued)

TABLE 8.1 *(continued)*

	All children				Children in Centers				Children in Homes			
	Intellectual		*Social Cognitive*		*Intellectual*		*Social Cognitive*		*Intellectual*		*Social Cognitive*	
Year	1	2	1	2	1	2	1	2	1	2	1	2
n =	144	127	144	127	62	92	62	92	119	97	119	97
Daytime Variables												
Caregiver's Qualifications												
Caregiver's education	.15	.24*	•	.26**	•	.32**	•	.15	.13	.20*	•	.19*
Caregiver's training in child care	.21**	.24**	•	.19*	.15	.24*	•	•	.16	.15	−.19	•
Caregiver's experience in child care	.19	.20**	•	•	•	•	•		•		•	
Caregiver's knowledge of development	•	•	•	•	•	•	•	•	•	•	•	•
Caregiver's age	•	•	•	•	•	•	•	•	•	•	•	•
Caregiver's traditional values	•	•	•	•	•	•	.36**	•	•	.36*	•	.28*
Caregiver's positive attitude toward child	•	•	•	•	.28*	•	•	•	•	•	•	•
Caregiver's expectations for child	•	•	.15	.16	•	•	•	•	•	•	.17	.33*
Caregiver's stability	•	•	•	•	•	•	•	•	•	•	•	•
School Activities/Group Education	.17	•	.18	•	•	.17*	•	.19*				
Caregiver teaching group	•	•	•	•	•	.16	•	•				
Caregiver talking to group	•	•	•	•	.17	.18	•	•	•	•	•	•
Child imitating caregiver	.33*	•	•	•	.37**	•	•	•	•	•	•	•
Showing object	•	•	•	•	−.19	•	•	•	•	•	•	•
Positive Caregiving									.43**	.31*	•	•
Caregiver reading or singing	.33**	.23*	.20*	.21**	.17	.16	.22	•	.40**	.26*	.20	.30
Caregiver offering choice	.17*	.17*	•	•	.30*	.17	•	•	.24**	.18	•	•
Caregiver Attention	•	•	•	•	•	−.20*	−.16	−.18*	.17	•	•	.15
Caregiver one-to-one talk	.15	.14	•	.24*	•	•	•	.19	.19	.18	•	.16
Caregiver touching	•	•	−.18*	•	•	−.27**	−.13	−.22*	•	.24*	•	•

(continued)

TABLE 8.1 (continued)

	Cognitive ability										
	All children				Children in Centers				Children in Homes			
	Intellectual		Social Cognitive		Intellectual		Social Cognitive		Intellectual		Social Cognitive	
Year	1	2	1	2	1	2	1	2	1	2	1	2
n =	144	127	144	127	62	92	62	92	119	97	119	97

Daytime Variables

Caregiver Attention (continued)

Caregiver affection
| | | | | | −.34** | | −.21* | | | | |

Caregiver playing
| | | −.24** | | | | | | | | −.19* | .15 |

Caregiver helping child
| | | −.24** | −.18* | | | | | | | −.25** | −.18 |

Caregiver's Teaching

Caregiver one-to-one teaching
| .15 | | | .26** | | | | .29** | | | | |

Caregiver teaching, proportion
| | | | | | | | .17 | | | | |

Caregiver giving lesson
| | | | .39** | | | | .30** | | | | .25* |

Caregiver's Discipline

Caregiver control
| | −.35* | | −.32** | | | | | | | | |

Caregiver demanding
| −.24** | −.23* | | −.18* | −.18 | | | | −.33** | −.14 | −.15 | −.20 |

Caregiver's Responsiveness

Caregiver appropriate response
| .16* | | | | .25 | | | | .21* | | −.19 | |

Caregiver giving object
| | | | | | | −.20 | | .16 | | | |

Caregiver verbal responsiveness
| .18* | .21* | | | | .20 | | | .20* | .17 | | |

Peers' Activities

Peer interaction
| | | | | | | | | | | | −.21* |

Child imitating peers
| | −.23* | | | | −.26* | | | −.23* | −.18 | | −.21* |

Child watching peers
| | | | | | | | | −.18 | | | −.17 |

Child watching caregiver
| −.16* | −.20* | | −.17* | | −.36** | | | −.20* | | −.13 | |

Peer talk
| .15 | | | | | | | | | | | |

Pretend play
| .20* | | | .17* | | | .35* | | .25* | | .21 | |

Parallel play
| | −.37* | | −.33* | | −.29* | | −.48* | .23* | | | |

(continued)

TABLE 8.1 *(continued)*

	Cognitive ability										
	All children				Children in Centers				Children in Homes			
		Social				Social				Social	
Intellectual		Cognitive		Intellectual		Cognitive		Intellectual		Cognitive	
Year 1	2	1	2	1	2	1	2	1	2	1	2
n = 144	127	144	127	62	92	62	92	119	97	119	97
Daytime Variables											
Peers' Activities (continued)											
Positive affect											
•	•	•	•	•	•	•	•	•	•	•	•
Peer aggression											
− .17*	•	− .37**	•	•	− .18	− .28*	•	− .19	•	− .34**	•
Negative affect											
•	•	− .20**	•	•	•	•	•	•	•	− .27**	•
Child's Activities											
Plays with object											
•	•	.15	•	•	.33*	.21	.17	•	.25*	•	•
Alone											
•	•	•	•	•	•	•	•	•	•	•	•
Watching TV											
− .20*	− .14	•	•					•	− .24*	− .19	•
Activities with (nonday-care) adults											
.23**	.14	•	•								
Activities with (nonday-care) peers											
•	•	•	•								
Mesh between family and day care											
				•	•	•	•	•	.62*	•	•
R^b											
.47**	.47**	.49***	.55***	.63*	.52*	.67*	.53*	.43**	.46*	.39**	.52*

[a]With child's age partialled out.

[b]These regression coefficients are for the regression analyses described in the text. The selected set of variables they included is listed there.

•$p > .10$. $^+p < .10$. *$p < .05$. **$p < .01$. ***$p < .001$. (two-tailed tests)

the class), and the degree of structure in the program and stimulation in the setting. In analyses of variance, there were no differences in cognition between children in the three different home arrangements (with mother, sitter, or day-care home provider); however, the mean differences in cognitive development between children in home care and in center care were significant [for intellectual ability $F(1, 142) = 6.2$ $(p < .01)$; for social cognition in Year 1 $F(1, 142) = 6.7$ $(p < .01)$, in Year 2 $F(1, 126) = 5.4$ $(p < .05)$].[1]

---

[1]This last difference was underestimated because of the selective subject attrition; children in parent care who dropped out scored lower on social cognition in Year 1.

Moreover, children who gained the most in cognition over the course of the study were those who, between Year 1 and Year 2 assessments, switched from a home-care arrangement to a center [ANCOVA, with family SES covaried out: $F(2,118) = 14.9$ ($p < .001$); M for gain in cognition = -1.4 for children who stayed in a home arrangement, $n = 28$; $M = -3.5$ for children who stayed in a center, $n = 51$; and $M = 5.77$ for children who switched from home to center, $n = 42$].

The finding that children attending center programs were more advanced than those in home settings reflects the advanced development of children in day-care and preschool programs that has been observed in numerous other studies (e.g., Burchinal et al., 1989; Kontos & Dunn, 1993; J. Robinson & Corley, 1989; Rubenstein & Howes, 1983; and see review by C. Hayes et al., 1990). Unlike these previous studies, however, in the present study we also analyzed the contribution of the family to the differences between children who were and were not attending day care and probed the particular aspects of the day-care experience that were related to children's advanced development.

To examine the contribution of the family to the advanced development of children in day-care centers, analyses of covariance were performed, covarying out the family's SES. In these analyses, the overall differences between day-care and nonday-care children remained significant. When partial correlations partialling out the family's SES were run for individual daytime variables, however, the level of correlations with caregivers' education and training dropped to marginal significance ($p < .10$).

Quality of Day Care

Unlike many previous studies, the present study went beyond simply comparing the abilities of children with and without day-care experience by analyzing how children's abilities were correlated with specific experiences in their daytime and day-care settings. As Table 8.1 reveals, there were a number of significant associations with the quality of daytime experiences. Children's cognitive performance was predicted by the neatness of the physical setting; the amount of reading or singing and lessons by the caregiver; the amount of time the children spent imitating the caregiver; and a style of caregiving that was responsive rather than controlling[2] and that involved individual (one-to-one) teaching rather than touching, playing, or helping.[3] These correlations, which reflect the child's experiences in the setting more directly than the demographic features of class size and caregiver training, were not reduced by partialling out the family's SES.

---

[2] These correlations with caregiver discipline were significant even with the individual child's demandingness partialled out.

[3] This was help initiated by the teacher; help that occurred in response to the child's requests was positively correlated with cognitive development [$rs = .27, .29$ ($p < .05$)].

These variables also were related to the child's development over time. Children who scored higher on cognition in Year 2, had caregivers who in Year 1 did more reading and one-to-one teaching and were more responsive and the children spent more time imitating them [rs with Year 1 cognition partialled out = .28, .29, .25, and .30 ($p < .05$)]. The correlations with cognition in Year 1 and these variables in Year 2 were approximately .00.

Regression analyses gave more evidence of the effect of the daytime experiences on the child's development: The multiple regression coefficient for cognition in Year 2 predicted from the set of these variables reflecting the quality of the child's daytime experience in Year 1 was .56 ($p < .001$), whereas the multiple regression coefficient connecting cognition in Year 1 with the same experiential variables in Year 2 was only .29 ($p < .10$).

The relations of children's cognitive development to caregiver reading and imitating the caregiver remained significant [rs = .23, .26 ($p < .05$)] even when correlations were calculated just for the samples of children who had any of these experiences (71% of the children for caregiver's reading and 51% of the children for imitating). For these variables, then, it is not simply having any of the experience, but having more of it that predicts development.

As we had done for family variables, we used regression analyses to look for curvilinear effects in all these associations. These analyses showed that a number of these relations, as well as being significant linearly, had significant curvilinear shapes (ps < .05). This was particularly true for school-like activities (reading, lessons, teaching a group). For these variables, the shape of the curve was an inverted U: There was a positive linear relation with development at low and moderate levels but at the highest levels children's development was less advanced. It is not likely that the negative association at the high end was a result of caregiver's responding to children's advanced development by reducing their frequency of reading, lessons, group education, because these variables did not decrease as children got older (Table A.3, appendix). For these variables, perhaps, the curvilinear results suggest that it is possible for children to have too much of a good thing.

There was also a significant curvilinear relation with the amount of one-to-one talk with the caregiver. As this variable was negatively related to the child's age, this association seems comparable to the curvilinear one observed with the frequency of the mothers' talking to the children at dinnertime. That is, children whose caregivers talk to them least include both those whose development is lagging because they are being ignored and those whose caregivers pay less attention to them because their development is advanced and they can function on their own. A similar phenomenon was observed for the caregiver's physical contact with the child. This was the only daytime variable that cross-time analyses suggested was the consequence of children's cognitive abilities rather than the cause. Children who were advanced in social cognition in Year 1 had caregivers who initiated less physical contact with them in Year 2 [$rs = -.34$ ($p < .05$)]. This finding suggests that the reason for the negative link between children's cognitive abilities and more physical contact with the caregiver is that caregivers respond to children's greater maturity by giving them more independence.

Interaction With Other Children

Another aspect of the child's daytime experience was the interaction the child had with other children. More advanced children were in care arrangements with older children and their interactions with these other children were more mature. They engaged in more pretend play and less parallel play and aggression with these other children.[4] Because only some of the children in the study engaged in pretend play (39%) or parallel play (42%) or experienced peer aggression (64%), we also analyzed the associations for just these samples of children. Parallel play and aggression were still negatively related to cognitive development even for these samples [$rs = -.25, -.22$ ($p < .05$)], suggesting that it is not just experiencing any aggression or parallel play that matters, but the amount. The amount of pretend play was not significantly related to cognition, which suggests either that this variable reflects the child's ability level and is more likely to occur with advanced development, or that experiencing any opportunities for pretend play is sufficient to promote cognitive development.

Children's cognitive abilities were not consistently related to the amount of interaction they had with other children, but a significant curvilinear relation was observed ($p < .05$). Cognitive development was positively related to more interaction with other children at low and moderate levels but at the highest levels cognitive development was less advanced. Paralleling this curvilinear association with the amount of interaction with other children were curvilinear relations with the number and variety of children in the care setting and the number of children for each caregiver. Clearly, although being with a number of other children predicts advanced development, being with a crowd of children does not. Whether this is because too much peer interaction in itself is not good for children's cognitive development or because being with a large number of children reduces the caregiver's attention to the child is a question we consider in later (regression) analyses when we combine the different daytime predictors.

Other Social Experiences

Of course, day care is not the only source of stimulation outside of the family. Children also go with their parents to visit shops and relatives,

---

[4]Although cognitive performance was also predicted by the SES of the children in the class, these correlations are not discussed because they were decreased to nonsignificance by partialling out the family's SES (only the correlation with intellectual ability in Year 1 remained significant).

friends and church groups. In this study, as Table 8.1 shows, children's cognitive development was also significantly correlated with having more frequent and varied social activities with other adults, outside of day care.

Combined Predictors

The next set of analyses performed was an attempt to separate out the contributions of different components of the day-care environment to children's cognitive development. As we had done with family variables, we identified a number of distinct aspects of the daytime environment, selected a small number of variables to represent each, and ran regression analyses to evaluate the combined and independent contributions of these aspects. The aspects (and variables) selected were the following:

1. caregivers' backgrounds (education and experience),
2. caregivers' behavior (playing, teaching, reading, responding, controlling),
3. the nature of the program (structure and toys), and
4. the child's interaction with peers (variety and age of peers, amount of interaction with peers).

The overall multiple regression coefficients for these analyses were highly significant (see Table 8.1), but not large in absolute terms (altogether, the multiple R accounted for only about 25% of the variance in children's cognition). The regression coefficients for each of the separate components were also significant: Caregivers' background [$Rs = .26, .27$ ($p < .05$) for intellectual ability, $Rs = .24, .27$ ($p < .05$) for social cognition]; caregivers' behavior [$Rs = .40$ ($p < .01$), .32 ($p < .05$), 37 ($p < .01$), .34 ($p < .05$)]; program [$Rs = .20$ ($p < .05$), .21 ($p < .05$), .30 ($p < .05$); .25 ($p < .05$)]; peers [$Rs = .22$ ($p < .05$), .23 ($p < .05$), .27 ($p < .05$), .26 ($p < .05$)].

The important thing revealed by these analyses, however, was not that these clusters of variables were significantly related to children's cognitive development (we already knew that from the correlational analyses), but how development was predicted by each cluster relative to the others. Not surprisingly, perhaps, the most strongly predictive component of the daytime environment was the caregivers' behavior. This cluster of variables also had a significant independent effect beyond the contributions of the other variables [Fs for independent effect = 2.5, 2.3 ($p < .05$) for intellectual ability, 3.2 ($p < .01$), 2.6 ($p < .05$) for social cognition]. Significant independent effects were also found for the nature of the program [Rs for social cognition = .35 ($p < .01$), .33 ($p < .05$); $Fs = 5.0, 3.6$ ($p < .01$)] and the child's interaction with peers [$Rs = .29, .30$ ($p < .05$); $Fs = 4.4, 2.0$ ($p < .05$)]. This suggests that interaction with other children and the physical environments in the daytime setting have direct effects on development, and are not just mediated through the caregiver's behavior.

Amount of Time in Day Care

When children's cognitive scores were correlated with the amount of time they had spent in day care for the sample of all the children in the study, including those who were not in day care at all, children's cognitive performance was found to be positively related to the number of hours per week they had spent in day care [for intellectual ability in Year 1 $r = .25$ ($p < .05$)]. However, this analysis is misleading. When only the subsample who were in day care was examined, the correlation with hours of day care was negative [$r = -.38$ ($p < .01$)]. Hours in day care were negatively related to cognitive development both for children in home day care [$r = -.59$ ($p < .001$)] and for children in center day care [$r = -.38$ ($p < .01$)].

Further analyses showed that the relation with the hours of day care for the total sample was curvilinear ($p < .01$). Table 8.2 presents the mean cognitive scores for children with different amounts of day care showing that the highest scores were observed for children with 10 to 30 hours of day care each week. This finding duplicates the one discussed earlier for hours of maternal work.

The question, then, is, whether these children receiving 10 to 30 hours of day care per week did best on our tests of cognition because (a) they came from the best homes, (b) they were in the best day care, or (c) being in day care either not at all or for more than 30 hours a week was disadvantageous for development. Children in day-care centers 10 to 30 hours/week were from families of higher SES than those who were not in day care [$F(1, 82) = 20.3$ ($p < .001$)], so it might appear at first glance that the difference in cognitive development was attributable to family characteristics. But the SES of children in 10 to 30 hours of day care was equivalent to that of children who were in day care more than 30 hours per week, so family characteristics did not account for the difference between these two groups.

TABLE 8.2
Mean Scores for Children with Different Amounts of Day Care

		Hours of Day Care Per Week					
	Year	None	10–30	30–40	>40	F	df
	1	n = 48	n = 36	n = 51	n = 9		3,140
	2	n = 23	n = 47	n = 49	n = 9		3,124
Social cognition	1	.19	.78	.61	.52	5.9***	
	2	−.23	.18	−.04	−.12	2.7*	
Intellectual ability	1	−.20	.50	−.11	−.51	9.7***	
	2	.04	.27	−.07	−.56	4.4**	
"Good day care"[a]	1	−3.8	1.7	−.36	−9.5	2.1[+]	
	2	11.5	36.8	28.6	30.6	11.7***	

[a]"Good day care" is a measure composed of caregiver education, talking, reading, offering choices, and program structure.

[+]$p < .10$. *$p < .05$. **$p < .01$. ***$p < .001$. (two-tailed tests)

It was also true that the caregivers in part-time care were more knowledgeable and better educated, talked more to the children, offered them more choices, and were less demanding than the caregivers in full-time care [$Fs(1, 94) = 1.7$ ($p < .10$) to 4.8 ($p < .05$)]. So it might be that the difference in cognitive development was attributable to the quality of care experienced by children in full-time and part-time care. But the difference appeared for children whose day care scored above the median on an index of good quality day care [a composite score combining structured activities and caregiver's education, talking, offering choices, reading, and (not) disciplining; $r = -.34$ ($p < .05$)] as well as for children in "not so good" day care [$r = -.29$ ($p < .05$)]. Partialling out the quality of care, using this index, did not reduce the significance of the association with hours of care [$r = -.41$ ($p < .01$) in Year 1, $r = -.52$ ($p < .01$) in Year 2]. Thus, it does appear that there is an optimal amount of day care for promoting children's cognitive development. It is not the case that more—even of a "good" thing—is necessarily better.

Further analyses showed that the more hours children were in day care the stronger were the predictions from the quality of that care—offering further evidence for the effects of day care. First, analysis of covariance revealed that hours in day care interacted significantly with a number of day-care variables in predicting cognitive development. Then dividing the group into part-time and full-time day-care attendees revealed that the cognitive scores of children who were in full-time day care were more highly predicted by these day-care variables than were the scores of children in day care only part time. The variables included the caregiver's reading [$rs = .38$ ($p < .05$) vs. .18 ns], talking [$rs = .42$ ($p < .05$) vs. −.15 ns], teaching [$rs = .64$ ($p < .01$) vs. .10 ns], and offering choices [$rs = .42$ ($p < .05$) vs. −.05 ns], and the child's passively watching other children [$rs = −.45$ ($p < .05$) vs. .00 ns]. The prediction of cognitive development from the summary measure of "good quality" day care, showed a higher correlation for children in full-time day care [$r = .42$ ($p < .05$)] than for children in part-time day care ($r = .01$ ns) , suggesting that the "effect" of day care was greater if children spent more hours there and if the quality was lower.

PREDICTORS OF COGNITIVE DEVELOPMENT IN DIFFERENT KINDS OF DAYTIME SETTINGS

What we have just discussed are associations with children's cognitive development across the broad spectrum of daytime environments, from home with a single caregiver, like mother, to being in an institutional setting with 500 other children. Now we look at how children's experiences within different kinds of care arrangements predict development. In chapter 4 we discussed the major distinction between settings, namely the distinction between home and center settings. We saw that children's experiences in these two kinds of setting were substantially different in a variety of ways. In this section we see whether the distinction between home and center settings should also be maintained in considering how specific aspects of the environment influence children's development.

Experiences in Day-Care Centers

In the first set of analyses we investigated links between children's development and their experiences and environments in center settings. The results of correlational and multiple regression analyses for children in centers are presented in the second column of Table 8.1.

Caregiver's Characteristics. Replicating the finding for the total sample, for the sample in day-care centers, children's cognitive development was positively related to the caregiver's qualifications (training and education). Advanced cognition in Year 2 was also predicted by being with a more highly trained teacher in Year 1 [$rs = .27$ ($p < .05$) vs. .03]. The size of the correlations with teachers' training and education was not reduced by partialling out the family's SES.[5] Previous research on teachers' qualifications support this finding of a link between children's cognitive development and their teacher's training (Ruopp et al., 1979).

We did not find that cognitive development was related to other caregiver characteristics—age, experience, attitude toward the child, expectations for the child—or to the number of caregivers in the class. We also did not find the negative effect of staff turnover on children's intellectual development revealed in National Day Care Staffing Study (Whitebook et al., 1989); in our study there was no relation between children's development and the length of time the lead teacher had worked at the center. But this discrepancy may be the result of the two different measures of staff stability in the two studies. Staff instability is probably related to poor outcomes for children not only because it reflects the fact that teachers leave (and new ones take their place) but also because it indicates that conditions in the center are bad enough to cause the teachers to leave. The index of staff instability used in the Whitebook et al. study—rate of teacher turnover—would reflect these bad conditions. Our measure of staff instability—the length of time an individual teacher had been in a particular center—would not necessarily reflect negative conditions.

Caregiver's Behavior. There were more associations in the present study with the caregiver's behavior than with these background characteristics. Children's cognitive development was advanced when

---

[5]In fact, none of the correlations for day-care center children in Table 8.1 were reduced by removing the effect of family SES.

teachers read to them and gave lessons in a group,[6] and also when they taught, talked, and responded to them individually. Their development was delayed if they spent their time simply passively watching the teacher, advanced if they spent more time imitating the teacher. There was a suggestion in the data that teachers were promoting children's development with these stimulating behaviors, not merely responding to children's advanced development. Advanced cognition in Year 2 and gains in cognition between Year 1 and Year 2 were predicted by more group education (reading, lessons, imitating caregiver) and a more structured program in the day-care class in Year 1 [rs = .35, .44 ($p < .05$)]. The relations with caregivers' behavior were especially clear in large classes[7] [rs for one-to-one interaction, group education = .32, .41 ($p < .05$) in large classes, .03, −.25 in small classes]. Relations with group education were higher for 4-year-olds than for younger children [average rs = .00 for 2-year-olds, −.02 for 3-year-olds, and .57 ($p < .001$) for 4-year-olds].[8]

When correlations were calculated for reading, lessons, and imitating the caregiver for just the subsamples of children for whom these behaviors occurred (they did not occur for every child), only imitating the caregiver remained significantly linked to cognitive ability [r = .35 ($p < .05$)]. For the other two variables, reading and lessons, apparently, within the range of variation observed in these day-care centers, the significant associations observed for the total sample were the result of having some of the experience versus having none of it.

A nonauthoritarian style of teaching that included relatively few demands and directions and more choices was also related to children's advanced cognitive ability, especially in small classes [r with teacher demanding = −.46 ($p < .05$)], and to greater gains in social cognitive development over the year of the study [r = −.55 ($p < .01$)]. But when the caregiver was affectionate, this was related to less cognitive ability; children with high cognitive scores received less physical contact and affection.

Our findings showing that children's cognitive performance was associated with teachers' behavior is consistent with the findings of other research for teachers' talking (Carew, 1980; Rubenstein & Howes, 1983; Phillips, Scarr, & McCartney, 1987), responsiveness (Fagot, 1973), physical affection (Fagot, 1973), and directiveness (Fagot, 1973; Rubenstein & Howes, 1979). Previous research has also shown, as we did, that children in programs with more lessons, stories, and teaching have advanced cog-

---

[6]In analyses of children in day-care centers, as in the analyses for the sample as a whole, these relations had an inverted-U curvilinear shape ($ps < .05$).

[7]To investigate the interactions of day-care center variables with the size of the class, analyses of covariance were performed and then correlations for children in large and small classes compared. The contrasts included in this discussion refer to the variables for which a significant interaction was found.

[8]This was the only age-related pattern that appeared in analyses of covariance for age X day-care center variables.

nitive development (Lazar et al., 1977; Miller & Dyer, 1975; Tizard et al., 1976). Results of the present study go beyond those of previous research, however, in suggesting that the effect of group education (reading, lessons, imitating the teacher) is more extreme in large classes. In our study, as well, lessons and reading had a curvilinear relation with cognitive development ($p < .05$). This finding may reflect the negative effect of too much pressure in preschool, an effect observed by Hirsh-Pasek et al. (1990), Sylva et al. (1980), and Miller and Dyer (1975). Our finding that children with advanced cognitive development spent less time passively watching the caregiver follows Sylva et al.'s (1980) observation that, in preschool, "rich" play was unlikely to occur when children were simply watching or waiting.

Interaction With Peers.   In terms of their interactions with peers, children with more advanced cognitive abilities had older, more diverse classmates, and spent more time in pretend play with them and less time playing in parallel or imitating them. The diversity of other children in the class was especially predictive of cognitive development for children in small classes [$r = .52$ ($p < .01$) for small classes vs. .07 for large classes]. There was no significant relation between children's cognitive development and the number of children in their class or the child–adult ratio in the contemporaneous correlations, but over time, children gained more in cognitive development when there were fewer children in the class, especially younger children, and the child watched and interacted with them less, especially in negative ways, in Year 1 [$rs = -.48, -.48, .22, -.42$ ($p < .05$), $-.67$ ($p < .01$), $-.51$ ($p < .05$)].

The similarities between our results and those of other research concerning the effects of the number and ages of other children in the class were limited. We found no relation between children's cognitive performance and the size of the class, the number of children the child interacted with, or the ratio of children to adults in the class in the contemporaneous correlations, although such links have been found in other research. The reason we did not observe these associations may be that the teachers of larger classes in our study were better trained and more highly educated than the teachers of smaller classes, compensating for the possible negative effects of large numbers of children in the class. Or perhaps these other studies included a larger range of class sizes than ours. In Whitebook et al.'s (1989) study, for example, the group sizes ranged from 2 to 37; in Ruopp et al.'s (1979) it was from 8 to 32. In our study, of the 157 classes observed, only 5 classes had more than 30 children (maximum = 33), only 11 had more than 25, and only 11 had fewer than 10 (minimum = 7).

In our study we did find that having the opportunity to interact with more diverse other people including older children was positively related to development, a finding supported by research in which preschool children randomly assigned to mixed-age classes increased in intelligence (Beller, 1974). Other research on children in a mixed-age class extends this finding by showing that 3- and 4-year-old children preferred 5-year-olds over their own age-mates in the class, interacting with them more positively and less negatively (Roopnarine & Johnson, 1984). Of relevance for understanding this finding, too, is Thomas, Due, and Wigger's (1987) demonstration that children are more likely to imitate competent children than incompetent children.

The finding that spending more time with peers—imitating, fighting, or playing alongside—was related to less advanced development probably reflects both a lack of adult supervision and a lower level of maturity on the part of the children. It has been suggested that conditions fostering a peer orientation may later interfere with academic—adult-oriented—success (Harper & Huie, 1987). Such interference may occur earlier than suspected. Our finding that children with advanced cognitive development spent more time in pretend play with peers is supported by Sylva et al.'s (1980) observation that rich play was more likely when the child was engaged in pretend as opposed to rough-and-tumble play.

Program. Program variables (the number of toys, decorations, degree of structure, etc.) were not related to children's cognitive development except in large classes [in which there were more toys and decorations; rs with intellectual ability = .34 ($p < .05$) for toys, .32 ($p < .05$) for decorations]. This finding that children in large classes do better cognitively if they are in classrooms with more varied toys echoes Holloway and Reichhart-Erickson's (1988) finding that children's social knowledge is related to being in classes with more varied, age-appropriate toys.

Children with higher levels of cognitive development spent more time in the center playing alone with toys. This finding is supported by Sylva et al.'s (1980) observation that rich play was more likely when the children were engaged in construction, art, or play with manipulatives, structured materials, or small-scale toys.

Combined Effects. To test whether all of these aspects of the children's experience in day-care centers were contributing to children's development equally, the same procedure was followed as had been used before for family and daytime variables. Small sets of variables were selected to represent the different aspects of experience in the day-care center and regression analyses were run to assess their combined and independent contributions. These analyses revealed that the teacher's behavior (reading to the children and offering them choices), and the characteristics of the children in the day-care center (older, more diverse, higher SES) had significant independent effects on children's cognitive development [e.g., for intellectual ability, F for independent effect of teacher behavior = 2.3 ($p < .05$); F of teacher reading = 12.9 ($p < .001$); F of teacher offering choices = 3.8 ($p < .05$); F of peer characteristics = 3.7 ($p < .01$)]. The teacher's background (education, training), the amount of money the parents paid for day care (a variable that was also positively related to children's cognitive performance), and the structural aspects of the program (toys, structure, decoration) did not have independent effects beyond the teacher's and peers' behavior. This finding that the variety of toys in the day-care center did not have an effect on development that was independent of other aspects of the child's experience in the center is supported by the observation in other studies that covarying out either characteristics of the child (Holloway & Reichhart-Erickson, 1988) or the teacher's behavior (Busse et al., 1972; Ruopp et al., 1979) reduced the size of the association with this aspect of the program.

Differences Related to Family SES.   Paralleling the analyses we did to compare the predictability of family variables for children who were in two kinds of daytime environments (day care and family care), the next set of analyses compared the predictability of day-care center variables for children who were in two kinds of nighttime environments (with parents of high SES or with parents of lower SES). It was expected that the quality of day-care would predict development more strongly for children from families of lower SES because the day-care setting would be more likely to offer them educational activities not available at home. Analyses of covariance were performed to identify significant interactions of day-care center variables and SES in predicting cognitive development. One index of day-care quality that was found to be more highly and positively related to cognitive development for children from families of lower SES was the teacher's qualifications [education and experience: average $rs = .47$ ($p < .01$) for lower SES children vs. $-.03$ ns for high SES children]. As there is no previous research literature with which to compare this finding, it must be considered as strictly exploratory. Perhaps the reason that lower-SES children were more influenced by the teacher's qualifications was that high-SES children already had caregivers—their parents—with high levels of education; perhaps it was simply that the educational levels of the teachers of the high SES children had reached ceiling levels.

Also confirming the hypothesis that the development of children from lower-SES families would be more affected by high quality day care than the children from high-SES families would be was the finding that the development of children from lower-SES families was related to being in a smaller class [r with number of children in class $= -.38$ ($p < .05$)], whereas children from families of high SES did better in larger classes [$r = .25$ ($p < .05$)].

On the other hand, the educational curriculum was not more predictive of cognitive development for children from families of lower SES. Although the development of high-SES children was related to receiving more formal group education and spending less time simply playing with other children in the day-care class, no such relations were observed for lower-SES children [$rs = .29$ ($p < .05$) vs. $.04$ for group education, $-.27$ ($p < .05$) vs. $.27$ for peer interaction].

Experiences in Home Settings During the Day

Parallel analyses to those conducted for day-care centers were carried out to identify predictors of advanced cognition in the daily experiences of children in home care—with mother, sitter, or day-care home provider (presented in the third column of Table 8.1). Multiple regression analyses showed significant levels of predictability from these variables.

Caregiver's Behavior. The highest relations observed were those between measures of cognitive development and positive caregiving—a factor reflecting the degree to which the caregiver read and offered choices to the child and was responsive rather than demanding and controlling.[9] Regression analyses showed that positive caregiving made a significant independent contribution to children's cognitive development [$Fs = 4.3$ ($p < .01$), 3.5 ($p < .05$)]. Reading was the single most highly predictive variable in this factor, significantly correlated with cognitive development [$r = .35$ ($p < .01$)] even when the sample of children whose caregivers did not read to them at all was eliminated from the analysis (52% of the observations). How much attention caregivers paid to the children (talking, touching, giving lessons) was also positively related to their cognitive development, especially for children who were alone with the caregiver.[10] Spending more time simply watching the caregiver or watching TV was related to lower cognitive ability, as was being helped by the caregiver.

Correlations with the gains children made in their cognitive scores and correlations between experience in Year 1 and cognition 1 year later suggested that caregivers' behavior was influencing children's development. Cognitive gains and cognition in Year 2 were related to more interaction with the caregiver in Year 1 [talking, playing, teaching, reading, responding; $rs = .19$ ($p < .05$) to .32 ($p < .001$), $M = .24$ ($p < .05$)].

There have not been many studies of how children's experiences in day-care homes are related to their development. In one of these few studies, Goelman and Pence (1987a) found that children's intelligence scores were related to being in day-care homes where they spent more time engaged in structured fine motor activity and less time watching TV, and where they received more information and story reading from the day-care provider. These relations are comparable to the ones obtained in the present

---

[9]This relation with responsive caregiving was especially strong for 2-year-olds [$r = .45$ ($p < .01$) for 2-year-olds, $r = .00$ for 3-year-olds, $r = -.10$ for 4-year-olds; significant interaction with age in analysis of covariance, $p < .01$]. In other research, too, it has been found that caregivers' responsiveness is more important early on in life and its significance diminishes with age (Clarke-Stewart et al., 1980).

[10]Analysis of covariance revealed that caregiver attention interacted with the presence of other children in the day-care setting. For children who were alone with the caregiver, attention was positively related to cognitive development [average $r = .37$ ($p < .05$)], whereas for children who had peers in the home setting there was no significant correlation ($r = .02$). This was the only significant interaction in the analyses of covariance for home variables.

study. Beyond this study, we must extrapolate from studies of influences on children's development observed in their own homes. Gadberry's (1980) observation that children's performance on intelligence tests improved when their television watching was restricted fits with our results. Previous findings that children's cognitive development was predicted by the amount the mother talked (Carew, 1980; Huttenlocher et al., 1991) and read to the child (Laosa, 1982), her responsiveness (Barnard et al., 1984; Bradley et al., 1989; Olson et al., 1986) and discipline (Barnard et al., 1984; Hess & McDevitt, 1984; Nelson, 1973), also paralleled the present results.

Caregiver's Background. Of the home caregiver's professional quali-fications (training, education, experience, knowledge) only the caregiver's education was significantly related to children's cognitive development. Gains in children's cognitive development over the year of the study were moderately related to the educational level of the caregiver in Year 1 [$r = .17$ ($p < .10$)]. However, regression analyses showed that the caregiver's background did not contribute independently to children's cognitive abil-ities beyond what was contributed by her behavior.

It did not matter if the caregiver in the home setting was the mother or another care provider: Analyses of variance contrasting the cognitive abil-ities of children at home with their mothers with those of children in homes with care providers were nonsignificant. However, for children who were with care providers, cognitive development was positively related to the "mesh" (agreement and similarity) between their parents and the provider.

Interaction With Other Children. Within the range of settings we ob-served, the number of children in the home-care arrangement did not predict children's cognitive development, but spending more time with peers (watching, interacting, imitating, or being the recipient of aggression) did. More frequent interaction with other children was negatively related to children's cognitive development.[11] The amount of peer aggression was even significantly negatively correlated with cognition when the children who did not experience any aggression (54%) were eliminated from the sample [$r = -.27$ ($p < .05$)]. Being with older children and engaging in pretend play with them was related to higher cognitive levels [and the more time playing, the higher the level; $r = .30$ ($p < .05$)]. Children with an infant present in the home-care arrangement had lower levels of social cognition [$F(1, 94) = 4.3$ ($p < .05$)]. Analyses over time further supported the link

---

[11]This was only true for children over 2 years old. For 2-year-olds, interacting with peers was positively related to social cognition. Analysis of covariance showed a significant inter-action between peer interaction and age for predicting cognitive development [$r = .26$ ($p < .05$) for 2-year-olds; $r = -.15$ for 3-year-olds; $r = -.30$ ($p < .05$) for 4-year-olds]. Cognitively advanced 2-year-olds may show their advanced level by playing more with peers because they are more able; cognitively advanced 4-year-olds may show their advanced levels by working on puzzles rather than playing with peers.

between peer interaction and cognitive development. Children who did better on the assessment of cognition in Year 2 and who gained more in cognitive development between Year 1 and Year 2 were in homes with fewer children and spent less time watching them in Year 1 [rs with Year 1 cognition partialled out = $-.30$ ($p < .10$), $-.42$ ($p < .05$)].

There have not been many studies of how children's experiences in day-care homes are related to their development. In the one study of day-care homes that included a measure of the characteristics of the children in the day-care home, Siegel-Gorelick et al. (1981b) observed that when there were older preschool children in care this enhanced the play maturity of the younger children. This finding fits with the results of the present study, as we, too, found that being with older children was related to advanced intellectual ability. Extending this finding, and paralleling the observation of children in mixed-age center classes, is Rothstein-Fisch and Howes' (1988) observation that toddlers in family day-care homes preferred slightly older children as playmates, watching them more often, imitating and talking to them more.

Studies of children's experiences at home with their mothers during the day also provide relevant comparisons with the findings from the present study. The observation by Nelson (1973) that children who spent more time with other children during the day had slower language development is confirmed by the correlations obtained with children's experiences during the day in the present study.

The Physical Environment.   Having a safer, more stimulating physical environment in the home setting (more toys and decorations, less mess and fewer hazards) was marginally related to higher cognitive ability. It was more strongly related over time; the variety of toys in Year 1 predicted gains in children's cognition over the year of the study [$r = .55$ ($p < .05$)]. Similarly, Goelman and Pence (1987a) found that children's intelligence scores were related to being in day-care homes with more learning materials.

Parallel Patterns in Different Settings

Many of these predictions of cognitive ability from children's experiences at home during the day paralleled those based on their experiences at home during the evening. In both settings, there were significant positive relations with adult stimulation (reading and lessons), adult sensitivity (responsiveness and choices), and a stimulating physical environment, and significant negative relations with discipline, passive watching, and the presence of a younger child.

Many of the relations between cognitive development and experiences in home care during the day were also similar to those based on children's experiences in centers. Again, in both settings, children's cognitive scores were predicted by positive caregiving—by more reading, responding and offering choices, less physical control, and fewer demands. In both settings, children with more advanced cognitive development spent more time in lessons and solitary play with objects and less time passively watching other people. In both settings, children with more advanced development were less likely to imitate or be involved in fights with peers and more likely to spend time in pretend play with older children.

These parallels were further confirmed in within-subject comparisons for children who spent some time each day in a home setting and in a center ($n = 40$ in Year 1; $n = 61$ in Year 2). Parallel correlations with intellectual ability scores were observed in centers and home settings for caregivers' training [$r = .20$ ($p < .10$) in centers; $r = .27$ ($p < .10$) in homes], education [$r = .28$ ($p < .05$); $r = .34$ ($p < .01$)], talking [$r = .28$ ($p < .10$); $r = .30$ ($p < .10$)], offering choices [$r = .25$ ($p < .10$); $r = .31$ ($p < .05$)], giving lessons [$r = .31$ ($p < .05$); $r = .33$ ($p < .01$)], and responding frequently [$r = .22$ ($p < .10$); $r = .21$ ($p < .10$)] and appropriately [$r = .23$ ($p < .10$); $r = .23$ ($p < .10$)], for the number of older children [$r = .20$ ($p < .10$); $r = .16$ ($p < .10$)] and the variety of children in the setting [$r = .54$ ($p < .01$); $r = .29$ ($p < .10$)], and for the frequency with which the child imitated the caregiver [$r = .29$ ($p < .10$); $r = .34$ ($p < .05$)].

Different Patterns in Different Settings

Although the patterns of prediction in the two kinds of home setting were similar, differences were also observed. What was different was that in the daytime observations positive relations with playing alone with toys or with older children and negative relations with watching TV and with watching or interacting with other children were found. During the dinner-time observations, in contrast, interacting with other children was positively related to cognitive ability.

There were also differences in predictions for the two kinds of daytime setting. In centers, relations with children's cognitive development were stronger for one-to-one teaching, varied toys, a structured program of activities, and a peer group of children from middle-class or professional-status families. In home-care arrangements, relations with children's cognitive development were stronger for discipline and television watching. In home-care arrangements, caregivers initiated more physical contact with more advanced children; in centers, they initiated less.

For the sample of children who were in both home care and center care, also, relations with children's cognitive development were stronger for varied toys and time spent playing with them in centers [$rs = .31$ ($p < .05$), .37 ($p < .01$) vs. .03 ns, −.21 ($p < .10$)]; relations with discipline were stronger in homes [$rs = −.38$ ($p < .05$) vs. −.15 ns]; and in homes caregivers initiated more physical contact with advanced children [$r = .29$ ($p < .05$)], whereas in centers they initiated less [$rs = −.49$ ($p < .01$)].

In addition, however, in this subsample of children who were in both home and center settings during the day, cognition was more positively related to reading by the adult caregiver and more negatively related to the number of children interacting, especially younger ones, in homes than in centers [rs = .34 (p < .05), −.56 (p < .01) vs. −.06, −.06 ns]. This finding is perhaps surprising; one might have expected these variables would be more predictive in centers, where they were more frequent, than in homes. But remember that these variables had curvilinear relations with cognition. It seems that these qualities are more predictive in homes, where they were less frequent and therefore more distinct and salient.

Different Patterns for Girls and Boys

Just as we had analyzed the interactions of family variables with the child's sex, we conducted analyses of covariance to find out whether daytime variables interacted with sex in predicting children's cognitive development. Again, significant interactions were rare. Basically, there was just one way in which associations with daytime experiences were different for boys and girls. Boys' development was more closely associated than girls' with being in a structured, formal educational program with a rich physical environment. This was true for the entire sample, for which it was observed that being in a day-care center was more highly predictive of cognitive development for boys than for girls [rs = .30 (p < .05) for boys and .10 for girls; interaction with sex t = 2.1 (p < .05)]. This finding is consistent with a finding by Larsen and Robinson (1989) that boys' language development was more affected than girls' by participation in a university preschool. Moreover, for the children in our study who were attending day-care centers, boys' cognitive development was more highly predicted than girls' by the frequency of group education in the class, the number of toys available in the class (remember that boys also spent more time than girls playing alone with toys), the degree of structure in the program, and the amount of reading the teacher did with the children [rs = .27 (p < .05) to .40 (p < .01) for boys and .02 to .09 for girls; ts for interaction = 1.8 (p < .10) to 3.8 (p < .001)]. Regression analysis showed that the caregiver's reading had a highly significant independent effect on cognitive development for boys only [F = 20.6 (p < .001)]. For children in home care, although reading was significantly correlated with intellectual ability for both boys and girls, for boys it was also correlated with social cognitive ability [r = .41 (p < .01)]. This pattern of boys' cognitive development being more highly predicted by educational activities and the availability of toys and materials parallels the one found in the dinnertime observations, when boys also were apparently more influenced by the amount of reading the mother did and the number of toys available in the home.

FAMILY AND DAY-CARE EXPERIENCES COMPARED
AND COMBINED

Our final questions concerning the prediction of children's cognitive development involved both comparing and combining the effects of the environments of home and day care: How much is development affected by experiences in day care and how much by experiences at home? How do the two environments combine to predict development?

Are Family and Day-Care Experiences Both
Important?

To answer questions concerning the relative contributions of family and day-care experiences to children's cognition we turned to regression analyses that included both sets of independent variables. Based on the results of the earlier regression analyses for family and daytime variables, two sets of variables were selected to represent the child's home and day-care environments. Identical variables were selected in order to compare equivalent processes in the two environments: adults' educational backgrounds and behavior (talking, teaching, demanding, and reading) and the stimulation in the physical setting (toys).

These regression analyses revealed that both family variables and daytime variables were significantly predictive of cognitive development [Rs = .47 ($p < .01$) for family variables, .38 ($p < .01$) for daytime variables].[12] Both also made independent contributions to cognitive development [F = 4.7 ($p < .001$) for family variables and F = 2.1 ($p < .05$) for daytime variables]. The results of identical analyses performed separately for children in day-care centers and children in home settings during the day paralleled these: For children in day-care centers, Rs = .48 for family variables and .32 for day-care variables [Fs for tests of independent effects = 2.1 and 2.1 ($p < .05$)]; for the sample in home care, Rs = .43 for family variables and .35 for day-care variables [Fs = 3.5 ($p < .01$) and 3.4 ($p < .01$)]. Thus, it seems that cognitive development is affected by both family and day-care environments.

The results of these regression analyses are consistent with those in previous research showing that children's cognitive development was advanced when they received high-quality care, stimulation, and encouragement in both home and day-care settings (Goelman & Pence, 1987b)—

---

[12]The multiple Rs reported in this section are for the analysis of intellectual ability in Year 1. Regression coefficients for intellectual ability in Year 2 and social cognition in Years 1 and 2 were just slightly smaller than these. The results of regression analyses including only measures of the mother's background and behavior to represent the home environment were identical to the ones reported for both parents.

but extend the earlier findings by establishing that the family and day-care environments make independent contributions to development.

Which Is More Influential?

As to the question of which source of influence—family or day care—contributes more, the results of these regression analyses suggest that there is only a small difference favoring families. When other researchers have weighed the relative contributions of day-care and family variables to cognitive development, as we discussed in chapter 1, their results have been inconsistent—because they have been comparing apples and oranges. Their results may reflect the higher predictiveness of more reliable measures or variables that more closely index the quality of children's actual experiences—mother's education or intelligence versus the type of day care (Desai et al., 1989; Melhuish et al., 1990; Tizard et al., 1976) or the caregiver's training (Goelman & Pence, 1987b), for example; or observed day-care quality versus parents' values (Phillips, Scarr, & McCartney, 1987). In the present study, "fairer" comparisons, using identical measures of background characteristics and observed interactions in family and day-care environments, suggest that children's cognitive ability is affected by both family and day-care experiences rather than that one or the other has clear predominance. The balance is tipped depending on how much time the child spends in day care and how different the family and day-care environments are.

How Are the Effects of Family and Day Care Combined?

The next question was how the influences of both these environments are combined. Are their effects simply additive or something more complex? Regression analyses, using these same variables, were carried out to compare three possible models illustrating ways that family and day-care environments might jointly contribute to children's cognitive development: An additive model in which the sum of the family and day-care variables were entered, a curvilinear model in which the square of the day-care variables was entered after the sum of the day-care and family variables, and an interactive model in which the product of day-care and family variables was entered after the sum of the day-care and family variables. The additive model was somewhat higher [$R = .51$ ($p < .001$)] than the model containing only family variables [$R = .47$ ($p < .01$)] or day-care variables alone [$R = .38$ ($p < .01$)]. The curvilinear and interactive terms did not increase the multiple R or make significant independent contributions ($Fs < 1$).

The additive model was further explored by dividing children in day-care centers into four groups based on summary scores for overall quality of family and day-care environments[13]—those from higher quality family environments attending higher quality day-care centers, those from higher quality family environments attending poorer quality day-care centers, those from poorer quality family environments attending higher quality day-care centers, and those from poorer quality family environments attending poorer quality day-care centers. Children attaining the highest cognitive scores, this comparison showed, were in higher quality family and day-care environments (M[14] = .63); those receiving the lowest scores were in poorer quality family and day-care environments (M = −.21). Children from poorer quality family environments attending higher quality day-care centers tended to have somewhat higher scores (M = .30) than those from higher quality family environments attending poorer quality day-care centers (M = −.01), but this difference was not statistically significant.

This finding gives only weak support to the suggestion that high-quality day care has a compensating effect for children from poor family environments (Long et al., 1985), or that low-quality day care has a detrimental effect for children from advantaged family environments—suggestions previously supported by research like that of Tizard et al. (1976), who observed that children from working-class families benefited from an educational day-care program and children from middle-class families suffered from a noneducational one, and Schlieker et al. (1989–1990), who found that the positive effects of day-care quality were greater for children from single-parent families than two-parent families. But our data were in the right direction to confirm the suggestion and might have proved significant if the range of family conditions in the study had been greater.

An Integrated Model

The final analyses in the domain of cognitive development were the most integrative and multivariate. These analyses were an attempt to examine the influences on cognitive development across time, identifying the model that was maximally predictive of cognitive development and included both family and day-care environments. Path analyses were used to put together experiences in family and day-care environments, in Year 1 and Year 2. We developed several conceptual models of the relations among children's environments and cognitive development and then selected specific measures to comprise the "latent variables" in these models. Our strategy in

---

[13]"High-quality day care," as before = above the median on a composite score combining structured activities and caregiver's education, talking, offering choices, reading, and (not) disciplining. "High-quality family care" = above the median on a composite score combining father's education, parents' knowledge of childrearing, reading, responsiveness, and (not) disciplining.

[14]Means for the three measures of cognitive ability.

selecting these measures was to include in a latent variable only those measures that the correlational analyses had suggested were the "best predictors" of cognitive development for that aspect of the environment. The latent variables (and specific measures) we used were the following: *parents' education* (mother's education); *stimulating family interaction* (father interacting, father reading, mother reading, discipline, time spent passively watching parents, variety of toys); *siblings* (brothers); and *stimulating day care* (caregiver's education/experience, caregiver reading, number of children, diversity, structure). We then tested several models based on these latent variables using EzPATH (a causal modeling program written for SYSTAT by Steiger, 1989).

The most significant and parsimonious model was the one presented in Fig. 8.1. This model was statistically significant [Steiger–Lind Adjusted Root Mean Square Index = .07 (90% confidence interval = .05 to .09), where values below .10 indicate a good fit, and the Adjusted Population Gamma = .92 (90% confidence interval = .86 to .93), where values above .90 indicate a good fit and values above .95 an excellent fit (Steiger, 1989)]. In the model, cognitive development was directly predicted by the presence of brothers, stimulating interactions with parents at home, and stimulating experiences in a day-care center. Mother's education was linked to cognitive development both directly and through the stimulating family interactions. There were also significant links between stimulating day care experiences and stimulating family interactions.[15]

Several alternative models were also tested. This model was superior to any model omitting one or more of these latent variables; to a model in which the direction of arrows was reversed so that the child's cognitive ability influenced the parents' stimulating interaction (Steiger–Lind RMS = .19, Adjusted Population Gamma = .60); and to a model in which mother's education was linked to stimulating day care (Steiger–Lind RMS = .14, Adjusted Population Gamma = .66). But this combined family and day care model was not better than a model based on family variables alone (Steiger–Lind RMS = .07, Adjusted Population Gamma = .92).

In brief, then, both path analyses and regression analyses point to the importance of family stimulation as a predictor of children's cognition, for children in day care as well as at home. These analyses also suggest that although day-care variables predict cognitive development, their influence is not as significant as that of the family. Regression analyses revealed that day care has a significant and independent effect that adds to the prediction from family variables, yet the influence of the family is somewhat greater than the influence of day care.

---

[15]Comparing the fit of the model for children in full-time day care with those in part-time day care revealed a slightly better fit for the children in full-time day care (Steiger–Lind Indexes = .14 vs. .16; Adjusted Population Gammas = .70 vs. .62).

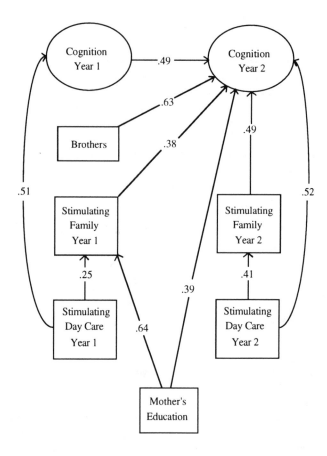

Key to Variables

Latent variable
Manifest variable (loading on the latent variable)

Cognition Year 1
Social cognition (.65)

Stimulating Family Year 1
Watching parents (-.48)
Toys (.82)
Mother reads (.45)
Father reads (.71)

Mother's Education (.48)

Brothers (.69)

Stimulating Day Care Year 1
Number of children (.96)
Diversity (.84)
Structure (.94).
Caregiver reads (.65)
Caregiver's experience (.79)

Cognition Year 2
Intellectual ability (.73)
Social cognition (.69)

Stimulating Family Year 2
Father interacts (.83)
Father reads (.83)
Mother physical contact (-.31)
Discipline (-.68)

Stimulating Day Care Year 2
Number of children (.81)
Diversity (.77)
Caregiver reads (.58)
Caregiver's training (.54)
Caregiver's education (.67)

FIG. 8.1. Best path model predicting cognition from family and daytime variables.

SUMMARY AND CONCLUSION

In this chapter and in chapter 7, a variety of analyses —correlations within and across time, regression analyses, and path analyses—provided ample evidence that children's cognitive development is directly influenced by their experiences at home and in day care. The results of analyses of the links between children's development and their experiences in the daytime echoed the theme that appeared in the analyses of family predictors; that is, the importance of education.

Recall that we saw in chapter 7 how children's cognitive development was linked to the educational level of their parents and the stimulating experiences the parents provided at home (more varied toys and playthings, more lessons and reading, more teaching by the father, more stimulating siblings). Paralleling this trend, during the daytime, cognitively advanced children attended day-care center programs, where they received more stimulation from the teacher—talking, teaching, reading, and group education. They spent more time at the center imitating the teacher and less time interacting with other children—watching, imitating, fighting, playing with or alongside. Their classes included playmates who were more stimulating—older, and, if they were in small classes, more diverse. If the children did not have the advantage of being in a day-care center during the day, their cognitive development was enhanced by the same kinds of stimulating interactions in their daytime home setting—more talking, reading, and giving lessons by the caregiver. More cognitively advanced children in home arrangements also spent less time watching TV and interacting with peers, unless the peers were older; then, they spent more time playing with them. All these specific relations paint a picture of greater stimulation, or education, enhancing children's cognitive development.

Just as we noted for the family predictions of cognitive development, the measure of cognitive development that most clearly showed the effects of these stimulating educational experiences was the more purely cognitive measure, the measure of children's memory and language comprehension. This variable was more strongly predicted than the measure of social cognition by having a trained teacher, more diverse classmates, spending less time imitating peers or passively watching the teacher in a day-care center. The positive correlations with school-like activities and negative relations with interacting with peers, it should also be noted, were higher for 4-year-olds than they were for 2- or 3-year-olds, suggesting that education is likely to become an increasingly important influence on cognitive performance as children get older.

These relations demonstrate clear parallels across settings in predictions of cognitive development. Whether at home or in day care, with parents or other caregivers, during the day or at night, children with advanced cognitive development had more frequent stimulating interactions with adults and older children and were less likely to be in environments in which the adult had to take care of an infant. In all settings, as well, children's cognitive development was more highly predicted by adults' behavior if there were no other children were present. In addition to these consistent links with educational stimulation, in all kinds of settings, children's cognitive development was enhanced when caregivers were less controlling and demanding, more responsive and likely to offer the child choices.

The significance of adults' reading and singing to the children as a source of cognitive stimulation was a particularly consistent part of the common pattern of prediction across settings. This variable, which was predictive for both fathers and mothers was also predictive in both centers and homes in the daytime. More reading and singing was significantly correlated with development within the group of children who heard any reading or singing as well as distinguishing between the cognitive level of this group and that of children who heard no stories or songs at all. It was related to cognitive development even when the effects of all other sources of stimulation were removed statistically.

There were only a few differences in the patterns of prediction in different settings. One difference was that in daytime settings, spending more time interacting with other children was generally associated with less cognitive progress, presumably because interacting with peers in these settings meant that the child was receiving less stimulating attention from an adult. At night, however, interacting more with other children was positively associated with cognitive development. Siblings, apparently, are part of a stimulating family constellation. Siblings are also better teachers according to research by Azmitia and Hesser (1993). Young children in their study were more likely to observe, imitate, and consult their older sibling and the older sibling provided more explanations and positive feedback compared to an older, familiar peer who was also asked to teach the young child to build a model.

A second difference was that in the daytime in centers more physical contact initiated by the caregiver was negatively related to children's cognitive development, whereas in the daytime in homes, physical contact with the caregiver was positively related to cognitive development. This difference reflects the different relations between adults and children in schools—where the teacher reads to a group of children in a circle, for example—and at home—where the caregiver reads to a child sitting on her lap.

The third and most notable difference between settings in the prediction of cognitive development concerned the educational backgrounds of the adult caregivers. Although children's cognitive development was positively related to the educational backgrounds of both parents and daytime caregivers (in homes or in day-care centers), this link was independent of the adults' behavior only for parents. The educational level of the daytime caregiver was not significantly predictive after the influence of her behavior was statistically controlled. This difference between parents and other caregivers is quite sensible; parents' education is a proxy for other—genetic—links between the cognitive abilities of parents and offspring; caregivers' education is not.

The links with the different kinds of stimulation we have described, at home and in day care, were, however, independent of caregivers' education and of each other. It was not the case that the parents' or caregivers' education was the basis for predictions of children's cognitive development and the other sources of stimulation were merely associated with it. Independent effects were found for mothers' backgrounds and for fathers' backgrounds; for stimulating interactions with mothers, with fathers, and with caregivers; for the presence of brothers and of diverse and older classmates; for involvement in structured activities and interactions with peers. Each of these sources of education contributed separately to the child's cognitive development.

Along with these linear predictions of cognitive development, the data in the present study also revealed some curvilinear relations. The curvilinear relation with the number of hours the mother worked outside the home was replicated in the analyses of the amount of time the child spent in day care. Children's cognitive development was promoted when mothers worked a moderate amount and the children spent a moderate amount of time in day care—10 to 30 hours a week. In addition to the possibility that we mentioned earlier that working part time is good for the mother, these data also suggest that being in day care more than 6 hours a day may not be good for children. Curvilinear relations with cognitive development were also observed for a number of the variables that positively predicted cognitive abilities at low and moderate levels but which in the extreme had negative effects. This was true for lessons and group education, number and variety of children, frequency of the caregiver's talking and responding and her level of expertise in child development. Even reading, that most significant source of stimulation, was curvilinearly related to cognition in centers, where it was more frequent.

As to the questions of whether being in day care reduces or eliminates the influence of the family on children's development and whether children's experiences at home or in day care are of greater significance, our analyses suggest that being in day care does not reduce the effect of the family and that children's cognitive abilities are affected by their experiences in both family and day-care settings. Family variables contributed significantly to cognitive development, and day care made a separate and significant contribution to predicting cognitive outcomes beyond the contribution of the family. How much day care contributes depended on how much time the child spent in day care—effects were stronger for children in full-time day care—and how different the family and day-care environments were—effects of center day care were more marked than effects of home day care.

9

Social Competence

In this chapter we turn to a different domain of development—the domain of children's social competence. We were interested in how development in the social domain was related to children's experiences and environments at night and in the daytime and whether the same patterns observed in the prediction of cognitive development would reappear for social development.

We had measured children's social competence in a wide variety of ways, for the domain of social competence is a broad one. In fact, our consideration of development in the social domain takes up the remainder of the book. In this chapter we consider a set of three variables that relate to children's social competence with adults. These three variables are the child's (a) *social competence with unfamiliar adults in the laboratory* (friendliness toward the researchers in the laboratory; cooperation in joint tasks; prosocial behavior when the researcher needed help or comfort; trust of the researcher in "dangerous" situations; and ratings by the researcher of the child's likability and social competence), (b) *social competence with an unfamiliar adult at home* (friendliness toward the researcher visiting the home; cooperation in joint tasks; prosocial behavior when the researcher needed help or comfort; trust of the researcher in "dangerous" situations; and appropriate and competent responses to requests), and (c) *independence from the mother in the laboratory* (physical contact and proximity to mother during play when mother and child were alone, with another mother and child, or with the researcher in the laboratory, and following brief separations from the mother).

This last variable reflecting the child's willingness to leave the mother's side and either play alone or interact with unfamiliar people is not a conventional measure of children's social competence. In fact, we had originally intended it to be a measure of the child's relationship with mother, not an index of social competence with unfamiliar adults. But it was included in this set of variables because of its conceptual relation to the other two variables (all reflect the child's social maturity in new situations, in unfamiliar surroundings or with unfamiliar people) and its high methodological overlap and empirical association with the measure of social competence with strangers in the laboratory [Table 6.1, $r = .50$ ($p < .001$)]. In addition, support for considering physical distance from mother in a new situation as a measure of social competence comes from previous research showing that as children get older they venture farther and farther away from mother when they allowed to explore freely (Rheingold & Eckerman, 1971). As we discussed in chapter 6, children who maintained more distance from their mothers in the laboratory also initiated less physical contact with them at home and refused more of their requests. The other two variables, both representing the child's ability to interact confidently with unfamiliar adults, were related to each other conceptually, procedurally, and empirically [Table 6.1, $r = .36$ ($p < .001$)]. Children who were socially competent with strangers in the structured assessments were less negative, difficult, and likely to initiate physical contact with their mothers or caregivers. Because the three variables representing children's social competence were interrelated, we expected to find similar patterns of association between them and the variables reflecting children's experiences and environments.

In chapters 7 and 8, in our attempt to understand the contributions of family and day care to children's cognitive development, we analyzed a broad set of variables reflecting children's experiences in day care and at home. In this chapter, we focus on those variables that we expected on the basis of theory or previous research would predict children's social competence with unfamiliar adults, in particular, children's social experiences, especially their interactions with adult caregivers, at home and in day care. The analyses we conducted paralleled those for cognitive development; as before, the child's age at the time of assessment, and when relevant, the family's SES level, were partialled out of the analyses.

FAMILY PREDICTORS

Correlation coefficients and multiple regression coefficients for the relations between the three measures of social competence and family variables are presented in Table 9.1.[1] Multiple regression coefficients, based on a subset of variables selected to reflect the parents' backgrounds, behavior, and attitudes (also indicated in Table 9.1), were significant but somewhat lower than those with cognitive development. Individual correlations also showed some parallels with the correlations observed for cognitive measures, albeit at lower levels. These parallels are not surprising, given that measures of cognition and social competence were significantly correlated

---

[1]Subanalyses for boys and girls, older and younger children, and children in higher and lower SES families revealed no consistent patterns.

TABLE 9.1
Correlations[a] Between Children's Social Competence and Family Variables

| | Social Competence | | | | | |
| | *Social Competence With Strangers*[b] | | *Social Competence With Visitor*[c] | | *Independence From Mother* | |
Family Variables	Year 1	Year 2	Year 1	Year 2	Year 1	Year 2
Family Background						
Socioeconomic status	•	•	•		•	•
Father's education	•	•	•		•	•
Father knowledge of development	•	.16	.25**		•	•
Working Mother	.17*	•	•	•	.16*	.21*
Mother's education	•	•	•		•	•
Mother's work hours	.13	− .16	•	•	.13	.21*
Mother's career orientation	•	•	•		•	•
Household help	.13	•	•		.19*	•
Money for day care/month	.19*		.13		.15	
Mother's traditional values	•	•	•		•	− .21*
Father's traditional values	•	•	•		− .17*	− .24**
Mother's involvement in care	•	•	•	•	•	− .17*
Father's Interaction						
Father playing	•	.14	•	.26*	•	.14
Father affection	•	•	•	•	.19*	•
Father talking	•	•	•	•	•	•
Mother's Physical Contact						
Mother touching	− .21**	•	•	•	− .15	
Mother affection	•	.18*	.13	.14	•	•
Mother helping child	•	•	•	•	•	.15
Mother's Interaction						
Mother playing	− .20**	•	•	•	•	•
Mother talking	•	•	•	•	•	•
Parents' Teaching	− .16*	•	•	− .18*	•	•
Parents' Responsiveness	•	•	•	.14	•	•
Parents' Discipline						
Parent offering choice	•	.17*	•	•	•	•
Mother demands	•	•	•	•	•	•
Mother demanding	•	•	•	•	.14	•
Mother control	•	•	− .30*	•	•	•
Father demands	•	•	•	•	•	•
Father demanding	.16*	•	•	•	.21*	•
Father control	•	− .18*	− .14	•	•	•
Negative affect	•	•	•	•	•	•
Positive affect	•	.15	•	.22*	.15	.15
Parents' Attitudes						
Father's expectations	•	•	•		•	•
Father's positive attitude	.21*	•	•		•	•
Mother's expectations	.12	•	.27***		•	•
Mother's positive attitude	.16*	•	.25*		.22**	.23**

(continued)

TABLE 9.1 *(continued)*

| | Social Competence | | | | | |
| | Social Competence With Strangers[b] | | Social Competence With Visitor[c] | | Independence From Mother | |
Family Variables	Year 1	Year 2	Year 1	Year 2	Year 1	Year 2
Mother's Satisfaction						
Satisfaction as mother	− .21**	.17*	•	.32**	•	•
Alienation	•	•	− .13	•	− .18*	•
Family Environment						
Number of adults at home	.20*	•	.18*	•	.20*	•
Extended family	•	•	•	•	•	− .18*
Child alone	•	− .16	•	•	•	•
Siblings	•	•	•	•	− .16	− .22*
R overall[d]	.52*	.40	.52***	.51***	.43*	.47*

[a]With child's age partialled out.
[b]Social competence with unfamiliar adults in the laboratory.
[c]Social competence with unfamiliar adult in the home.
[d]Regression coefficients from regression analyses of the following variables: father's knowledge of development; working mother factor; mother's affection, talking, and demanding; father's affection, talking, and demanding; mother's positive attitude.
•$p > .10$. *$p < .05$. **$p < .01$. ***$p < .001$. (two-tailed tests)

(see Table 6.1). Nevertheless, statistically controlling for children's cognitive (intellectual) ability in these analyses (through partial correlation) did not, by and large, eliminate the significance of the correlations obtained. There is no reason to believe that the observed relations with social competence were simply the result of children's underlying cognitive abilities.

Playful Fathers

One of the ways in which the correlations for social competence paralleled those for cognitive development was in the father's play. Like children who were advanced in cognitive development, more socially competent children had fathers who interacted with them more in positive ways. They played and offered choices more and were less likely to use physical control and punishment.[2]

Working Mothers

Like the children who were advanced in social cognition, too, more socially competent children had working mothers. Children whose mothers worked were more independent of them in the assessments in Year 1 [$t =$

---

[2]Correlations with father playing and control were significant even when cases with zero values were eliminated from the analysis.

1.9 $(p < .05)$] and Year 2 [t = 2.0 $(p < .05)$], and regression analyses indicated that mother's work status made an independent contribution to the children's independence beyond the contribution of other family variables [F = 6.5 $(p < .01)$]. The parents of more independent children had more household help, held nontraditional values, and spent more money on child care. Their mothers were less involved in their day-care arrangements. Their mothers also felt less alienated; that is, they preferred to spend less of their time alone and disagreed with statements like "Most of my life is spent doing meaningless things." "I feel no need to try my best for it makes no difference anyhow." When mothers worked more hours each week, their children were even more independent. In fact, when mothers worked more hours in Year 1 their children were more independent in Year 2 [r = .18 $(p < .05)$], suggesting that mother's work might be causally related to the child's independence.

The relation between mother's work and the child's social competence with strangers was not as clear. There was a trend for the relation with the hours the mother worked to be positive in Year 1 and negative in Year 2. Analyses of the associations between social competence and day-care participation discussed later in the chapter throw more light on this complex relation.

Although our measures of social competence were original, they are conceptually similar to measures other researchers have used, measures of social confidence, self-sufficiency, self-reliance, social responsiveness and responsibility, empathy, and sociability. What is more, the patterns of prediction other researchers have found using these other measures are quite similar to those observed in the present study. Schachter (1981) observed that children with working mothers were more self-sufficient, paralleling our finding for children's independence from the mother in the unfamiliar playroom. A. E. Gottfried et al. (1988) and Hoffman (1989) found that working mothers were more likely to encourage and teach their children independence. But our findings go beyond this simple comparison to suggest that these more independent children came from family situations themselves characterized by independence—mothers who worked more hours and had less family-oriented values.

Educational Families

One clear difference between social competence and cognitive development was in the relation of these two aspects of development to the educational atmosphere of the family. Unlike social cognition, social competence was not related to the mother's career orientation; unlike intellectual ability it was not related to higher levels of parental stimulation (parents reading, teaching, child spending less time passively watching parents). The strong linear relation with SES, and particularly mother's education, observed for cognitive ability was not found for social competence: Children who were most competent with strangers had mothers with a moderate level of education (the curvilinear analysis was significant, $p < .05$).

Social Partners

Another difference was observed in the social partners with whom the child interacted at home. More cognitively advanced children, as we discussed in chapter 7, were more likely to interact with father and brother and less likely to interact with mother during the dinnertime observation. Cognitive development was not related to the number of relatives the child had or the number of people who were in the home during the observation. More socially competent and independent children, in contrast, did not interact more with siblings or father or less with mother. They were, in fact, less likely to have siblings, and their social competence was not related to how much they interacted with either parent. The negative link between social competence and family size was especially strong for children who were home with mother all day. Although they did not have siblings, more socially competent children did have more adults in the home during the dinner hour. This offered them opportunities to interact with nonparental, probably unrelated, adults. Perhaps these opportunities allowed them to develop the ability to interact with other adults without the mother which showed up in our assessments.

Positive Parents

But perhaps the clearest difference between cognitive and social development was the relation of these abilities to parents' positive attitudes and behavior. Cognitive abilities were unrelated to the mother's positive attitude; they were negatively related to her positive (affectionate) behavior and to the father's positive attitude. In contrast, children's social competence was consistently related to parents' positive attitudes and behavior. It was positively related to both father's and mother's positive attitudes, to the amount of physical affection expressed by both father and mother, and to the positive affect observed during the dinnertime observation. The mother's positive attitude and affectionate behavior were both found to make independent contributions to the child's social competence beyond the contributions of other family variables [$Fs = 4.3$ ($p < .01$) to 8.2 ($p < .01$)]. These relations were especially strong for children who were home with mother all day.

To some extent, of course, social competence and positive parental attitudes are confounded because they both involve the child's likability. How much the researchers liked the child was part of our measure of social competence with strangers, and how much the parents liked the child was implicit in their ratings of the child which constituted our measure of positive attitude. But our measure of the child's independence from mother was not methodologically or logically linked to likability, and the parents' positive attitudes were backed up by their positive behaviors. So it does seem that the relation between children's social competence and their parents' positive attitudes is not tautological.

Other researchers have also found measures of social competence and confidence to be predicted by warm and responsive mother–child conversations (Levenstein, 1986; Olson et al., 1984) and more empathic mothering (Zahn-Waxler et al., 1979). They have also found that measures of social incompetence (withdrawal) were predicted by more controlling, authoritarian discipline (Baumrind, 1967; Baumrind & Black, 1967).

Authoritative Discipline

This last finding raises the issue of the relevance of parental discipline for the development of children's social competence and independence. The strong and consistent negative relation with parental discipline (demanding, controlling, punishing) that was found for cognition was not observed for social competence. Although the physical control parents exerted was negatively related to children's social competence, as it had been to their cognitive development, social competence was also related to a more demanding parental style rather than a less demanding one. Children who were most socially competent received a moderate number of parental demands (a significant, $p < .01$, curvilinear relation was found between the number of maternal demands and the child's social competence with the visitor), and their mothers' and fathers' styles of interaction contained relatively more demands than responses. Father's demanding style, in fact, made a significant independent contribution to children's social competence beyond the other family variables [$F = 4.7$ ($p < .01$)].

If we combine this disciplinary style involving frequent demands and infrequent physical control with the more positive attitudes and affectionate behavior toward the child noted earlier, our findings replicate well the pattern of authoritative parenting first identified by Baumrind (1967) as the key to predicting children's social competence. When parents' behavior offers a balance of warmth and control, she found, the children's behavior is characterized by a balance of independence and sociability. In this study a similar pattern was observed. More socially competent and independent children came from families in which they experienced both closeness and distance, both fondness and firmness. Their fathers also were more knowledgeable about childrearing as judged by our questionnaire about how children should be disciplined in hypothetical problem situations. [This variable, in fact, made an independent contribution to children's social competence beyond the contribution of other family variables; $t = 7.4$ ($p < .01$).] On this questionnaire, "correct" answers collected from the experts usually reflected authoritative discipline.

To test the association between social competence and authoritative discipline, further analyses were conducted. A variable combining mother's positive attitude and father's demanding style was created. This variable was more highly related to social competence, particularly independence, than was either positive maternal attitude or demanding paternal style alone [$r = .28$ ($p < .001$)]. In addition, analyses of variance revealed significant differences among groups based on the combination of positive maternal attitudes and demanding paternal style [$F(1, 140) = 7.2$ ($p < .001$) Year 1, $F(1, 124) = 7.6$ ($p < .001$) Year 2]. Children with less positive mothers and less demanding fathers were the least independent ($M = -.45$ Year 1, $M = -.37$ Year 2); children with more positive mothers and more demanding fathers were the most independent ($M = .36$ Year 1, $M = .58$ Year 2). In between were children with positive mothers and undemanding fathers ($M = .08$ Year 1, $M = -.02$ Year 2) and children with negative mothers and demanding dads ($M = .14$ Year 1, $M = -.15$ Year 2). Thus, we see confirmation of Baumrind's findings in a study of younger children, using entirely different measures of children's social competence and parents' childrearing styles. This association appears to be robust.

Cross-Time Relations

When we examined the correlations between authoritative discipline (positive attitude + demanding style) and social competence with strangers across time and examined the predictors of gains in social competence between Year 1 and Year 2, the analyses did not reveal strong cross-time links. Across time, social competence was related only to the positive emotional component of the authoritative pattern [r between social competence in Year 2 and mother's affection in Year 1 $=.20$ ($p < .05$)] and to the lack of physical control and punishment [$r = -.25$ ($p < .05$)] but not to authoritative discipline per se. The cross-time correlations between authoritative discipline and independence from mother were strong in both directions [$rs = .25$ ($p < .01$) and .25 ($p < .01$)]. It was therefore not possible to determine whether authoritative discipline from parents was the cause or consequence of children's independence. There was, however, a suggestion that children's social competence was affecting the mother's feelings. Children who were more independent and more socially competent with strangers in Year 1 had mothers who were more satisfied with their roles as mothers in Year 2 [$rs = .17$ ($p < .05$), .22 ($p < .01$)].

DAILY EXPERIENCES AND ENVIRONMENTS
AS PREDICTORS

In the next set of analyses we examined the prediction of children's social competence from their experiences during the day. Multiple regression analyses performed on a subset of variables selected to reflect caregivers' backgrounds and behavior, structured activities, and the child's contact with peers showed that these experiences accounted for about 20% of the variance in children's social competence. These multiple regression coefficients and the individual correlations between the measures of social competence and the daytime variables are presented in Table 9.2. Many of these correlations, like those with the family variables, were similar to the relations obtained for measures of cognitive development. Like those relations, their significance was not reduced when children's cognitive ability was controlled statistically through partial correlation.

Being in Day Care

Both social competence and cognitive development were related to the child's participation in day care. As was true for cognitive ability, social competence was positively related to being in day care. Children in day care, specifically in center day care, were significantly more competent with strangers and independent of mother in the unfamiliar playroom. This was evident in the significant correlations with the child-care arrangement and also in analyses of variance contrasting children in different care arrangements. There were no significant effects of being in home day care; differences in social competence between children in parent care and sitter care (in the child's own home or a day-care home) were nonsignificant ($Fs < 1$). This suggests that social competence with unfamiliar adults is not just the result of knowing one nonparental adult well. However, there were significant differences between being in home care and being in center care [in analyses of variance controlling for SES, $Fs(1,142; 1,126) = 6.9$ ($p < .01$); 4.6 ($p < .05$) for independence, 6.0 ($p < .05$); 3.8 ($p < .05$) for social competence with strangers, 5.8 ($p < .05$) for social competence with visitor].

These differences are reflected throughout the correlational analyses. More socially competent children were in care arrangements with more children, of greater diversity, in programs that provided more structured and planned activities including songs, stories, and lessons. They had caregivers with more professional experience in child care. They received less play, affection, physical contact, and physical control from these caregivers.

These relations between social competence and children's experiences during the daytime simply reflect the fact that more socially competent children were in day-care centers. Other research also suggests that children who attend day-care center programs are less timid and distressed in new and unfamiliar situations (Cochran, 1977b; Kagan et al., 1978; Moskowitz et al., 1977), more independent of their mothers in the lab (Wynn, 1979), and more socially mature and self-reliant according to their mothers' reports at age 10 (Larner, Gunnarsson, Cochran, & Hagglund, 1989). Although such relations have not been observed in every study (Schenk & Grusec, 1987), there does seem to be a growing body of evidence suggesting that children with experience in day care are more socially competent than children without this experience.

Being in Good Day Care.   But social competence was not just related to being in any kind of day care, or even any kind of center day care. It was related to being in "better" day care.

For children in center care, this meant that the caregivers did less touching, hugging, and playing, gave more lessons, and exerted less physical control (see Table 9.2). These relations parallel those for cognitive development. Unlike the patterns for cognitive development, however, it did not seem to matter for children's social competence how diverse their social contacts in the class were, how qualified their teachers, how frequently they heard stories or songs or engaged in structured activities. These seem to be more cognitively oriented features of the day-care program. In fact, relations of social competence with one of these variables was in the opposite direction: Among children in centers, more socially competent children had caregivers with lower levels of education.

For children in home-care arrangements, however, caregivers' qualifications were positively predictive of greater social competence. More socially competent children were in home care with caregivers who had more training, experience, education, and knowledge. In contrast to center caregivers, these home caregivers read, touched, and played with socially competent children more and had higher expectations for them. Like the center caregivers, they gave the children more lessons. These associations in home care were generally stronger than those observed with the same variables for cognitive development.

Many of the differences in the correlational patterns predicting social competence from experiences in home care and experiences in centers can be explained in terms of social competence being related to optimal levels of experience. This is so for the level of caregivers' professional qualifications—education, training, experience, knowledge—which were positively related in homes (in which the average level of professional qualifications was lower) and negatively related in centers (in which the average level of professional qualifications was higher). It was so for the amount the caregiver read to the child, which was positively related only in homes (where, on average, it occurred less).

But curvilinear relations do not explain all the differences observed between the correlational patterns in home care and center care. In addition, in centers, more socially competent children were touched and played with

TABLE 9.2

Correlations[a] Between Children's Social Competence and Daytime Variables

	Social Competence																	
	All Children						*Children in Centers*						*Children in Homes*					
	Social Competence Stranger		*Social Competence Visitor*		*Independence Mother*		*Social Competence Stranger*		*Social Competence Visitor*		*Independence Mother*		*Social Competence Stranger*		*Social Competence Visitor*		*Independence Mother*	
Daytime Variables	*Year 1*	*2*	*Year 1*	*2*	*Year 1*	*2*	*Year 1*	*2*	*Year 1*	*2*	*Year 1*	*2*	*Year 1*	*2*	*Year 1*	*2*	*Year 1*	*2*
Child-Care Arrangement	.25**	•	.23**	•	.22**	.17*	•	•	•	•	•	•	•	•	•	•	•	•
Children in care arrangement	.26**	.17*	.16*	•	.23**	.14	•	•	•	•	•	•	•	•	•	•	•	•
Child-caregiver ratio	.22**	.25**	•	•	.14	•	•	.20*	•	•	•	•	.15	.16	•	•	•	•
Diversity	.19*	.23**	•	•	.26**	.14	•	•	•	•	•	•	•	•	•	•	•	•
Number of caregivers	•	.18*	.18*	•	.19*	.14	•	−.21*	•	•	•	•	.18*	•	•	•	•	.27**
Amount of interaction with any nonparental caregiver	.27**	•	.22**	.29**	.17*	•	•	•	•	•	•	•	•	•	•	•	•	•
Program	.24**	.17*	.19*	•	.27**	•	•	•	•	•	•	•	•	•	•	•	•	•

Caregiver's Qualifications

Caregiver's education
.17* .14 • • • • • • • • .16 • • .19*

Caregiver's training in child care
.18* • • • −.29* • • • .18* • • • • •

Caregiver's experience in child care
.25** .18* .23** • • • • .25** • .22* • • •

Caregiver's knowledge of development
• .19* .14 • • • • • • .24** .20* • •

Caregiver's age
.13 .15 • • • • .17 • • • • .15

Caregiver's positive attitude toward child
.15 .21** .14 .20* .32** .19 .31* .21 .28* .16 .16 .20 .32** .23*

Caregiver's expectations for child
.15 .14 .15 .13 .15 • • • • • • .25** .26** •

Caregiver Behavior

Caregiver reading or singing
.20* .18* .20* .17* .20* • • • .22* .16* .20* .20* .23*

Caregiver offering choice
−.17* • −.22** −.24* • −.21* −.29* • • −.20* • • •

Caregiver one-to-one talk
• .16* .14 • • • • • • .25* .29**

(continued)

TABLE 9.2 (continued)

	All Children						Children in Centers						Children in Homes					
	Social Competence Stranger		Social Competence Visitor		Independence Mother		Social Competence Stranger		Social Competence Visitor		Independence Mother		Social Competence Stranger		Social Competence Visitor		Independence Mother	
	Year		*Year*		*Year*		*Year*		*Year*		*Year*		*Year*		*Year*		*Year*	
	1	*2*	*1*	*2*	*1*	*2*	*1*	*2*	*1*	*2*	*1*	*2*	*1*	*2*	*1*	*2*	*1*	*2*
Daytime Variables																		
Caregiver Behavior (continued)																		
Caregiver touching	-.14	•	•	•	-.15	•	-.20	-.17*	-.25	-.27**	•	•	.17	•	.22*	.26**	.15	.20*
Caregiver affection	-.22*	•	•	-.15	•	•	-.21	•	-.17	•	•	•	-.20*	•	•	•	•	•
Caregiver playing	-.19*	-.19*	•	-.24**	•	•	-.20*	•	•	-.24*	•	-.22*	•	.20*	.24**	•	•	.15
Caregiver giving lesson	•	.16*	.16*	•	.17*	.26**	.22	•	•	•	.21	.22*	•	.20*	.18*	•	.15	.30**
Caregiver control	-.20*	•	•	•	•	•	•	•	•	•	•	-.32**	•	•	•	•	•	•
Caregiver demanding	.16*	•	•	•	.21**	•	.23	•	•	•	.20*	.21*	.21*	•	•	•	•	•
Caregiver verbal responsiveness	.16	•	.22*	•	•	-.23**	•	•	•	•	•	•	.19*	.20*	•	.25**	-.25**	-.31**

Peer Activities

Younger children present	−.14	−.15	−.14		−.14												−.25**
Child imitating, watching, or talking to peers		−.19	−.21														•
Peer aggression (if peer present)	−.23	−.25	−.22		−.14	.29*	.25*				−.31**	−.30**	−.22*	−.25**	−.19*		−.25**
											−.31**	−.30**	−.35**		−.18		−.25**

Child Activities

Child alone		.17		.20													
Child activities with adults						.28**						.20*	.17	.19*			
Mesh between family and day care																	
R^b	.44**	.46**	.42**	.46**	.49**	.38+	.57*	.41+	.63**	.50*	.57**	.38	.28	.45+	.35+	.44*	.29	.47*

[a]With child's age partialled out.

[b]These regression coefficients are based on regression analyses of sets of variables selected to reflect caregivers' backgrounds (education, experience) and behavior (reading, playing, lessons, demanding), structured activities (program), and the child's contact with peers (number, interaction).

•$p > .10$. *$p < .05$. **$p < .01$. ***$p < .001$. (two-tailed tests) less by the caregiver (i.e., they were given more independence); in homes, more socially competent children received more touching, playing, and one-to-one talk from the caregiver (i.e., they were given more attention).

Unfortunately, there are no other studies with which to compare the results of these analyses. Other researchers have investigated general relations between children's social competence and global indexes of day-care quality, but their measures and their results are not comparable with each other or with those of the present study. In these other investigations, Lamb et al. (1988) found that children's social skills with an unfamiliar adult were related to lower day-care quality (in Sweden); Howes and Stewart (1987) found that children in higher quality day-care homes were more socially competent with adult caregivers; and Phillips, McCartney, and Scarr (1987; Phillips, Scarr, & McCartney, 1987) found that children in high-quality day-care centers were more communicative, considerate, and sociable according to teachers' and parents' ratings. The present study dug deeper to identify specific processes at work in different kinds of day care.

How Much Day Care Is Good Day Care?   So we know that being in day care is predictive of increased social competence and that the quality of the day care matters as well, but does it make a difference how much time the child spends in the day-care setting? Can we say how much day care is good for the child's development? As we have already mentioned, children who were more independent of their mothers in Year 2 had mothers who worked more hours in Year 1. Paralleling this finding, in a stepwise regression analysis, the single most predictive variable for independence from mother was the length of time the child had spent in day care. Both months in day care and daily hours in day care were significantly correlated with independence [$rs = .28$ ($p < .001$), $.26$ ($p < .01$)], whether day care occurred in a home or center setting (see also means in Table 9.3), and with the gain in children's independence from Year 1 to Year 2 [$rs = .19$ ($p < .05$), $.19$ ($p < .05$)]. In terms of children's independence from mother, then, more time in day care advanced development. The opposite relation was found for cognitive development.

Links were also found between children's social competence with strangers and the amount of time they had spent in day care, but the associations were not as simple. The months and hours children spent in day care were correlated with social competence with strangers differently for children in home care and in center care. For children in home day care, those who had spent more time in day care were more socially competent [$rs = .20$ ($p < .05$), $.21$ ($p < .01$)]; for children in center care, months and hours of care were related to lower social competence [$rs = -.30$ ($p < .01$), $-.29$ ($p < .01$)]. The reason for this difference between home and center day care may also be the curvilinear relations described earlier. Paralleling the results for cognitive development, the most socially competent children had some day care (10 to 30 hours a week; see Table 9.3). For social

TABLE 9.3

Mean Social Competence for Children with Differing Amounts of Day Care

Outcome Measure	Year	Hours of Day Care Per Week				F df	F linear trend df
		None	10–30	30–40	>40		
	1	n = 48	n = 36	n = 51	n = 9	3,140	1,140
	2	n = 23	n = 47	n = 49	n = 9	3,124	1,124
Social competence	1	− .29	.28	.06	.15	3.5*	ns
with strangers	2	− .23	.27	− .12	− .16	2.1⁺	ns
Social competence	1	− .18	.28	.01	− .13	2.3⁺	ns
with visitor							
Independence	1	− .48	.24	.23	.41	2.3⁺	2.8*
from mother	2	− -.66	− .28	.45	.63	2.9*	4.0**

$^+p < .10.$ $^*p < .05.$ $^{**}p < .01.$

competence with strangers, then, as for cognitive abilities, a moderate amount of day care may be optimal.

Other Social Partners

An aspect of the child's daytime experience that was of particular interest for predicting social competence was the child's opportunity to interact with different social partners in the daytime. Here some differences in the patterns of predictions were found for social competence as compared with cognitive development.

Adults. Overall, more socially competent children had more different adults with whom to interact in the daytime, and they spent more time interacting with these caregivers who were not their parents. One might infer therefore that experience with a range of adult partners fostered children's ability to interact with an unfamiliar adult in our research. This finding, however, was a result of the fact that children in day-care centers—where there were more caregivers—were more socially competent than children in home care. Looking at the samples of children in day-care centers and in home care separately revealed that the number of caregivers in home care was not related to children's social competence, and in centers, the relation with number of caregivers was negative: More socially competent children had fewer caregivers. Perhaps the overall positive relation with number of caregivers can be explained in terms of social competence being related to interacting with a moderate number of caregivers. But no significant curvilinear relations were found for this variable. More likely, the number of caregivers is irrelevant for social competence and the positive relation for the whole sample was a result of other aspects of the experience of being in a day-care center. Regression analyses showed that after other distinctive features of being in a day-care center (program, lessons, reading) were removed, the relation with number of caregivers was no longer significant. Children's social competence was not related to the frequency and variety of their social activities with nonrelated adults outside of day care; this variable significantly predicted cognitive development (see Table 8.1) but not, as might have been expected, sociability with strangers.

Peers.   In both home and day-care center settings, social competence was related to the opportunity to interact with more different children under the supervision of a single adult. Positive correlations with social competence were significant for the number of children present in home-care arrangements and for the number of children per caregiver in center classes. For two other peer variables, relations were different in the two kinds of daytime setting. In home care, more socially competent children had a more diverse set of other children to play with; in centers, diversity of playmates was not related to the child's social competence. Because diversity was substantially greater in center classes than in home arrangements, this suggests that a moderately diverse set of playmates may be optimal for social competence; this suggestion was supported by a significant (inverted U-shaped) curvilinear relation between social competence with strangers and diversity in Year 1 ($p < .003$). A second difference between settings was found in the amount of time the child spent playing with other children. More socially competent children in home care spent less time playing with other children; more socially competent children in centers spent more time playing with other children. A curvilinear relation with social competence with strangers in Year 1 for the total sample was also found for this variable ($p < .06$).

Time Alone.   One consistent association in homes and in centers was between children's social competence and how much time they spent alone. Whether they were in home care or centers, more socially competent children spent more time alone. Perhaps this is a demonstration of their independence.

Positive Caregivers

The distinctive pattern of association between social competence and parents' positive attitudes toward child was paralleled in the analyses of variables reflecting children's experiences during the daytime. Like their parents, children's daily caregivers expressed more positive attitudes toward children who were more socially competent. This was true for both children in center care and children in home care. Because the caregivers in home-care arrangements included both mothers and unrelated sitters, analyses were done to find out whether the relations with caregiver's attitude were different depending on who the caregiver was. Analyses of covariance demonstrated that they were not. What is different from the pattern noted for parents is that the daily caregivers of more socially competent children did not, as parents did, express more affection to them; in fact, they expressed less. This finding underscores the difference noted earlier that children's interactions with their parents are more emotional than their interactions with other caregivers.

Discipline in the Daytime: Love and Limits Again

The distinctive pattern of association between social competence and parents' authoritative discipline also reappeared in the daytime observations. More socially competent children had caregivers whose management style was demanding but not physically controlling. They received relatively more demands and fewer choices from caregivers (relations that were in the opposite direction from those observed with cognitive development). This was true for children in center care and for children in home care. Combining the caregiver's positive attitude and her demanding style into a new variable reflecting authoritative discipline increased the size of the correlation coefficients with social competence to .29 ($p < .001$) for independence from mother, to .22 ($p < .01$) for social competence with strangers, and to .23 ($p < .01$) for social competence with the visitor, for the entire sample; to .37 ($p < .01$) for social competence with strangers, .38 ($p < .01$) for independence from mother, for children in day-care centers). Backing up the link with authoritative discipline was the finding that the caregivers of more socially competent children scored higher on our test of childrearing knowledge, which, you will recall, tapped the respondent's positive attitude toward authoritative disciplinary strategies in hypothetical problem situations.

Daytime Predictors Compared

To compare the contributions to children's social competence of all the different aspects of the child's daytime experiences we carried out multiple regression analyses. The variables included were caregiver's background (education, experience in child care), behavior (giving lessons, making demands), and attitude (positive attitude toward the child), the structure in the program, and the child's interaction with peers (number of children in the class and amount of time spent interacting with them). These analyses showed that the caregiver's behavior and attitude were the most significant and consistent contributors to competence and had independent effects for all three measures in both years [$Rs = .37; .32, Fs = 2.4$ ($p < .05$); 2.1 ($p < .10$) for independence; $Rs = .34; .23, Fs = 2.1$ ($p < .05$); 2.1 ($p < .05$) for social competence with strangers; $Rs = .30; .20, Fs = 3.0$ ($p < .01$); 2.1 ($p < .05$) for social competence with visitor]. More specifically, the combination of positive attitude and demanding discipline that we have identified as reflecting an authoritative management style was significantly and independently predictive of all three measures of social competence when all other aspects of experience were statistically controlled [$Fs = 4.7$ ($p < .01$), 6.4 ($p < .01$), 6.8

($p < .01$) for the three measures of social competence in Year 1]. The other aspects of the environment (the caregiver's background, the program, interaction with peers) did not make independent contributions to children's social competence.[3] Recall that these factors were independently predictive of cognitive development.

Cross-Time Relations

When we examined the correlations with authoritative discipline across time we did not find a strong cross-time link with social competence with strangers. Nor were gains in social competence with strangers between Year 1 and Year 2 related to caregivers' authoritative discipline in Year 1. Gains and Year 2 social competence were related only to the positive emotional component of the authoritative pattern [rs with caregiver's positive attitude = .26 ($p < .01$) and affection =.18 ($p < .05$)].

Cross-time correlations with independence from the mother did reveal significant relations with authoritative discipline. Children with more authoritative caregivers made greater gains in independence between Year 1 and Year 2 [$r = .18$ ($p < .05$)]. But the cross-time correlations with authoritative discipline (positive attitude + demanding) were strong in both directions [$rs = .45$ ($p < .001$) vs .30 ($p < .01$)]; it was not possible to determine whether authoritative discipline from caregivers was the cause or consequence of children's independence. There was a suggestion that children's independence affected their caregiver's opinions: Caregivers of children who were more independent in Year 1 had higher expectations for them in Year 2 [$r = .21$ ($p < .01$)]. These cross-time patterns for independence from mother and social competence with strangers are remarkably similar to those observed with parent's authoritative discipline discussed earlier.

COMBINED EFFECTS OF FAMILY AND DAYTIME EXPERIENCES

The variables reflecting the child's daily experiences made a significant independent contribution beyond the contribution of family variables for all three measures of social competence except independence from mother in Year 2 [$Fs = 2.0$ ($p < .05$) to 2.3 ($p < .05$)]. In fact, daytime experiences were the major predictors of independence from mother in Year 1 and social competence with strangers in Year 2; family variables did not make a

---

[3]The prediction of social competence from daily experiences was stronger for boys than for girls. For example, the correlation between being in day care and being more socially competent with strangers was .38 ($p < .05$) for boys and .10 for girls. Stronger effects of day-care participation on boys' independence from mother in the laboratory were also observed by Moskowitz et al. (1977). In their study, boys without day-care experience stayed closer to their mothers than did boys with day-care experience, but no differences were observed for girls with and without day-care experience.

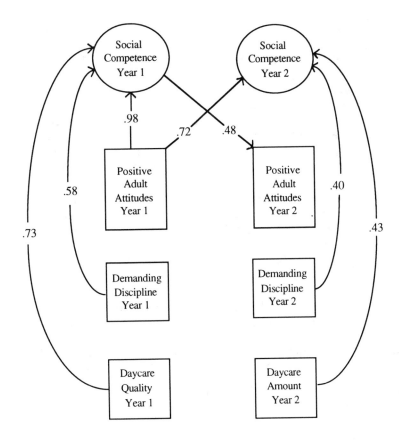

Key to Variables

Latent variable
Manifest variable (loading on the latent variable)

Social Competence Year 1
Social competence with stranger (.57)
Independence from mother (.58)

Positive Adult Attitudes Year 1
Mother's positive attitude (.50)
Caregiver's positive attitude (.65)

Demanding Discipline Year 1
Father demanding (.69)
Caregiver demanding (.59)

Day-Care Quality Year 1
Day-care structure (.93)
Lessons (.80)
Caregiver's experience (.82)

Social Competence Year 2
Social competence with stranger (.38)
Independence from mother (.80)

Positive Adult Attitudes Year 2
Mother's affection (.48)
Caregiver's positive attitude (.67)

Demanding Discipline Year 2
Father demanding (.40)
Caregiver demanding (.48)

Day-Care Amount Year 2
Months in day care (.68)
Hours in day care (.91)
Mother's work hours (.76)

FIG. 9.1. Best path model for combined variables predicting children's social competence.

contribution beyond that of daytime experiences for these measures. For a combined index of social competence, an additive regression model including both family and daytime variables was more significant [$R = .60$ ($p < .01$)] than models including only family variables [$R = .48$ ($p < .05$)] or day-care variables [$R = .44$ ($p < .05$)].

In the final analyses, models relating the associations with social competence that we have discussed were tested. These path analyses showed that the data best fit the model pictured in Fig. 9.1. The fit for this model, which brought together the significant associations with social competence into a single, coherent pattern, was quite good [Steiger–Lind RMS Index = .09 (.07 – .10); Adjusted Population Gamma = .89 (.84 – .96)]. In the model, a latent variable representing children's social competence (social competence with strangers and independence from mother) was predicted by latent variables reflecting adults' positive attitudes to the child (mother's and caregiver's positive attitudes and mother's affectionate behavior), demanding discipline (father's and caregiver's demanding styles of interaction), day-care quality (program structure, lessons, and caregiver's experience), and the amount of time the child had spent in day care (months and hours in day care, hours mother worked). The model included contemporaneous links between social competence and demanding discipline and between social competence and day care in Year 1 and in Year 2; it included contemporaneous links between social competence and positive adult attitudes in Year 1 and links between social competence and positive attitudes across time from Year 1 to Year 2 (in both directions). Note that the strongest paths in the model were between positive adult attitudes in Year 1 and social competence in Year 1 and Year 2.

This model provided a better fit for the data than the following models:

1. a model based on family variables alone;
2. a model based on daytime variables alone;
3. a model including cross-time links between social competence and demanding discipline;
4. a model with cross-time links between social competence and day-care quality;
5. a model in which positive attitudes and demanding discipline were combined to form a latent variable of authoritative discipline;
6. a model not containing demanding discipline;
7. a model not containing positive attitudes;
8. a model not containing day-care participation;
9. a model with no cross-time connections between social competence and positive attitudes;
10. a model with no cross-time connection between social competence in Year 1 and positive attitudes in Year 2;
11. a model with no cross-time connection between positive attitudes in Year 1 and social competence in Year 2.

For all these models the Steiger–Lind RMS Index was > .1 and the Adjusted Population Gamma was < .81.

These results suggest that children's social competence is fostered by participation in day care, particularly high-quality day care, and by positive and affectionate attitudes and interactions from the adults in their lives. They also indicate that children's social competence encourages further positive actions and attitudes by those adults. They show that social competence is associated with a more demanding style of discipline, but it is not clear whether this is a cause or a consequence of children's advanced social competence.

SUMMARY AND CONCLUSION

Despite the fact that children's social competence was moderately correlated with their cognitive abilities, the pattern of prediction from children's experiences was quite different. Unlike cognition, social competence was not linearly related to mother's education or parents' stimulation (talking or reading) or to receiving less demanding discipline. The prediction of social competence from stimulation in the daytime (reading, lessons) was not as strong as the prediction of cognition, and social competence was not independently related to being in a more educational program.

What social competence was related to was a distinctive pattern of experience that involved love and limits: Positive attitudes and affectionate behavior combined with moderate discipline—demanding but not physically controlling. Like Baumrind's authoritative discipline, this pattern predicted both social responsiveness (social competence with an unfamiliar adult) and independence (physical distance from the mother in the laboratory playroom). In our study, children's social competence was linked to authoritative discipline both at home at night and in day care during the day. The only difference between the two settings was that at home more socially competent children received more physical affection from the adults, but in day care they did not. Perhaps this was because of the different roles of parental and nonparental caregivers; perhaps it was the consequence of setting differences. In centers, the study revealed, caregivers touched and played less with socially competent children; in homes, they touched and played with them more.

Causal analyses suggested that some aspects of the authoritative pattern were not just linked to children's social competence with strangers but were actually influencing it. Less physical control at dinnertime and a more positive attitude from the caregiver in the daytime led to increased social competence with strangers over the course of the study. But the adults' demanding style of interaction was not causally linked to social competence. Thus, it may be positive interaction with adults rather than demanding discipline that fosters social competence. Even so, it should be noted, based on our analyses, the relation between social competence and positive adult attitudes and behavior is likely to be reciprocal, a consequence as well as a cause of social competence.

Children's experience in day care added significantly and independently to the prediction of their social competence beyond these associations with authoritative discipline. Social competence with strangers was predicted by being in a day-care center and spending a moderate amount of time there (10 to 30 hours per week), whereas independence from the mother was related to spending more time in day care. Time in day care, in fact, was the single most significant predictor of independence from the mother. Paralleling their children's behavior, the mothers of more independent children were themselves more independent: They worked more hours, held less traditional family values, and had smaller families.

10

Sociability With Mother

In this chapter we consider another aspect of development: the child's relationship with his or her mother. This relationship is, of course, of critical concern for children who are separated from their mothers for large parts of the day. Researchers as well as parents have been alarmed by the possibility that children attending day care for many hours every week will have less than optimal relationships with their mothers. In particular, they have suggested that day-care attendance may impair the formation of a secure attachment bond between the child and the mother (e.g., Belsky, 1988). They worry that children in day care will not feel as close to their mothers and, as a result, will have emotional problems later in life. Although the children in the present study had not started day care until they were at least 2 years old, after their attachments to their mothers had formed, the issue of the quality of their relationships with their mothers is still of concern.

In this study we assessed the quality of the child's relationship with the mother in a number of ways during our laboratory sessions each year. The variable reflecting the child's relationship with mother that we created from these observations included the following measures: the child's positive and reciprocal interaction with mother during free play; cooperation with the mother in a structured task (drawing a face together); positive interaction and greeting of the mother after brief separations (rather than avoiding, turning away from, or acting angry toward the mother); and initiation of prosocial acts when mother was "hurt."

This variable was only modestly correlated with the child's cognition and social competence (see Table 6.1). The one measure of competence with which sociability with mother was quite strongly associated was the measure of the child's social competence with strangers in the laboratory. This association was probably a result of the fact that the two measures were assessed in the same laboratory session and that each reflects the child's ability to interact with adult partners in a friendly, cooperative, positive way. Children who were high in social reciprocity with their mothers in the laboratory also talked to them more at home.

FAMILY PREDICTORS

Despite this overlap with general sociability, we expected that our measure of the child's sociability with mother would prove to be a distinct child development "outcome" that would be related specifically to the child's experiences interacting with the mother at home. We expected that it would be correlated with the mother's characteristics and behavior with the child, and not with the child's experiences with father, siblings, or in day care. Regression analyses and correlations of sociability with the family variables (presented in Table 10.1) supported this hypothesis. Significant regression coefficients [$R = .41$ ($p < .05$) in Year 1; $R = .39$ ($p < .10$) in Year 2] were obtained when maternal variables were analyzed, but regression coefficients for father and sibling variables were nonsignificant and very low [Rs = .05 and .19 for father variables (amount of interaction with the father, physical control exerted by the father, father's positive attitude); .16 and .09 for sibling variables (number of siblings, amount of interaction with siblings)]. The only paternal variables that were related at all to children's sociability to the mother were variables for which the fathers' behavior or attitude was correlated with the mother's. These variables were physical control, verbal responsiveness, positive expectations, and attitudes. Partialling out the identical maternal behaviors reduced these correlations to nonsignificance.

   In terms of specific correlations, children who were more sociable with their mothers in the laboratory had mothers who interacted more with them at home at dinnertime (talking, teaching, reading, showing affection), and were less controlling and more responsive. They also worked fewer hours, had more positive attitudes toward the child, and were less alienated from life and other people in general. More positive affect was expressed in family interactions at dinnertime, and the children spent less time at home alone or playing with objects. In brief, children's positive relationships with their mothers were reflected in positive interactions at dinnertime and bedtime as well as in our laboratory assessment. This association with the mother's behavior held up even for children in day care full time [rs for positive interaction with mother = .28 ($p < .05$) in Year 1, .24 ($p < .05$) in Year 2].

TABLE 10.1
Correlations[a] Between Children's Sociability with Mother and Family Variables

Family variables	Sociability With Mother	
	Year 1	Year 2
Family Background		
Socioeconomic status	•	•
Working Mother		
Mother's education	•	•
Mother's work hours	− .15	− .18*
Mother's career orientation	•	•
Household help	.14	•
Mother's traditional values	•	.14
Mother's Childrearing Expertise		
Mother's child-care training	•	•
Mother's child-care experience	•	•
Mother's knowledge of development	•	•
Father's Interaction		
Father's playing	•	•
Father talking	•	•
Father touching	•	•
Father affection	•	•
Mother's Physical Contact		
Mother touching	•	•
Mother touching, proportion	•	•
Mother affection	•	.25**
Mother helping child	•	•
Mother's Interaction		
Mother playing	.16	•
Mother talking	.28**	•
Mother teaching	.20*	•
Mother reading	•	.21*
Parents' Discipline		
Mother demanding	− .16	•
Mother control	•	− .44 +
Father demanding	•	•
Father control	•	− .50+
Parents' Responsiveness	.21**	.20**
Positive affect	.14	.29**
Parents' Attitudes		
Father's expectations for child	.20*	•
Father's positive attitude	.17	•
Mother's positive attitude	.21**	•
Mother's Satisfaction		
Mother's overall role satisfaction	•	•
Mother's satisfaction as mother	•	•
Mother's alienation	− .18*	•
Child's Activities		
Child alone	•	− .16
Child playing with object	•	− .20*

(continued)

TABLE 10.1 *(continued)*

Family variables	Sociability With Mother	
	Year 1	Year 2
Family Environment		
Siblings	•	•
Sibling interaction	•	•
R^b	.46**	.45**

[a]With child's age partialled out.

[b]These regression coefficients are for the following sets of variables: maternal variables (mother's talking, teaching, controlling, and positive attitude); paternal variables (father's interaction, physical control, positive attitude); sibling variables (number of siblings, amount of interaction with siblings).

$^+p < .10.$ $^*p < .05.$ $^{**}p < .01.$ $^{***}p < .001.$ (two-tailed tests)

When Children Were at Home All Day

In addition to this association with positive interaction with the mother which showed up for all children, several other relations appeared in the dinnertime observations for children who were at home with their mothers all day. Among these children, those with more positive relationships with their mothers, as expressed in the laboratory, had mothers who were more highly educated [$r = .28$ $(p < .05)$], experienced in child care [$r = .30$ $(p < .05)$], knowledgeable about childrearing [$r = .30$ $(p < .05)$], and had more help with housework [$r = .36$ $(p < .01)$]. Their interactions with the child were more likely to include physical contact [$r = .39$ $(p < .05)$]. For children who spent the most time with their mothers, then, the associations with the mother's qualities included her "qualifications" as a caregiver (knowledge, experience, availability) and her frequent, close physical interactions.

Differences in SES

One reason that there were few significant correlations with paternal variables was that the correlational patterns for interaction with the father were different for different socioeconomic levels. Analyses of covariance revealed that there were significant interactions of the paternal variables with SES for several variables. More frequent positive interaction with the father (touching, playing, showing affection) was related to higher sociability with the mother in high-SES families [$r = .31$ $(p < .01)$] but lower sociability with mother in lower-SES families [$r = -.26$ $(p < .05)$]. In high-SES families, interaction with father at dinnertime may have included the mother; in lower-SES families it may have excluded the mother. Reanalyzing the links between maternal and paternal behavior for higher- and lower-SES families separately revealed that, in lower-SES families, the amounts the mother and father interacted positively with the child, especially in interaction involving physical contact, were negatively correlated [$rs = -.28$ ($p < .05$), $-.33$ ($p < .05$)]; whereas in high-SES families, the amounts the mother and father interacted positively with the child were positively correlated [$rs = .27$ ($p < .05$), $.31$ ($p < .01$)]. What these results indicate once again is that it is interaction with the mother, not with anyone else, that is the key to the quality of the child's relationship with her.

DAYTIME PREDICTORS

This statement that the child's sociability with mother depends on the child's interaction with her rather than with anyone else may seem obvious. But it has been suggested that if children are in day care their relationship with mother will be improved by positive interaction with their substitute caregiver, that good quality day care will promote a more secure attachment to mother. In this study, however, there was no evidence that would support this speculation. Regression analyses including day-care variables supported the hypothesis that children's sociability with their mothers would be associated primarily with qualities of the mother and her interaction with the child not with other aspects of experience. After maternal variables (talking, teaching, controlling, and positive attitude) were entered into a regression analyses, there were no significant effects for the daytime variables (being in a day-care center, having a more qualified caregiver, interacting more with peers, receiving better care—hearing more stories, being given more choices, getting more affection). In fact, Rs for daytime variables, even without removing maternal variables, were all nonsignificant (for all subjects, for subjects in day-care centers only, and for subjects in home-care settings only). Nor were individual correlations with these variables significant. Children in day care had as good relationships with their mothers as children who were home with the mother all day ($Fs < 1$), and even though sociability was related to the number of hours the mother worked, it was not related to the number of hours the child spent in day care.

RELATIONS OVER TIME

Path analyses indicated that the best fitting model for the child's sociability to mother was the one presented in Fig. 10.1. In this model, sociability was predicted by positive interaction with the mother (responsiveness, talking, playing, positive affect, affection) and by the mother's positive attitude. The goodness of fit for this model [Steiger–Lind RMS Index = .11 (.09 − .14); Adjusted Population Gamma = .87 (.80 − .92)] was somewhat better than that for a model in which the direction of the arrows was reversed so that the child's sociability predicted the mother's positive interaction and attitude (Steiger–Lind RMS Index = .16, Adjusted Population Gamma = .77). It was also better than a model that included the mother's work hours (Steiger–Lind = .15, Adjusted Population Gamma = .73), or a model in which the link between the mother's attitude and the child's sociability was mediated through her positive interaction (Steiger–Lind RMS Index = .17, Adjusted Population Gamma = .71). The key to a good relationship with mother, thus, appears to be a positive mother.

Although no significant relations between sociability with mother and enrollment in day care appeared in the contemporaneous correlations,

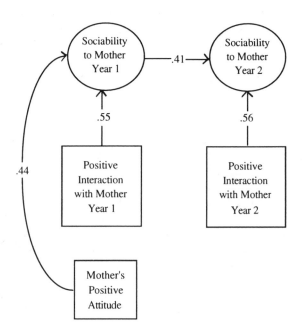

Key to Variables

Latent variable
Manifest variable (loading on the latent variable)

Sociability to Mother Year 1
Sociability to mother (.64)

Positive Interaction with Mother Year 1
Mother's responsiveness (.45)
Mother's talk and play (.67)
Positive affect at dinnertime (.53)

Mother's Positive Attitude
Mother's expectations (.77)

Sociability to Mother Year 2
Sociablity to mother (.64)

Positive Interaction with Mother Year 2
Mother's responsiveness (.69)
Mother reading (.23)
Positive affect at dinnertime (.99)

FIG. 10.1.   Best path model for predicting sociability to mother.

there was one significant association across time: Children who were most sociable with their mothers in Year 1 were in home care both years (M = 1.2); children in center care both years were moderately sociable with the mothers in Year 1 (M = .40); children who were least sociable with their mothers in Year 1 were in home care in Year 1 and center care in Year 2 [M = −.86; $F(2, 118)$ = 6.4 (p < .01)]. This relation suggests that the child's relationship with mother could affect the parents' selection of day care: Mothers whose relations with the child at 2 – 3 years were least warm and sociable were more likely to place the child in day care within the year. This interpretation is supported by Melhuish et al. (1991) and Blurton Jones et al.'s (1980) findings that women who went to work felt more remote from their children even before they placed them in day care. Alternatively, perhaps the mother's anticipation of putting the child in day care had already created a less sociable relationship.

SUMMARY AND CONCLUSION

Unlike the other child development outcomes discussed in previous chapters, children's sociability with their mothers was not predicted by participation in day care. It was neither enhanced nor impaired by being in a day-care center, even one of the highest quality. This index of the positive and reciprocal quality of the mother–child relationship was consistently and significantly related only to the mother's attitude and behavior. Mothers of more sociable children interacted with them more at dinnertime—playing, talking, teaching, reading, hugging, kissing, responding, laughing—and had more positive attitudes toward them. This association appeared both for children who were at home all day with their mothers and for children who were away from their mothers in day care during the day.

Unfortunately, there is not a research literature with which to compare these observed predictors of children's sociable and reciprocal relations with their mothers. The closest literature would be the research on children's attachment relationships. This literature also documents links between the quality of the child's relationship with the mother (security of attachment) demonstrated in a laboratory procedure and mother's sensitivity, responsiveness, and affection (Bates, Maslin, & Frankel, 1985; Belsky, Rovine, & Taylor, 1984; Crockenberg, 1981; Egeland & Farber, 1984; Gaensbauer et al., 1985; Grossmann, Grossmann, Spangler, Suess, & Unzner, 1985; Smith & Pederson, 1983). Although our measure of the mother–child relationship was based on positive, reciprocal, empathic interaction and is not strictly equivalent to the measure of attachment in the Strange Situation, it does have similarities to this measure (both conceptually and methodologically). Parallels with these results for attachment, therefore, are not surprising. What is most important about the relations demonstrated in the present study is that they suggest that there are strong and significant associations between the quality of the child's relationship with mother and her behavior and attitude toward the child—even for children in day care.

11

Compliance

In this chapter we turn to the prediction of another important aspect of development: children's willingness to comply with adults' orders or requests. This kind of behavior is of interest to researchers and parents alike. In the study, we had identified three variables reflecting children's compliance. One was a variable assessing the child's "general competence at home." This variable was based on the observer's ratings of the child's general compliance and overall good behavior (sociability, playfulness, cheerfulness, nonaggressiveness) in the unstructured observations made at home at dinnertime. This variable clearly includes a broader range of behavior than simply compliance with adult requests; it includes other social competencies as well as obedience. It was included in the set of variables discussed in this chapter because it was correlated with our other measure of compliance with parents (see Table 6.1) and because it exhibited similar correlational patterns with variables representing the child's experiences. The second variable, "compliance with parents," was based on observed rates of direct compliance with specific demands and requests made by parents during the dinnertime observations. It consisted of the proportion of the parents' demands during the dinnertime observation with which the child complied. The third variable, "compliance with requests," combined two measures: likelihood of the child's direct compliance with mother's and researchers' requests to put away toys in the laboratory and at home in structured observations; and parents' ratings of the child's usual level of compliance (the child is obedient, no trouble; not assertive, adventurous, or disobedient).

These three measures (as Table 6.1 shows) were moderately interrelated. As we already mentioned, children whom observers found to be more competent and cooperative overall at home were more likely to comply with their parents' direct requests at dinnertime and bedtime. Children who were more likely to comply with their parents' naturally occurring requests at home were also more likely to comply with their parents' and the researchers' requests in the laboratory. Children who were compliant with parents and researchers in the laboratory and with their parents at night were more compliant with their daytime caregivers as well. Children who were more compliant in the laboratory or at home at dinnertime were less difficult, negative, and demanding and more compliant in their daytime observations as well.

The three measures of compliance were, however, as Table 6.1 also shows, related to children's development in different ways. Higher levels of general competence and compliance with parents at home were related to advanced social cognition and competence, whereas compliance with a standard set of requests in the laboratory was related to less social competence. It is clear that these measures reflect somewhat different facets of children's compliance, that compliance is not a single dimension of behavior (cf. Sternberg et al., 1991), and that compliance does not inevitably reflect behavior that is more competent (cf. Crockenberg, 1991).

FAMILY PREDICTORS

Parents' Behavior

Despite these differences among the three variables representing children's compliance, there were commonalities in the correlational patterns relating them to the child's experiences in the family (see Table 11.1). Most striking was the strong and consistent association between children's compliance and parents' discipline: Children who were more compliant received less discipline—fewer demands, less physical control, more choices; more disobedient children got more discipline. This association appeared for all three measures of compliance, in both years. It was not reduced when the child's demandingness or the family's SES[1] was partialled out. The association was significant for both mothers and fathers, and the discipline each parent exerted contributed independently to the child's compliance after the other family predictors were statistically controlled [Fs for tests of independent effects = 18.8 ($p < .001$) for compliance with parents; 2.8 ($p < .05$) for general competence; 2.2 ($p < .10$) for compliance with requests].

A second clear link was observed with parental behavior that was complementary to discipline; that is, with parental responsiveness. More compliant children had parents who were more responsive, even when the frequency of the child's demands were partialled out.

The third kind of parental behavior associated with children's compliance was the teaching and explaining parents did. Children whose parents were more likely to interact with them in this instructive way were more compliant with the researchers' requests and generally more competent at

---

[1]Correlations coefficient reported in Table 9.1 were not changed significantly when the family's SES was partialled out; changes all less than +/- .03.

TABLE 11.1
Correlations[a] Between Children's Compliance and Family Variables

| | Compliance | | | | | |
| | General Competence at Home | | Compliance With Requests | | Compliance With Parents | |
Family Variables	Year 1	2	1	2	1	2
Family Background						
Socioeconomic status	•	.14	•	.18*	•	.21*
Father education	•	•	.22**	.22*	.19*	.14
Working Mother	.18*	•	•	.14	•	•
Mother's education	•	•	•	.16	•	•
Mother's work hours	.15	•	•	.17*	−.13	•
Mother's career orientation	.15	•	•	.23*	−.22*	−.18
Household help	.19*	•	•	•	•	−.17
Parents' Childrearing Expertise	•	•	•	•	•	•
Mother's child-care training	•	•	•	•	•	.14
Mother's child-care experience	•	•	•	•	−.15	•
Mother's knowledge of development	•	•	•	•	•	•
Father's knowledge of development	•	•	•	•	.14	•
Father's Interaction	•	•	•	•	•	•
Father playing	•	•	•	•	•	•
Father talking	•	•	•	•	•	.24**
Father affection	•	•	•	•	•	.18*
Father touching	•	.15	•	•	•	.16
Father touching, proportion	•	•	−.20**	−.22*	•	•
Mother's Interaction	•	•	•	•	•	•
Mother playing	.17*	•	•	•	•	•
Mother talking	•	•	•	•	•	•
Mother affection	•	•	•	•	•	•
Mother touching	•	•	•	•	•	•
Mother touching, proportion	•	•	•	•	•	•
Mother helping child	•	•	•	•	•	•
Parents' Discipline	−.21**	•	−.21**	−.17*	−.48**	−.68**
Parent offering choice	•	•	•	•	.29**	.49**
Mother demands	•	•	−.17*	•	−.40**	−.51**
Mother demanding	−.16*	•	−.16*	−.17*	−.34**	−.62**
Mother control	−.19*	•	•	−.19*	−.28**	−.40**
Father demands	•	•	•	−.17*	−.27**	•
Father demanding	•	•	−.20**	−.25**	−.30**	−.47**
Father control	−.23**	•	•	•	−.31**	−.24**
Parents' Teaching	•	.30**	.14	•	•	−.27**
Mother teaching	•	.18*	•	•	•	−.20*
Mother teaching, proportion	•	.21*	•	•	•	−.30**
Father teaching	•	.24**	.20**	•	•	•
Father teaching, proportion	•	.29**	.22**	•	•	−.27**
Parent giving lesson	•	.23*	•	•	−.16	−.21*

(continued)

TABLE 11.1 *(continued)*

Family Variables	General Competence at Home Year 1	2	Compliance With Requests 1	2	Compliance With Parents 1	2
Parents' Responsiveness	•	•	•	•	.36**	.39**
Parent appropriate responses	•	•	•	•	.26**	.40**
Parent verbal responsiveness	.21**	•	.20*	•	.24**	.43**
Parent giving object	•	•	•	•	.21**	.25**
Parents' Attitudes						
Father's positive attitude	•	•	•	•	−.18*	•
Mother's positive attitude	•	•	−.27**	•	−.30**	•
Mother's Satisfaction	•	.19*	.14	•	•	•
Role satisfaction	•	.20*	•	•	•	•
Satisfaction as mother	.15	•	.22**	•	•	•
Alienation	•	−.16	•	•	•	•
Child's Activities						
Child alone	•	•	•	•	•	−.25*
Child watching parent	•	•	•	•	•	.24**
Family Environment						
Number of people at home	•	•	•	•	.−.16*	−.23*
Older siblings	−.26*	•	•	−.15	•	−.17*
Younger siblings	•	•	.17*	.18*	•	•
Negative affect	−.28**	−.26**	•	•	•	−.20*
R^b	.51**	.49**	.48**	.41	.65**	.77**

[a]With child's age partialled out.

[b]These regression coefficients are for regression analyses including the following variables: mother's behavior (demanding, controlling), father's behavior (demanding, controlling), parents' backgrounds (education), mother's work (status, hours).

$+p < .10.$ $*p < .05.$ $**p < .01.$ $***p < .001.$ (two-tailed tests)

home. They were, however, also less compliant with the parents' specific requests during the observation. Perhaps this was because these parents were teaching and explaining more in response to the children's noncompliance during the dinnertime observation.

In previous research, researchers have found that children's compliance is predicted by greater maternal responsiveness (Lay et al., 1989; Parpal & Maccoby, 1985), the use of less powerful methods of control (Crockenberg & Litman, 1990), and generally high quality parental care (Prodromidis, Lamb, Sternberg, Hwang, & Broberg, 1993; Sternberg et al., 1991). These findings are consistent with the results of the present study.

Family Context

Children who were more compliant in the dinnertime observations also spent less time alone and more time watching their parents. Less negative affect was observed during the observations of these families at dinner. These children were more likely to have younger siblings and less likely to have older ones. Perhaps this suggests that more compliant children were operating in a family milieu where there were no older siblings to model disobedient behavior.

Family Background

In addition to these links with parents' behavior and the sibling situation at home, there were significant links observed between children's compliance and their parents' backgrounds. More compliant children came from higher SES families, with more educated fathers. These variables contributed independently to children's compliance after the effects of other family predictors had been statistically controlled [F for test of independence = 4.7 ($p < .05$)]. Compliance was not significantly related to the mother's or father's childrearing "expertise," however. Knowing how experts think children should be disciplined or having more experience in child care did not make parents more effective at eliciting their children's compliance.

Parents with more negative attitudes had children who were more compliant, especially at home: These children, perhaps, knew they had to toe the line. Mothers' satisfaction with their maternal role was curvilinearly related to their children's compliance generally ($ps < .001, .05$); the most satisfied mothers had children who were moderately compliant.

The relation of children's compliance to their mother's work history was quite complex. If mothers were employed, this did not affect the child's general competence or their compliance with requests by parents at home. But the children of working mothers were more compliant in the laboratory [$t = 2.0$ ($p < .05$)]. When mothers were more career oriented and worked more hours, children were not only more likely to go along with requests to tidy up in the laboratory but they were also rated as more competent at home. On the other hand, they were less compliant with their parents' specific requests at the end of the day. The mother's work (status, hours) also had a significant independent effect for all three measures of compliance in Year 1 [$ts = 8.0$ ($p < .01$), 5.1 ($p < .05$), 9.1 ($p < .01$)]. This finding of links between children's compliance and mothers' employment raises a familiar issue in discussions of day-care effects. This issue is discussed next.

DAYTIME PREDICTORS

Being in Day Care

In several studies of day care, researchers have observed that children in day care were less compliant than children who were not in day care—in a boring task (Rubenstein et al., 1981; Rubenstein & Howes, 1983), while cleaning up (Sternberg et al., 1991), or according to their mothers' reports of their behavior at bedtime or when the mother is doing housework or trying to talk to her husband (Rabinovich et al., 1987). In the present study, however, as the relations with maternal employment suggested, the links between day care and compliance were more complicated. General competence and compliance at home in the evening and compliance with researchers' and parents' requests to put away toys in the laboratory were related to day-care attendance in the opposite direction from these previous studies: These forms of compliance were higher for children in day care than for children at home with their mothers [$Fs(1, 142) = 3.0$ ($p < .10$); 3.8 ($p < .05$)]. What is more, just as they were related to how much the mother worked, these measures of compliance were positively related to the number of hours the child spent in day care—home care or center care—every week and the number of months the child had been in day care over the previous year [$rs = .16$ ($p < .10$) to $.30$ ($p < .01$)].

There was only one measure of compliance that supported the previous findings. Compliance with parents' specific requests in the dinnertime observations was higher for children in maternal care than for children in day care [$F(1, 142) = 2.3$ ($p < .05$), Year 1]. This difference was especially marked for children who were in day-care centers (negative correlation with day-care center factor) and who were in day care more than 40 hours a week [mean level of compliance with parents = .53 for children who were not in day care, .57 for children in care 10 to 30 hours per week, .46 for children in care 30 to 40 hours, and .35 for over 40 hours; $F(3, 140) = 3.1$ ($p < .10$)]. Hours in day care (like the hours the mother worked) were negatively correlated with this measure of compliance [$r = -.17$ ($p < .05$) Year 1].

These different correlational patterns for the different measures of compliance are not the result simply of children's maturity; remember it was compliance with the researcher that was the least mature kind of compliance, not compliance with parents. A more likely explanation seems to be that children who were with their mother more of the time were more compliant with her, but not with other adults or overall, whereas children who spent more time with other caregivers were more broadly competent and compliant. It may also be that children who spent more time in day care were more accustomed to the specific task of putting toys away after an activity and thus were especially compliant with this situation in the laboratory. This somewhat complicated, but reasonable, pattern of associations is missed when researchers combine different indices of compliance into a single composite score. Prodromidis et al. (1993) did not find a composite measure of compliance to be related to day-care participation (or, indeed to any variables reflecting the child's day-care history or experience).

Caregivers' Behavior

To find out how the quality of experiences children had during the day, whether in day care or not, predicted compliance, we correlated the three measures of compliance with the variables shown in Table 11.2. These analyses revealed that during the daytime, as at home at dinnertime, more compliant children received less discipline—less control, fewer demands, more choices. In fact, they received less individual attention of any kind from their caregivers. Again, this pattern was a consistent one, which appeared for children in home care arrangements and in centers. It appeared both for children who were with their mothers during the daytime observations and for children who were with other caregivers.

Previous research on the prediction of compliance from children's experiences in day care has been limited to examination of more general links between compliance and day-care quality. These studies suggest that children in high-quality day care are more compliant than those in low quality day care (Howes & Olenick, 1986; Sternberg et al., 1991). But, unfortunately, we cannot use these results to support or disconfirm our results because of differences in the ways both compliance and day-care experiences were assessed.

Daily Context

As at home also, more compliant children spent less time alone and more time watching other people interacting, and their interactions involved more positive and less negative affect. These correlational patterns were generally similar for children in home care and center care, but, in centers, in addition to these relations, more compliant children were in smaller classes.

Caregivers' Backgrounds

More compliant children also had caregivers who were younger, better educated, with more training in child development. But these caregivers were less likely to agree with experts about discipline.

COMBINED PREDICTORS

In the next set of analyses we examined the relative and combined contributions of family and daytime variables to children's compliance. Regression analyses were conducted to compare the weights of family variables (father's education, parents' discipline and teaching, younger and older siblings) and the equivalent day-care variables (caregiver's education, discipline and teaching, younger and older classmates). Combining the two sets of variables increased the multiple regression coefficients beyond what they were for either set of variables alone [$Rs = .55$ ($p < .01$) to $.81$ ($p < .001$) vs. $.41$ to $.77$ ($p < .01$) for family variables and $.31$ to $.47$ ($p < .05$) for daytime variables]. But comparing the contributions of each set suggested that parents had a greater influence than day care on two of the three measures of compliance. Although both family and day-care variables contributed

TABLE 11.2

Correlations[a] between Children's Compliance and Daytime Variables

Daytime Variables	All Children						Children in Centers						Children in Homes					
	General Competence		Comply With Requests		Comply With Parents		General Competence		Comply With Requests		Comply With Parents		General Competence		Comply With Requests		Comply With Parents	
	Year 1	Year 2	Year 1	Year 2	Year 1	Year 2	Year 1	Year 2	Year 1	Year 2	Year 1	Year 2	Year 1	Year 2	Year 1	Year 2	Year 1	Year 2
Day-care Center	.13		.13			−.20												
Caregiver's Qualifications																		
Caregiver's education			.17*												.19*		.31*	
Caregiver's training in child care										.22*						.25*		
Caregiver's knowledge of development		−.21*						−.19						−.18	−.24*			
Caregiver's age	−.17*			−.14			−.20	−.19		−.29*			−.17					
Caregiver's Attitudes																		
Caregiver's positive attitude toward child					−.14					−.24								−.19
Caregiver's Behavior																		
Caregiver attention to individual child	−.14	−.16	−.13	−.14			−.33*	−.18		−.20		−.22*		−.19*			−.27**	−.18
Caregiver discipline (controlling, demanding, not giving choices)	−.14	−.26*	−.14	−.24*				−.24							−.18	−.25*		−.36*

Caregiver talking to group	.24*	.19*	.28*	•	•	.18	•	•	•	•	.17	.18*	.29*	•	.18
Peers															
Children in class	•	•	•	•	−.20*	•	−.21	•	•	•	•	•	•	•	
Child watching interactions	.14	.14	.15	•	•	•	•	•	•	•	•	.20*	•	•	
Positive affect	•	.13	•	•	.21	•	•	•	.22*	•	•	•	•	•	
Negative affect	−.14	•	•	−.25*	−.32*	•	−.29*	•	−.20*	•	•	•	−.16	•	
Child Activities															
Child alone	•	−.18*	−.19	•	−.35*	•	−.20*	•	−.20*	•	•	•	•	•	
R^b	.42**	.46**	.36+	.41*	.31	.47*	.48*	.38	.44	.44+	.48+	.44+	.35*	.41*	.30	.29	.41**	.27

[a]With child's age partialled out.

[b]These regression coefficients are for regression analyses of the following variables: caregiver's discipline (controlling, demanding), caregiver's attention, time alone.

$+ p < .10.$ $* p < .05.$ $** p < .01.$ $*** p < .001.$ (two-tailed tests) independently to the child's general competence at home [Fs = 2.4 (p < .001) for family, 2.1 (p < .05) for day care], only family variables had significant independent effects on children's compliance with requests [Fs = 2.2 (p < .01) vs. 1.3] and compliance with parents [Fs = 7.8 (p < .001) vs.< 1].

Further evidence of the greater significance of family variables for predicting these two measures of compliance was seen in an analysis of variance comparing the compliance of four groups of children: Group A, children with "higher quality" family environments (above the median on a composite variable consisting of father's education, parents' responsiveness, and discipline) and "higher quality" day-care environments (above the median on a composite variable consisting of caregiver's education, responsiveness, and discipline); Group B, poorer quality family and day-care environments; Group C, higher quality family and poorer quality day-care environments; and Group D, poorer quality family and higher quality day-care environments. Children in Group C were more compliant than children in Group D (see Table 11.3), significantly so for compliance with parents [Fs = 3.4 (p < .01), 4.4 (p < .001)].

TABLE 11.3
Differences in Compliance for Children in Different Family/Day Care Combinations

	Mean Compliance Scores			
Family/Day-Care Combination	Compliance With Requests Year 1	Compliance With Requests Year 2	Compliance With Parents Year 1	Compliance With Parents Year 2
High-quality family environment/ high-quality day care[a] (n = 48 Year 1, 38 Year 2)	.31	.28	.37	.44
High-quality family environment/ poor quality day care (n = 27 Year 1, 23 Year 2)	.11	.06	.26	.86
Poor quality family environment/ high-quality day care (n = 26 Year 1, 26 Year 2)	−.19	−.03	−.38	−.47
Poor quality family environment/ poor quality day care (n = 43 Year 1, 38 Year 2)	−.32	−.24	−.36	−.55
F	3.4*	ns	6.4***	13.3***

[a]"Higher quality" family environments are above the median on a composite variable consisting of father's education, parents' responsiveness, and discipline; "higher quality" day-care environments are above the median on a composite variable consisting of caregiver's education, responsiveness, and discipline.

*p < .05. **p < .01. ***p < .001. (two-tailed tests)

RELATIONS OVER TIME

But were the parents creating their children's compliant behavior—or responding to it? Was day-care attendance preceding or merely contemporaneous with increased compliance with requests? Cross-time correlations with compliance with requests (the only measure of compliance that was stable from Year 1 to Year 2) were examined in an attempt to find out whether children's experiences at home and in day care were causes or consequences of their compliance.

These analyses provided evidence that children's compliance with requests was related to preceding day-care participation: Greater compliance with requests in Year 2 was related to spending more hours in day care or more hours with mother working [rs = .30 ($p < .01$)], specifically in a day-care center [r with more children in the setting = .38 ($p < .001$)] in Year 1 (rs in the opposite direction were nonsignificant). Once again, the findings contradicted the general assumption that day care leads to problems with compliance.

There was also evidence in the cross-time analyses that adults were responding to the children's compliant behavior with less control rather than that their lax discipline was fostering compliance. Children's compliance with requests in Year 1 predicted less authoritarian discipline from both parents and daytime caregivers in Year 2 [rs = −.20 ($p < .05$); rs in the opposite direction were nonsignificant].

In the final analyses of compliance, path analyses were used to try to confirm this direction of influence, from child's behavior to adults' discipline. These path analyses (combining the contributions of parents' and caregivers' discipline) also suggested that the direction was from child to adult: The model in which Year 1 compliance was linked to Year 2 control provided a better fit than the model linking Year 1 control and Year 2 compliance [Fig. 11.1, Steiger–Lind RMS Index = .11 (.08 − .14); Adjusted Population Gamma = .88 (.81 − .93) vs. Fig. 11.2, Steiger–Lind RMS Index = .11 (.08 − .14); Adjusted Population Gamma = .88 (.82 − .93)]. But in a third model we included a connection between discipline in Year 1 and Year 2, and discovered that the fit was even better [Fig. 11.3, Steiger–Lind RMS Index = .07 (.03 − .10); Adjusted Population Gamma = .95 (.90 − .99)], and the paths between compliance and control—in either direction, within or across time—were reduced to nonsignificance.

The most reasonable interpretation of our findings concerning the prediction of children's compliance, then, would seem to be that, by the time these children were observed at 2 to 4 years of age, compliance and control had formed a stable system, which was probably influenced by the child's willingness to comply in the first place (see Lewis, 1981). Parents and day-care providers were able to discipline more compliant children less, it seemed, because they needed it less. Support for this suggestion comes from work by Anderson, Lytton, and Romney (1986), who found that when

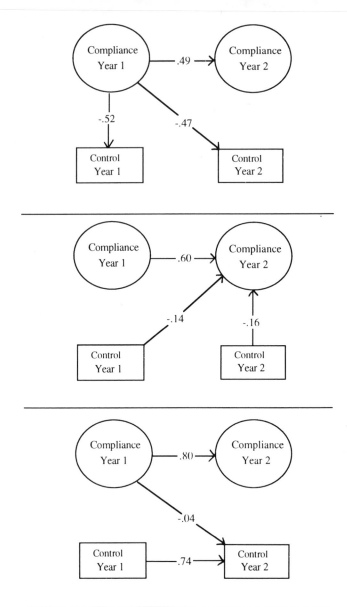

Key to Variables

Latent variable
Manifest variable (loading on the latent variable)

Compliance Year 1
Compliance with requests (.97)

Control Year 1
Parent discipline (.65)
Caregiver discipline (.40)
Parent responsiveness (-.59)

Compliance Year 2
Compliance with requests (.75)

Control Year 2
Parent discipline (.89)
Caregiver discipline (.53)
Parent responsiveness (-.51)

FIG. 11.1. Top panel: Path model for compliance predicting control. Middle panel: Path model for control predicting compliance. Bottom panel: Path model for compliance predicting control with cross-time stability of compliance and control.

mothers interacted with their own and other children, some of whom were conduct disordered, they were more demanding and negative with the conducted disordered (i.e., noncompliant) children. Even in their initial encounters with an adult, then, more disobedient children get more discipline.

So parents can be positive and responsive and highly educated and put their children in day care—and all these things predict greater compliance. In fact, the effect of maternal responsiveness on children's compliance has even been demonstrated experimentally (Lay et al., 1989; Parpal & Maccoby, 1985). But there are limits to what parents can do to promote their children's obedience. As research by Crockenberg and Litman (1990) demonstrated, if mothers respond negatively to their child's disobedience, they can be sure of worse to come, but if the mothers respond positively, although there is an increased probability that the child will comply, the adult's positive behavior is no guarantee that compliance will be the outcome.

SUMMARY AND CONCLUSION

The major predictor of children's compliance in this study was adult control: More disobedient children got more discipline from their parents and other caregivers; more compliant children were disciplined and directed less. Analyses suggested that children's compliance led to less control by these caregivers rather than the other way around. Compliance did seem to be increased by caregivers' responsiveness and general levels of education, but, disappointingly, perhaps, not by their childrearing expertise—their agreement with experts about how to discipline children or their training in child development.

Despite the widely held belief that participation in day care makes children less compliant, we did not find that day care caused noncompliance in any general way. On the contrary, children who were in day care were generally better behaved at home and complied more with specific requests made by the researcher in the laboratory, and the more months they had been in day care, the more compliant they were in these ways. However, children who were in day care were less compliant with specific requests made by their parents during the dinnertime observations, and the more hours they spent in day care, the more they refused or ignored these requests. Thus, it appears that children who were with the mother more of the time were more compliant with her but not with other adults or overall, whereas children who spent more time with other caregivers were more broadly competent and compliant. Mothers whose children were moderately compliant, both in general at home and with their specific requests at dinnertime, were most satisfied with their maternal role.

12

Peer Relations

Finally, in this chapter we turn to the prediction of the children's ability to interact with other children—a skill one might expect would be highly influenced by participation in day care and perhaps by interactions with children at home as well. We had identified four variables that reflected different facets of the child's social abilities with peers—positive and negative interaction, with familiar and unfamiliar peers. Because these variables were not intercorrelated (see Table 6.1), we discuss the prediction of each separately in this chapter.

POSITIVE SOCIAL BEHAVIOR WITH AN UNFAMILIAR PEER

We begin with the measure of the child's positive social behavior with another child in the laboratory playroom, a variable reflecting the child's social competence with an unfamiliar peer. This measure was based on observations of the frequency with which the child talked, played, imitated, gave, shared, cooperated, and showed affection or positive affect toward an unfamiliar agemate, both during free play (with toys, blocks, a jack-in-the-box, and without toys) and during structured activities (building a tower and a road with blocks, coloring a picture, playing "train"). The measure was significantly related to the child's age and to his or her social competence with adult strangers. It was also strongly related to the frequency with which the child talked to other children during the daytime observations [$r = .52$ ($p < .001$)] and negatively related to the amount the child touched these other children [$r = -.21$ ($p < .01$); see Table 6.1]. Thus, it appears that this variable is an index of the child's developmental maturity and level of social skill rather than simply an individual difference in gregariousness.

Family Predictors

Table 12.1 presents the correlations[1] between social competence with peers and variables representing the child's experiences in the family.

Parents' Behavior and Characteristics.   Not surprisingly, given its identity as an index of social competence, the child's positive interaction with an unfamiliar peer was related to experiences in the family that were similar to those we have discussed for social competence with adults. Children who interacted more positively and cooperatively with the unfamiliar peer came from families of higher SES, with more positive, satisfied, and career-minded mothers. In fact, even if the mother was not working, her career orientation was related to the child's social competence with peers $[r = .40\ (p < .05)$, Year 2]. These socially competent children's parents were more likely to respond to them verbally, but their fathers were less likely to teach them and their mothers were less likely to initiate physical or affectionate contact with them.

Examining the cross-time correlations with these family predictors revealed that the child's social competence with an unfamiliar peer in Year 2 was predicted by the hours the mother worked $[r = .33\ (p < .001)]$ and her responsiveness $[r = .51\ (p < .001)]$ and teaching $[r = .25\ (p < .01)]$ in Year 1. The same family variables predicted a gain in the child's social competence with peers between Year 1 and Year 2 assessments $[rs = .22\ (p < .05)$ for mother's work, $.48\ (p < .001)$ for responsiveness, $.22\ (p < .05)$ for teaching]. In addition, a significant predictor of the gain in social competence was higher SES $[r = .40\ (p < .01)]$. These findings suggest that the mother's behavior (teaching and responding rather than holding or touching) and background (being highly educated and involved in work) contribute to the child's development of social skills with unfamiliar peers. [Regression analysis showed that the mother's behavior had an independent effect on social competence beyond the contribution of SES; $F = 5.4\ (p < .01)]$.

Correlations with the characteristics of the home environment suggested that children were more socially competent if their homes were more stimulating (lots of toys) but also more messy. Perhaps such homes provided a setting in which the children could play freely with other children. We turn to this possibility next.

Interactions With Other Children at Home.   Of particular interest in predicting children's social competence with other children, of course, were their experiences with other children at home. One might imagine that having frequent and positive interactions with a sibling or another regular

---

[1]Partialling out the family SES did not change the correlations presented in Table 12.1 significantly (except, of course, the correlation with mother's education was reduced to nonsignificance).

TABLE 12.1

Correlations[a] Between Children's Interaction With Peers and Family Variables

		Interaction With Peers						
		Social Competence With Peer		Social Competence With Friend	Negative Behavior With Peer		Aggression Toward Peers	
Family Variables	Year	1	2	1 + 2	1	2	1	2
Family Background								
Socioeconomic status		•	.31**	•	•	•	•	•
Father's education		•	.27**	•	•	− .21*	•	•
Working Mother		•	.32**	•	.29**	− .18*	•	•
Mother's education		•	.23**	•	.16*	•	•	•
Mother's work hours		•	.14	•	.21**	•	•	•
Mother's career orientation		.15	.15	•	.23**	•	•	•
Mother's Child-Rearing Expertise		.17*	•	•	.28**	•	•	•
Parents' Interaction								
Father interacting		•	•	− .22**	•	•	− .20*	− .35**
Father teaching		− .20*	•	− .21**	•	•	•	•
Mother talking		•	•	•	•	.20*	•	•
Mother physical contact/ affection		− .19*	•	.25**	•	•	•	•
Mother helping child		•	•	•	.16*	.15	.29**	.22
Mother teaching		•	•	− .25**	.13	.20*	•	•
Parents' Discipline		•	•	•	•	.22*	.22*	.25*
Parents' Responsiveness		.22**	•	•	•	•	•	•
Giving object		•	•	•	•	.25*	•	.21
Parents' Attitudes								
Father's positive attitude		•	•	•	•	•	•	•
Mother's positive attitude		•	.21*	•	.16*	•	•	•
Mother's Satisfaction								
Mother's role satisfaction		•	.25**	.20*	− .28**	•	•	.29*
Mother's alienation		•	•	•	•	•	.20*	•
Family Environment								
Number of people at home		•	− .16*	•	•	•	•	•
Extended family		•	•	− .19*	•	.22*	.27*	•
Older siblings		•	− .20*	•	•	•	•	•
Younger siblings		•	•	•	•	•	•	•
Sibling interaction (including none)		•	•	.20*	•	− .16	•	•
Sibling interaction (if has sibling)		•	•	.19	•	•	•	•
Sibling aggression		.18*	•	− .19*	− .22**	•	•	.23*
Negative affect		•	•	•	− .22**	•	.18	.23*
Positive affect		•	•	.19*	•	•	•	•
Physical Environment								
Stimulating home		•	.26**	•	.13	•	− .21*	•
Mess		.18	•	•	•	•	.23*	.27**
R [b]		.39	.53**	.46**	.51**	.39*	.41	.65**

[a]With child's age partialled out.

[b]These regression coefficients are for the regression analyses described in the text. The selected set of variables they included is listed there.

*$p < .05$. **$p < .01$. (two-tailed tests)

playmate at home would increase the children's ability to interact with a new child. This was not the case. Social competence with the unfamiliar peer was not related to having siblings or interacting with them more frequently. Nor was it related to having more positive exchanges with them at dinnertime. In fact, more socially skilled children were less likely to have an older sibling—so they were apparently not learning social skills from that potential source. Moreover, if they did have a sibling, they were more often the target of the sibling's aggression in Year 1. Regression analyses revealed that sibling aggression had a nearly significant independent effect on social competence with peers beyond the contributions of the mother's behavior and background [$F = 3.2, p < .07$]. But cross-time analyses showed that sibling aggression (in Year 1) was not related to later social competence (in Year 2). So it appears unlikely that being the victim of sibling aggression is causing children's sociability. Perhaps more socially outgoing children simply run into more aggressive encounters with their siblings, especially when they are younger (in Year 1).

There have been few studies on the family predictors of children's social competence with unfamiliar peers at this age. One comparable study, of 33-month-olds, was done by Snow et al. (1981). They found, as we did, that only children and first-born children (i.e., children with no older siblings) were most sociable and assertive with an unfamiliar peer.

Prediction from Daytime Experiences

So, more socially competent children are not learning how to interact with an unfamiliar peer from their siblings. Perhaps they are picking up their skills with peers by interacting with other children in the daytime. It would make even more sense that children would learn how to interact with a new child from having repeated experiences with new playmates in day care rather than having repeated interactions with siblings and familiar playmates at home. When we assessed the effect of the child's experiences in the daytime on their social competence with an unfamiliar peer we found that these experiences were indeed associated with development. Adding daytime variables to the regression equation predicting children's social competence with peers from their experiences at home increased the level of predictability: The multiple R for daytime and family variables combined [$R = .61$ ($p < .001$)] was greater than that for either family variables or daytime variables alone. Both family and daytime variables had significant independent effects on the child's social competence with peers [$Fs = 3.9$ to 4.9 ($ps < .05$)].

Being in Day Care. As we had expected, children in day care were more socially competent with an unfamiliar peer [in ANCOVA for children in day care vs. those at home with mother, with family SES covaried out: $F(1, 142)= 6.7$ ($p < .05$)]. The difference was especially marked for children

in day-care centers—with more caregivers and more children, more structured and educational activities, more educated and experienced caregivers
[ANCOVA for children in day-care centers vs. in home-care arrangements,
with family SES covaried out: $F(1, 142) = 2.7$ $(p < .10)$ in Year 1, $F(1, 126) =$
11.1 $(p < .001)$ in Year 2; and see the results of the correlational analyses
relating social competence with unfamiliar peers to the child's daytime
experiences in Table 12.2].[2]

But was the difference the result of the fact that children in day care, and
particularly in day-care centers, had more practice interacting with other
children? Regression analyses revealed significant independent effects on
children's sociability with the unfamiliar peer for the caregiver's background [$F = 3.9$ $(p < .05)$] and behavior [$F = 2.6$ $(p < .05)$], the day-care
program [$F = 3.8$ $(p < .01)$], and the number of children in the setting [$F =$
3.5 $(p < .10)$]. There was no independent effect of interaction with peers. It
was not simply the case that advanced social skills with peers came from
spending more time playing with other children; other aspects of the
day-care experience seemed to be more significant.

Examination of correlations across time suggested that these significant
aspects of the day-care experience were influencing the development of
children's social skills, not just associated with it. Social competence with
the unfamiliar peer in Year 2 (with social competence in Year 1 covaried
out) was predicted by being in a day-care center [$r = .29$ $(p < .01)$], interacting
with more children [$r = .18$ $(p < .05)$] of greater diversity [$r = .23$ $(p < .01)$],
and being in a more structured program [$r = .28$ $(p < .01)$] in Year 1. The
overall regression coefficient for predicting social competence with an
unfamiliar peer in Year 2 from daytime experiences in Year 1 was highly
significant [$R = .53$ $(p < .01)$]. There were no significant correlations between
children's social competence with peers in Year 1 and their experiences in
Year 2, and the multiple regression coefficient was $< .10$. Thus, there is some
suggestion that being in a day-care center program was not only related to
children's social competence but was a positive influence on it.

Supporting this suggestion that children's experience in day-care centers
was positively influencing their social competence with peers, children
who gained most in social competence with peers between Year 1 and Year
2 were more likely to be in center care than home care [$F(1, 126) = 3.8$ $(p <$
.05)], especially full-time center care [$F(1, 65) = 9.8$ $(p < .01)$]. They interacted
with more different children [$r = .17$ $(p < .05)$], spent less time alone [$r = -.19$
$(p < .05)$] or watching TV [$r = -.32$ $(p < .001)$], and were involved in more
structured activities [$r = .25$ $(p < .01)$].

In other research, too, children with more experience in day care
have been found to be more socially skilled and outgoing with an

---

[2]Partialling out the family SES reduced the correlations in the table only slightly (changes
were $< .05$).

unfamiliar child (Wille & Jacobson, 1984; Wynn, 1979). This relation seems sensible and robust.

Spending More Time in Day Care.   These other researchers have not related children's social competence to the degree or length of their day-care experience, however. In the present study, children who were more socially competent with unfamiliar peers in Year 2 not only were currently in day care but they had been in day care longer [$r = .30$ ($p < .01$)] and spent more hours there every day [$r = .31$ ($p < .01$)]. This finding suggests that the effect of experience in a day-care program on children's social competence is cumulative. This was true for children in day-care centers: Among these children, more socially competent children spent more time in the day-care center every day and had been there longer [rs (with age partialled out, as usual) = .18, .28 ($p < .05$)]. For the sample of children who were in home environments during the day, there also was a positive relation with the amount of (home) day-care experience [$r = .33$ ($p < .05$) for months in day care, .35 ($p < .01$) for hours]. This suggests that it is not just center experience that boosts children's social skills, but day-care experience of any kind. But the correlations with time in home day care were reduced to nonsignificance when the family's SES was partialled out. Moreover, when just the sample of children in home day care was examined, not including the children who were home with their mothers, the length of time the child had been in day care was negatively associated with social competence with peers [$r = -.30$ ($p < .05$)]. Apparently for children in home care the boost to social skills comes from any participation in a day-care program rather than from continued or more extensive experience there.

Characteristics of the Day-Care Program

So what is it about participating in day care, in a home or a center, that is associated with more advanced social skills with peers? To answer this question we examined the correlations with characteristics of experience in the two kinds of settings (see Table 12.2).

Day-Care Centers.   For children in centers, more socially competent children were in settings with a lower child–adult ratio, that is, with fewer children per caregiver. They interacted with a smaller number of children, and the children they interacted with were more likely to be older. They spent more time watching and listening to these other children and more time in group (school-like) activities with them. They spent less time with them in parallel play (in Year 1) or pretend play (in Year 2). These more socially skilled children also received more individual attention and discipline from the teacher. In fact, when the teacher's behavior was removed in a regression analysis, the peer variables were no longer significantly related to the child's social competence with an unfamiliar child.

TABLE 12.2
Correlations[a] Between Children's Interaction With Peers and Daytime Variables

	All Children			Interaction With Peers					
				Children in Centers			Children in Homes		
	Social Competence With Peer		Social Competence With Friend	Social Competence With Peer		Social Competence With Friend	Social Competence With Peer		Social Competence With Friend
	1	2	1 + 2	1	2	1 + 2	1	2	1 + 2
Year	.13	.41**	.15						
Daytime Variables									
Child-Care Arrangement									
Amount of interaction with any nonparental caregiver	.22**	.23**	•		•	•		•	•
Day-Care Center	•	.28**	.18*	•	•	•	•	•	•
Number of People									
Number of caregivers	•	.20*	•	•	•	•	•	•	•
Children in class	.14	.35**	.21**	•	•	•	•	•	•
Child-caregiver ratio	•	.16	.13	−.22			.21*	.40*	•
Number of children interacting	•	.19*	.19*	−.30*	•	•	•	•	•
Diversity	•	.23**	.16*	•	•	•	•	•	•
Older children present	•	.15	.22**	.20*	•	.26*	•	•	.39**

Younger children present	-.16*	•	-.19*	•	•	•	-.17*	•	•
Middle-class peers	•	•	.15	•	•	•	•	•	.21*
Setting/Program									
Program	.21**	.27**	.21**	•	•	•	•	.28**	.17*
Structure	•	.22*	.16	•	•	•	•	.22*	.17*
Toys	•	.19*	.15	•	•	•	•	.21*	•
Decoration	•	-.18*	-.19*	•	•	-.21	•	-.23*	•
Mess/hazards	•	-.16	-.21**	•	•	•	•	-.17	-.17*
Caregiver's Background									
Caregiver's qualifications (education, training, experience)	.25**	.26**	•	•	•	•	.22*	•	•
Caregiver's age	•	.15	•	•	•	.28*	•	.24*	•
Caregiver's expectations for child	.13	.31**	•	•	•	•	•	•	•
Caregiver's Behavior									
School activities	•	.30**	.19*	.22	•	•	.16	•	.18*
Attention	•	•	•	.20	•	•	.16	.18	•
Discipline	•	•	-.17*	.26*	.18	•	.16	•	.19*
Responsiveness	•	•	•	•	•	•	-.16	-.22*	•

(continued)

TABLE 12.2 (continued)

	Interaction With Peers								
	All Children			Children in Centers			Children in Homes		
	Social Competence With Peer		Social Competence With Friend	Social Competence With Peer		Social Competence With Friend	Social Competence With Peer		Social Competence With Friend
Year	1	2	1 + 2	1	2	1 + 2	1	2	1 + 2
Daytime Variables									
Peer Activities									
Amount of interaction	•	•	.19*	•	•	•	•	•	•
Peer talk (if peer there)	•	•	•	•	•	•	-.26**	-.24**	•
Child imitating peers (if peer there)	•	•	•	•	.18	•	-.18*	-.20*	•
Child watching peer/interactions	•	•	.13	•	•	.32**	-.22*	-.26**	•
Pretend play (if peer there)	•	•	•	.21	.17	.24	-.18*	-.22*	•
Parallel play (if peer there)	-.21*	•	•	-.24	-.24*	•	•	-.18	•
Peer aggression (if peer there)	-.13	•	-.17*	-.24	•	-.35**	•	•	•
Negative affect	•	•	-.25**	•	•	•	-.18*	-.17	-.28**
Positive affect	•	•	.17*	•	•	•	•	-.21*	-.17*

Child's Activities									
Child's Activities									
Child alone	•	−.28**				.25*		•	•
Child watching TV		−.28**	•	•	•	•	•	•	•
Child activities with peers	•	•	•			•			
R^b	.49**	.51**	.51*	.53	.42	.65**	.31	.49*	.38**

[a]With child's age partialled out.

[b]These regression coefficients are for the regression analyses described in the text. The selected set of variables they included is listed there.

*$p < .05$. **$p < .01$. ***$p < .001$. (two-tailed tests)

Looking at the relations with these variables reflecting children's experiences in day-care centers over time, we found that children who were more socially competent with the unfamiliar peer in Year 2, and who gained more in social competence between Year 1 and Year 2, had received more teacher attention [rs = .41 (p < .01), .33 (p < .05)] in Year 1. The teacher's education was also significantly correlated with the gain in children's social competence from Year 1 to Year 2 [r = .26 (p < .05)]. Cross-time relations showed no association between social competence and the variables reflecting the child's interaction with other children in the day-care center.

Other researchers have related children's social competence with peers to the quality of day care. In one study, Vandell et al. (1988) found that children in high-quality day-care centers where they experienced more positive interaction with the caregiver were most socially skilled with an unfamiliar peer at 8 years of age. This parallels our finding that social competence with the unfamiliar peer was related to receiving more attention from the day-care center caregiver at an earlier time (in Year 1). The surprising finding in our data perhaps was the lack of association between social competence with the peer assessed in a structured laboratory situation and the child's naturally occurring interactions with other children.

Home Care.   In home care, more socially competent children were in more child-oriented physical settings (with more structure and toys, less mess and fewer hazards and adult decorations) with fewer younger children. Their caregivers were more educated, had more professional experience, and offered the child more school-like activities and individual attention. They were less likely to be demanding and controlling.

Again, the associations between children's social competence with peers and their experience with peers did not fit our expectation that social skills would be enhanced by having more experience interacting with other children. Although children in home settings with more other children present were more socially competent than children in home settings with no other children, more competent children spent less time interacting with the peer in any way—watching, imitating, listening, or playing—not more. Regression analyses to test the separate effects of interaction with peers and caregivers' behavior showed that only caregiver behavior had an independent effect for social competence [F = 2.2 (p < .10)]. So this difference in peer interaction seems to be the by-product of caregiver attention rather than a negative effect of interacting with peers per se.

Across time, the same relations appeared. Cross-time correlations for children who stayed in home care with other children showed negative associations with social competence with peers in Year 2 related to watching [r = −.44 (p < .05)], imitating [r = −.56 (p < .05)], and interacting with [r = −.32 (p < .05)] children, and positive effects of individual attention from the caregiver [r = .38 (p < .05)] in Year 1. But in a cross-time regression analysis, only the caregiver's behavior contributed to children's competence significantly and independently [$F = 2.9$ ($p < .05$)].

Similar Effects of Daytime and Home Experiences

Contrary to the common expectation that children's social competence with an unfamiliar peer would be predicted by more extensive and positive experience with other children, the results of these analyses suggested that it was adults who made the critical difference for children's social skills with other children. This pattern appeared when we considered the child's experiences in the daytime and at night. Children who had spent more time in the daytime in a day-care center were more socially competent, but apparently this was not just because day care afforded them more opportunities to interact with more other children. Among the children who were in centers, those who were more socially competent interacted with fewer children not a larger group; they did not spend more of their time playing with other children. What best predicted their social competence was attention and instruction from an educated teacher. For children in home care, more socially competent children were in arrangements with more children, but they spent less time interacting with these playmates. What best predicted their social competence was attention and instruction from an educated caregiver. In their own homes at night, more socially competent children, again, did not interact more or more positively with other children; in fact their interactions with their siblings were more aggressive. What best predicted their social competence was attention and instruction from a more educated mother. The results of this study suggest that mere exposure to peers does not promote social competence with an unfamiliar peer. The amount the child interacted with other children outside of day care, also, was not related to social competence. It was the opportunity to interact with a small number of—older—children in an educational context with an attentive caregiver rather than the chance for free play with a gang of kids that best predicted an increase in children's social competence with peers.

SOCIAL INTERACTION WITH A FRIEND

But interacting with an unfamiliar peer in a laboratory setting is not the only way children demonstrate their social skills with other children. The second measure of the child's social interaction with peers included in the study was a measure of the child's positive interaction with a familiar playmate at home. As in the laboratory assessment of the child's social competence with an unfamiliar peer, this variable was based on the observation of the frequency of positive social interaction (talking, playing, cooperating, showing affection, etc.) during free play (with a stacking toy and blocks) and in a more structured task (building a road together with blocks). Even though similar assessment procedures were followed for the two variables, however, the measure of the child's interaction with the friend at home did not turn out to be correlated with positive interaction with the unfamiliar peer in the laboratory. It seems to reflect a separate facet of sociability with peers, the ability to maintain social interaction with a "friend." One might expect that a somewhat different pattern of predictors would be found for this facet of the child's sociability with peers. This variable also was not related to the child's age or to other measures of development, so it does not seem to be a reflection of developmental competence in the same way as the first measure of social skill with an unfamiliar peer.

Family Predictors

Table 12.1 presents the correlations between the child's social interaction with the friend and the family variables.[3]

Parents' Characteristics and Behavior. Unlike the measure of social competence with an unfamiliar child, this measure of the child's social behavior was not significantly correlated with family background—SES, mother's work status, career orientation, childrearing expertise. Unlike the relations for social competence with the unfamiliar peer, also, children who were more sociable with a friend spent less time being taught by their mothers and more time in physical and affectionate contact with their mothers. The only relation with family variables that paralleled the ones found for social competence with the unfamiliar peer was that these children also experienced less interaction with their fathers.

In research in Sweden, too, Lamb and his colleagues (1988) observed that children's social skills with a friend at home were predicted by less involvement by the father. Relations with mothers' positive control and encouragement of prosocial behavior observed in other studies (Iannotti, Cummings, Pierrehumbert, Zahn-Waxler, & Milano, 1989; Stevenson-Hinde et al., 1986) were not observed in the present study, but are not incompatible with the picture that appears in our results. That picture is one of physically close and affectionate mother–child interactions that exclude the father. This pattern is distinct from the pattern observed for sociability with the unfamiliar peer and completely different from those obtained for cognitive development and social competence with adults.

Interactions With Other Children. Of particular interest among the relations with family variables were the relations with the child's experience

---

[3]Because this dependent variable was correlated with the friend's age [$r = .24$ ($p < .01$)], all correlations presented in this discussion have the friend's age partialled out.

with other children. Here we found that interaction with siblings was positively related to the child's social skills with a friend. Children who were more sociable with the friend spent more time interacting with their siblings or neighborhood children (perhaps including the friend) at dinner-time. Their interactions with these children were more positive and less aggressive. For this index of sociability, then, the expected association with experience with other children was found.

Daytime Predictors

Being in Day Care.   But was the child's sociability with a friend related solely to this experience at home, or was it related to participating in day care, in the same way the measure of sociability with an unfamiliar peer was? Parallel patterns linking sociability with the friend and sociability with the unfamiliar peer to participation in day care were indeed found. Children who were more sociable with their friend were more likely to be in day care [$F(1, 142) = 4.0$ ($p < .05$)]. They spent their day with more children and interacted with more different playmates. The children with whom they had an opportunity to interact were more diverse and older. Children who were more sociable with a friend were in more structured and child-oriented environments (more routines, toys; fewer decorations, hazards, messes).

Unlike the child's social competence with unfamiliar peer, sociability with a friend was not related to the caregiver's educational background or experience in child care. It was more closely related to the children's interaction with other children. More sociable children had more frequent and positive interactions, less aggression or parallel play.

Part-Time Day Care.   Another clear difference between the predictors of sociability with an unfamiliar peer and sociability with a friend was that children who were most sociable with the friend were most likely to be in day care only part time (Ms for children with no day care = $-.40$, for children in part-time day care = $.61$, for children in day care full time = $-.10$; $F(3, 140)$ = 2.5 ($p < .10$)]. Social competence with unfamiliar peer, recall, was related to spending more time in day care. More specifically, these children who were more sociable with a friend were likely to be in centers part time (for children in day-care centers full time $M = -.09$, for children in day-care centers part time $M = .56$).

Perhaps the advantage of part-time day care arrangement for children's social interaction with friends was that it allowed the children the oppor-tunity to make friends (in the morning at nursery school) and the time to play with them (in the afternoon at home). Sociability with the friend was indeed found to be related to more interaction with peers in the nursery school class [$r = .33$ ($p < .05$) for peer fun], and although it was not related to more peer interaction in the afternoon (home) observations of the nursery school children in Year 1 ($r = .01$), it was significantly related in Year 2 [$r = .42$ ($p < .01$)].

Our findings linking sociability to children's participation in day care are supported to some extent by other studies. They are supported by studies demonstrating that children who attended nursery school were more cooperative with peers (Herwig, 1989) and more popular in kindergarten (Allen & Masling, 1957). They are also supported by Wille and Jacobson's (1984) observation that children in part-time day care were more positive with a peer than children without this experience. They are supported by research showing that children's social relations with friends were not related to the type of day care they attended (i.e., homes or centers; Golden et al., 1978; Lamb et al., 1988). We found that children in centers part time were more sociable—but there was not a difference in sociability related to center care per se.

Quality of the Day-Care Center Program.   The major difference between our findings and those of previous research, however, is that other researchers have found that children in higher quality centers (with smaller classes and more frequent adult–child interactions) were more socially skilled with their familiar playmates (Holloway & Reichhart-Erickson, 1989; Howes & Stewart, 1987; Owen & Henderson, 1989). We did not find that our measure of children's sociability with a familiar playmate was related to the quality of care for the children who were in day-care centers. Our main predictors in the day-care center environment had to do with the nature of the interactions with other children that the child experienced, rather than overall program quality. Children who were more sociable with the friend were in day-care center programs with older children and spent more time watching and imitating these children. They were not in programs with more highly qualified teachers or a more educational program.

To account for this difference with previous research, it is important to note that, in the other studies, children's sociability with friends was observed in the day-care setting, rather than in an independent setting (in our case, at home). It would stand to reason that children's interactions in the day-care setting would be influenced by the quality of the day-care program. Our finding that more sociable children had more older classmates with whom to interact during the day is similar to Logue's (1989) finding that children in mixed-age classes, in comparison to those in single-age classes, were more likely to chat and share toys with other children and less likely to engage in dominance activities, including hitting.

Which Matters More—Interactions at Home or in Day Care? Interactions With Peers or Adults?

Regression analyses combining the significant daytime predictors of sociability with the friend (less caregiver discipline, more older children, more peer interaction, less peer aggression) with the significant family predictors (less interaction with the father, more physical affection from the mother, more sibling interaction, less sibling aggression) confirmed that both home and day-care variables were significantly related to children's sociability [Rs = .34 ($p < .01$) for family variables and .35 ($p < .01$) for daytime variables]. However, when the relative contributions of daytime and family predictors were compared, only the daytime variables had a significant independent effect [$F = 2.5$ ($p < .05$)]; family predictors did not contribute after the effect of the daytime variables had been removed. And when the relative contributions of adult variables (discipline, interaction, affection) were compared with peer variables (interaction and aggression with peers and siblings), only the peer variables had a significant independent effect [$F = 2.4$ ($p < .05$)]. Not surprisingly, the conclusion that must be drawn from these analyses is that what matters most for predicting how children act with a friend is positive social interaction with other children in the daytime. Note that these results are quite different from those for children's social competence with a child they had never met before; children apparently learn those social skills earlier if they have adult guidance.

NEGATIVE BEHAVIOR WITH THE UNFAMILIAR PEER

The third index of the child's social abilities with peers was the measure of children's uncooperative, unpleasant, and avoidant behavior with the unfamiliar peer in the laboratory playroom. During the same episodes of free play and structured play that the child's positive behavior toward the unfamiliar peer were recorded, these negative behaviors toward the peer were also coded. The measure consisted of the frequency of the child's taking away toys from the peer, physically controlling the peer's actions, saying negative things, refusing the peer's overtures or requests, withdrawing from or avoiding the peer. (Hitting was not observed in any laboratory session.) This variable was not correlated with the other measures of the child's interaction with peers, so we anticipated finding yet another pattern of family and day-care predictions. In fact, we expected to find two patterns, because the measures of negative interaction with the peer taken in the first and second years of the study were not correlated.

Predictors of Negative Behavior With Peers in Year 1[4]

The patterns of correlations with negative behavior with peers in the first year are presented in Tables 10.1 and 10.3.

---

[4]In Year 1, for girls, negative behavior with the peer was related to being more competent [more independent and more competent with parents, with strangers in the laboratory, and with a friend at home; rs = .18 to .24 ($p < .05$)]. For boys, correlations were in the opposite direction. Boys whose behavior with the unfamiliar peer was more negative were less independent of mother and less socially competent with parents, adult strangers, and a friend [rs = −.14 to −.20 ($p < .05$)]. Despite the differences between boys' and girls' negative behavior

Family Features.   The correlations between this index of the child's negative behavior with the unfamiliar peer and variables reflecting the child's experiences in the family are easy to summarize but difficult to understand. Children who were more negative with the unfamiliar peer had mothers who were better educated, worked more hours, were more career-minded and knowledgeable about childrearing. Because these variables reflecting the mother's involvement in work also predicted the child's positive interaction with the unfamiliar peer recorded at the same time, analyses were done to partial out the child's social competence with the unfamiliar peer from the relation between mother's work and negative behavior with the peer. The correlation between the child's negative behavior with the peer and the mother's work remained equally strong. This relation is apparently not the result of any methodological confounding of negative behavior to the peer with positive behavior to the peer. It is also not simply the result of the mothers of more negative children working more hours; even with work hours partialled out, the relation with the mother's education and career orientation remained strong. The mothers of children who behaved more negatively with the unfamiliar peer also initiated more help to their children during the dinnertime observation; they were positive and accepting in their attitudes toward the child, but expressed less satisfaction with their own roles as mothers (and workers). These relations seem somewhat inconsistent, with each other and common sense.

Another surprise was uncovered when we examined the relations between the child's negative behavior with the unfamiliar peer and the child's experience with other children at home. More negative children, it turned out, were less likely to have negative (aggressive) interactions with their siblings or other children in the home during the dinnertime observation. The reverse might have been expected.

Clearly, then, children were not behaving negatively with the unfamiliar peer in our laboratory assessment because their mothers were uneducated or negative or because their siblings picked on them.

Day-Care Experiences.   Were they behaving more negatively because they were in day care? The suggestion has been made more than once that children in day care are more aggressive with their peers than children who stay home with their mothers. This particular measure of negative behavior to the unfamiliar peer was not a measure of aggression—because the children did not act aggressively in the laboratory situation. But it did reflect other kinds of negative behavior to peers, and it might have been expected to have been predicted by the same experiences as aggression. In

peer, however, there were essentially no sex differences in correlational patterns with family or daytime experiences (no significant interaction with sex in analyses of covariance). Correlations are therefore presented for both sexes together.

fact, children who behaved more negatively with the unfamiliar peer in the laboratory were more likely to be in day care. This association appeared both for children in home day care [ANCOVA for home with mother vs. home with sitter, with family SES covaried out, $F(1, 94) = 5.9$ $(p < .05)$] and for children in center day care [ANCOVA for home with mother vs. full-time center care, with family SES covaried out, $F(1, 142) = 5.2$ $(p < .05)$]. What is more, these more negative children had been in day care longer [$r = .21$ $(p < .05)$] and spent more hours there every day [$r = .21$ $(p < .05)$; M for children with no day care $= -.37$; with 10–30 hours of day care $= .02$; with 30–40 hours per week $= .19$; with over 40 hours per week $= .93$; $F(3, 140) = 9.7$ $(p < .01)$].

There was also some indication that the kinds of interactions the children had in day care might have reflected or contributed to their more negative style of interacting with peers. More negative children had less opportunity to interact with older children, and their interactions with other children involved less imitation, less positive affect, and less aggression. Although again we might have expected these negative children to be more aggressive with their peers in day care, this pattern suggests that their interactions with peers were simply not intimate or intense. Their behavior of not imitating, laughing with or even occasionally hitting other children in day care, then, does seem to parallel their unfriendly (withdrawn and uncooperative) behavior in the laboratory.

In addition, the interaction these negative children had with caregivers in the daytime was more negative: They received more disciplinary interaction and less responsive, attentive, or instructive interaction.

An additive regression model, in which daytime and family variables were included, was significant [$R = .80$ $(p < .001)$] and demonstrated significant independent effects on children's negative behavior with the peer for both daytime [$F = 3.1$ $(p < .001)$] and family variables [$F = 2.3$ $(p < .01)$]. Significant independent effects were found for both caregiver's behavior [$F = 5.8$ $(p < .001)$] and interactions with peers [$F = 4.8$ $(p < .001)$]— unlike the associations found for the child's positive behavior with an unfamiliar peer (related only to caregiver's behavior) or with a familiar peer (related only to peer interaction).

Center Qualities.   Most of the significant correlations for the sample as a whole also appeared for the sample of children who were in centers (see Table 12.3): More negative children had been in their day-care centers longer [$r = .25$ $(p < .05)$] and attended for more hours every day [$r = .24$ $(p < .05)$]. Their caregivers were less attentive, responsive, and instructive, more demanding and controlling. The children were in classes with fewer older children. They had fewer interactions with peers that involved imitation or positive affect. In addition, more negative children in day-care centers had teachers with less training in child development.

TABLE 12.3

Correlations[a] Between Children's Interaction with Peers and Daytime Variables

Interaction With Peers (spans Children in Centers and Children in Homes)

Daytime Variables	All Children				Children in Centers				Children in Homes			
	Negative Behavior With Peer		*Aggression Toward Peers*		*Negative Behavior With Peer*		*Aggression Toward Peers*		*Negative Behavior With Peer*		*Aggression Toward Peers*	
Year	1	2	1	2	1	2	1	2	1	2	1	2
Daytime Variables	•		•		•		•		•		•	
Child-Care Arrangement												
Child-Care Arrangement	.16*	•	•	•	•	•	•	•	•	•	•	•
Amount of interaction with any nonparental caregiver	.28**	•	•	•	•	•	•	•	•	•	•	•
Day-care center	•	•	•	•	•	•	•	•	•	•	•	•
Number of people												
Number of caregivers	•	−.23**	•	•	•	•	•	•	•	•	•	•
Children in class	−.13	−.14	•	•	•	•	•	•	−.21*	−.41**	•	.35**
Caregiver – child ratio	•	•	•	•	•	−.18	•	•	−.16	•	−.28*	•
Number of children interacting	•	•	•	•	.20	•	•	−.24	•	•	•	•
Diversity	.18*	−.13	−.14	−.19	•	•	−.25	−.32	−.24**	−.31**	•	−.31*
Older children present	−.21**	•	•	•	•	•	•	•	•	•	•	•
Younger children present	•	•	−.21	•	−.20	•	•	−.30	•	•	•	−.26*

Middle-class peers	−.20*	•	•	•	•	•	•	•	•	•	•	•	•
Setting/Program													
Program	•	•	•	•	•	•	•	•	•	•	•	•	•
Structure	•	•	•	•	−.20*	−.30	•	•	−.20	•	−.40**	•	•
Toys	•	•	•	•	−.22*	•	•	•	−.35*	•	−.20	•	•
Decoration	•	•	•	•	•	•	•	•	•	•	•	•	•
Mess/hazards	.19	•	−.34**	•	.27**	•	•	•	•	•	•	•	.29*
Caregiver's Qualifications													
Caregiver's education	•	•	•	−.18	•	.26	•	•	22	•	.21	•	•
Caregiver's training in child care	−.19	•	−.23	−.18	•	−.25	•	•	•	•	•	•	•
Caregiver's experience in child care	−.17	•	•	•	.20*	•	•	•	−.20	•	•	•	•
Caregiver's knowledge of development	•	−.21	•	•	•	•	•	•	•	•	•	•	•
Caregiver's age	.20*	•	•	•	.30**	•	•	•	•	•	•	•	•
Caregiver's expectations for child	.22**	•	.20	•	.21*	•	.23*	•	•	•	.21	•	•
Caregiver's Behavior													
School activities	.17*	•	•	•	•	•	•	•	•	•	•	•	•
Attention	−.16*	.23*	−.31*	−.23*	•	.25	.36*	•	.19	•	.21	•	•

(continued)

TABLE 12.3 (continued)

Interaction With Peers

	All Children				Children in Centers				Children in Homes			
	Negative Behavior With Peer		Aggression Toward Peers		Negative Behavior With Peer		Aggression Toward Peers		Negative Behavior With Peer		Aggression Toward Peers	
Year	1	2	1	2	1	2	1	2	1	2	1	2
Daytime Variables												
Caregiver's Behavior (continued)												
Helping child	.21**	-.19*	.20	•	•	-.24*	•	•	.23*	•	•	•
Teaching	-.30**	•	-.23*	•	-.45**	-.20*	•	-.30	-.20*	•	•	-.25*
Discipline	.24**	.14	.18	.42**	.20	•	•	•	.16	.17	•	•
Responsiveness	-.22**	•	•	-.29*	-.21	•	•	-.30	-.19*	•	•	-.24
Peer Activities												
Amount of interaction	•	•	•	.19	•	.27**	•	•	•	•	•	.21
Peer talk (if peer there)	.15	.14	•	.17	.21	.25*	•	•	•	•	•	.21
Child imitating peers (if peer there)	-.16*	•	•	•	-.29*	•	•	•	-.19*	•	•	•
Child watching peer/interactions	•	.14	•	-.23*	•	.24*	.38*	-.35*	•	•	•	-.24
Pretend play (if peer there)	•	•	•	.18	•	•	•	•	•	-.20*	•	•
Parallel play (if peer there)	•	•	•	.29*	•	•	•	.31	-.20*	•	•	•

Peer aggression (if peer there)											
−.17*	•	.44**	.43**	•	•	.49**	.40*	−.19*	•	.41**	.38**
Negative affect											
•	.17*	.23*	.22	•	•	.25	.30	•	.17	.24*	.28*
Positive affect											
−.22**	•	•	•	−.21	•	•	•	−.19*	.21*	•	•
Child's Activities											
Child plays with object											
•	•	−.15	−.21	•	•	•	−.39*	•	•	•	•
Child alone											
•	•	•	•	•	•	•	−.19	•	−.33**.	22	.27*
Child watching TV											
•	−.23**	•	•	•	•	•	•	•	.23*	•	•
Child activities with peers											
•	.19*	•	•	•	•	•	•	•	•	•	•
R^b											
.59***	.37+	.54**	.69**	.65**	.47*	.72**	.63**	.56**	.50	.54	.36

[a]With child's age partialled out.

[b]These regression coefficients are for the regression analyses described in the text. The selected set of variables they included is listed there.

*p < .05. **p < .01. ***p < .001. (two-tailed tests)

In regression analyses for children in centers, only the caregiver's background and behavior had an independent effect $[F = 2.8\ (p < .01)]$ on children's negative behavior with the unfamiliar peer; characteristics of the child's interaction with peers did not $(Fs < 1)$.[5] These findings suggest that negative interaction with an unfamiliar peer is related to spending a lot of time in day care of low "quality" (less teacher training and attention).

The importance of day-care quality was further demonstrated when we compared children who had different combinations of family and day-care experiences: Children who were in poorer quality day-care centers (less educated teachers, offering less attention and structured activities and using more authoritarian control) and came from less adequate families (with less educated parents, less stimulating homes and interactions, and more authoritarian control) were most negative toward the peer $(M = .67)$; second most negative were children from higher quality family environments who were in poorer quality day-care centers $(M = .44)$; somewhat less negative were children from higher quality family environments in higher quality day-care centers $(M = -.21)$; least negative were children from poorer quality family environments who were in higher quality day-care centers $[M = -.60; F(3, 88) = 7.1\ (p < .01)]$.

Qualities of Home Care. The relations between negative behavior to the peer and experiences in home care were quite similar to those in center care. Among children in home care, as well as those in centers, more negative children had fewer older children to interact with and were less likely to interact with peers in ways that involved imitation, play or aggression. In fact, children who were more negative with an unfamiliar peer were in care arrangements with no other children $[M$ for children with peer present $= -.33$; with no peer present $= .26; F(1, 117) = 2.0\ (p < .05)]$. More negative children also experienced more discipline and less instruction and responsiveness from their caregivers, as they did in centers.

In brief, children whose interactions with an unfamiliar peer in the laboratory were more negative—avoidant and uncooperative—were not engaged with peers in their daily settings; they were in settings without other children, or, if they were in settings with other children, their interactions were not emotional. They were also not engaged with their caregivers; they were ignored by the caregivers except for being disciplined.

Predictors of Negative Behavior With the Peer in Year 2

The patterns we have just discussed for negative behavior exhibited by 2- and 3-year-olds in the laboratory were quite different from those revealed for the second assessment when they were 3 and 4 years old. Negative

[5]The associations with the caregiver's behavior were particularly high for children who were in day care full time (e.g., for caregiver teaching $r = -.65$ $[p < .01]$ for children in full-time day care, $-.24$ for children in part-time care).

behavior with the unfamiliar peer was negatively correlated with children's age, so by the time the children were 4 years old, avoiding and not cooperating with a peer took on a different meaning. This different meaning was apparent in the correlations observed with experiences at home and in day care.

Family Features.   Clearly different associations were found in the family variables. Children whose behavior with the unfamiliar peer was more negative had fathers with lower levels of education (children who were negative in Year 1, recall, had mothers with higher levels of education). Their mothers were less likely to be working, not more. They interacted more with their mothers and received more discipline. There was a tendency for them to interact less with siblings (Table 12.1).

Day-Care Experiences.   The strongest predictor of children's negative behavior with the peer in the second year was the number of caregivers they had in the daytime (Table 12.3). More negative children had fewer caregivers. That is, they were in home-care arrangements with a single caregiver (mother or sitter) rather than in day-care centers. In their home-care arrangements, they spent less time alone and more time watching TV. Their interactions were accompanied by more negative affect. How negative children were with the unfamiliar peer in the laboratory was not related to how much aggressive interaction they had with peers in the daytime, or, for that matter, to how much interaction of any kind they had with peers in the daytime observations. Nor was it related to the frequency and variety of activities with peers outside of day care. But children who were more negative with unfamiliar peers in Year 2 were less likely to have been in day-care centers in Year 1 [$r = -.24$ ($p < .05$)] and had spent fewer months in day care of any kind [$rs = -.22$ ($p < .01$) for any day care, $-.24$ ($p < .05$) for center day care, $-.48$ ($p < .05$) for home day care]. Clearly, as 4-year-olds, being uncooperative with a new acquaintance was related to lack of experience with other children in the larger world that day care provides. More negative children were still in home care rather than centers, and among children in home care, more negative children had interacted with fewer children in Year 1 [$r = -.39$ ($p < .05$)].

Center Qualities.   Among the children who were in day-care centers, more negative children got less attention and teaching from their caregivers and their teachers tended to have less training in child development. These relations with poor quality day care were consistent with the ones observed in Year 1. In addition, children who were more negative toward the unfamiliar peer in the laboratory tended to be in smaller classes and to spend more of their time at the center watching and interacting with peers. However, regression analyses revealed that these interactions with peers did not contribute to children's negativity beyond the contribution of the teacher's—less attentive—behavior [Fs = 3.9 (p < .01) for teacher's behavior, <1 for peer interaction]. So the most important predictor of negative behavior with an unfamiliar peer was being ignored by a teacher who did not know how to promote positive interactions or give enough attention to do so.

Consistent and Inconsistent Patterns

In the first year's assessment, children (especially 2-year-olds) who acted more negatively toward the peer came from families with higher levels of education and had spent more time in poorer quality day care (less caregiver attention, responsiveness, teaching). In Year 2, children (especially 4-year-olds) who acted more negatively toward the peer were from families with lower levels of education and had spent less time in day care of high quality. The common pattern of prediction across the two years was that more negative children received more discipline (from caregivers in Year 1 and parents in Year 2). Another consistent association across settings was that children who were more negative with the new acquaintance in the laboratory were observed to interact with fewer children, especially older children, and to be less positively engaged with peers. At night, they were less likely to interact with a sibling; in the daytime, they were in arrangements without other children, or, if there were other children, they experienced less intense interactions with them. A third consistent but puzzling finding for negative interaction in Years 1 and 2 (and in homes and centers) was that caregivers had higher expectations for these negative children. That is, they thought that these children would know more about the world before they started school. Unfortunately, there are no equivalent studies with which to compare these results concerning children's negative behavior with an unfamiliar peer. They must be considered strictly exploratory.

AGGRESSION TOWARD PEERS

The final measure of children's social behavior with peers was the aggressiveness they displayed with familiar peers. We used this measure to represent children's aggressiveness because aggressive acts were not observed during our semistructured observations of peer interaction, either with the unfamiliar peer in the laboratory or with the familiar playmate at home. The measure we used was the frequency of aggressive acts by the child—hitting, kicking, pinching, biting, threatening, grabbing a toy away—directed toward peers during the daytime observation (when there was a peer present).

This variable was strongly correlated in the two daytime observations 1 year apart. It was the only measure of the child's social skill with peers that was stable across the year of the study. Because it was related to lower levels of cognitive development, less social competence with the unfamiliar visitor to the home, and less compliance with parents (Table 6.1), this variable does seem to reflect less adequate—or at least less desirable—development.

Family Predictors of Aggression

Correlations of children's aggression with their experiences at home with their families are presented in Table 12.1.

Parental Discipline. These correlations show that more aggressive children interacted less with their fathers and received more discipline from both their parents. The correlations with parental discipline were significant even with the frequency of the child's demands partialled out. They were especially high for fathers' physical control, for children from families of lower SES, and for children who were not in day care (significant interaction terms in analyses of covariance for these variables). Regression analyses showed that both mother's and father's discipline had significant independent effects on children's aggression [for mothers, $F = 4.0$ $(p < .01)$, for fathers $F = 6.4$ $(p < .001)$].

The link between parental discipline and children's aggression also appeared in correlations across time, suggesting that high levels of discipline may have contributed to children's aggressiveness [the correlation between discipline in Year 1 and aggression in Year 2, with aggression in Year 1 partialled out = .19 $(p < .05)$; the correlation between aggression in Year 1 and discipline in Year 2 = .05)]. On the other hand, children's aggression may have led to less interaction with the father: The fathers of children who were more aggressive in Year 1 interacted with them less in Year 2 $[r = -.32 \ (p < .01)]$.

The link we observed between aggression and negative parental control was also observed in research by Pettit (1991) and by Hinde and Stevenson-Hinde (1986; Stevenson-Hinde et al., 1986). These researchers found negative parental control to be a significant predictor of children's hostility to their peers at nursery school and kindergarten and to their squabbling with siblings at home. Mothers of these more aggressive children, they observed, were more controlling and hostile to the child, less accepting of the child's wishes. Harsh parental discipline early in life has also been related to later aggressiveness in school-aged children, even when other contributors such as the child's temperament and the parents' SES were taken in consideration (Weiss, Dodge, Bates, & Pettit, 1992).

In the present study, the mothers of more aggressive children were also more alienated themselves. Their attitude toward their children was not necessarily more negative though. A significant interaction with the child's sex was found for the mother's attitude toward the child. Mothers of more aggressive boys had more negative attitudes toward them $[r = -.24 \ (p < .05)]$; mothers of more aggressive girls felt more positive about them $[r = $

.46 ($p < .05$); significant interaction with sex in analysis of covariance]. This was probably because boys in this study, as in the rest of life, were more aggressive than girls [$F(1, 142) = 2.2$ ($p < .05$); see chapter 4].

Interaction With Other Children.   In addition to these relations with parental discipline, we also found associations with the child's interactions with other children at home. More aggressive children with siblings, not surprisingly, were more likely to be targets of their sibling's aggression. This experience, however, did not have a significant independent effect on the child's aggressiveness during the daytime beyond the effect of the parents' discipline.

Home Environments.   Differences in the physical environments of more aggressive children were also observed. Their homes were messier and less stimulating. These features would seem to provide a suitable context for developing aggressive ways of interacting with other children. They did make a significant independent contribution to the child's aggressiveness after parents' discipline had been removed [$Fs = 8.6$ ($p < .01$) in Year 1, 8.3 ($p < .01$) in Year 2]. Prodromidis et al. (1993) also found that children in homes with higher HOME scores were less aggressive.

Daytime Predictors of Aggression

Being in Poor Day Care.   It is a commonly reported finding that children who are or who have been in day care (centers) are more aggressive than those reared exclusively at home (Bates et al., 1991; Haskins, 1985; Park & Honig, 1991; Thornburg et al., 1990; Vandell & Corasaniti, 1990). It might have been expected that the same would hold true in the present study. In this study, however, children's aggression was not related to being in a day-care center or a day-care home—even though that is the setting where the aggression was being assessed. Aggression was not related to the children's contemporaneous care arrangement; analyses of variance for child-care arrangement were all nonsignificant. This parallels the finding by Prodromidis et al. (1993) for children in day care in Sweden.

Nor was children's aggression in our study related to having been in a day-care center or day-care home longer. In fact, the trend was in the opposite direction: Children who displayed more aggressive behavior had been in day care for a shorter time [$rs = -.17$ ($p < .10$) for all children, Year 1, $-.48$ ($p < .05$) for children in home day care, Year 1; $-.22$ ($p < .10$) for children in day-care centers, Year 2]. These newcomers to day care had apparently not yet learned to get what they wanted without hitting and grabbing. The more hours the child was currently spending in day care did predict greater aggression for children in day-care homes [$r = .44$ ($p < .10$), Year 2]. Perhaps spending so many hours in day care was frustrating for these children. But the hours spent in day care did not make a difference for children in day-care centers (maybe because centers provided more activities to keep the children occupied and more toys to go around).

There was some suggestion that aggression was more likely to be observed in poor quality day care. Children displayed more aggression if their caregivers had less training and knowledge in child development and less experience in child care, and if the caregivers did less teaching and were less responsive to the children. Note, however, that although these caregivers were not specifically "experts" in child care, they were more highly educated than the caregivers of less aggressive children (this was true for both center teachers and home-care providers.) So even this suggestion that more aggressive children were in poor quality care is not entirely consistent with the usual definition of poor quality. Among children in homes, more aggressive children were in settings with less structure, fewer scheduled activities, fewer toys, and more mess. These features of home care do seem to represent poor quality.

Other researchers studying links between aggression and the quality of day care have typically studied children in day-care centers rather than day-care homes. But the results are similar to these for day-care homes. They have found, for example, that children are less aggressive in classes with more structured activities (Huston-Stein, Friedrich, & Susman, 1977). The benefit of program structure may appear only at the time, however. In an experiment by Connolly and Smith (1978), when children who had been in a highly structured program were switched to a moderately structured one, their aggression increased. Children who had been in an unstructured program to begin with, when switched to the moderately structured program were better able to resolve peer conflicts without resorting to aggression.

Interaction With Caregivers. Beyond these links with day-care quality, aggression was related to the specific kinds of interaction the child had with caregivers. The link with the caregiver's discipline was especially strong and predicted increased aggression across time. Caregivers supervising more aggressive children gave them more attention and discipline at the time (when aggression was being assessed), and when caregivers gave more physical control and punishment in Year 1, children were more aggressive in Year 2 [$r = .38$ ($p < .05$) for children in centers, .31 ($p < .05$) for children in homes; rs in the opposite direction = .00]. Regression analyses revealed that the caregiver's behavior made an independent contribution to the prediction of children's aggression [$F = 3.5$ ($p < .01$)].

Interactions With Peers. Aggressive children spent more of their time interacting with peers and, not surprisingly, as these were the interactions in which the target children's aggression was assessed, their interactions involved more negative affect and more aggression from the other children.

Regression analyses revealed that interaction with peers made an independent contribution to children's aggression beyond the contribution of the caregiver's behavior or the quality of the program [F = 4.5 ($p < .01$)].

The children these more aggressive children played with were less likely to be older. Other researchers have found that children are less aggressive in classes in which they have the opportunity to interact with older children (Logue, 1989). Among children in centers, in addition, more aggressive children were in classes with a higher proportion of lower SES children (this association was significant even with the child's own SES partialled out). Surprisingly, perhaps, children were not more aggressive if they were with a larger group of children; a trend in the opposite direction was suggested. Among children in homes, more aggressive children were in settings with fewer children, they interacted with fewer children and spent more time alone; in centers, more aggressive children were with fewer children per caregiver and a less diverse group of children. It may be that in larger classes caregivers work harder at curbing children's antisocial behavior—because to ignore such behavior could lead to kiddy chaos. In Allhusen's (1992) study, caregivers with the largest groups and the worst adult–child ratios were lowest on all measures of caregiving except for promoting children's social development (encouraging children to play and share together, mediating peer conflicts, etc.).

Combining Family and Daytime Predictors of Aggression

An additive regression model including both family and day-care variables was more predictive than models for either family or day variables alone [R = .81 ($p < .01$)], but when the relative contributions of family and day-care variables were compared, only the daytime variables were found to make an independent contribution to the child's aggression [F = 2.5 ($p < .05$)]. In a further analysis to confirm this finding, analysis of variance was performed for children from higher and lower quality families and from higher and lower quality day-care environments. Children were divided into high-quality and low-quality groups by median splits on the composite scores for adults' educational backgrounds, stimulation, and discipline. High-quality parents were of higher SES, more stimulating and less controlling; high-quality day-care caregivers had more training, were more stimulating and less controlling. The ANOVA differentiating between children in high-quality day care and low-quality day care was significant [$F(3, 124)$ = 3.5 ($p < .05$); Ms for children in high-quality day care = .63 for children from poorer quality family environments, .52 for children from higher quality family environments; Ms for children in low-quality day care = 1.1 for children from poorer quality family environments, 1.1 for children in higher quality family environments]. These results suggest, then, that in the present study the strongest predictors of children's aggression were their experiences in day care rather than their experiences at home.

SUMMARY AND CONCLUSIONS

The major theme that appears in the results of the analyses relating children's social behavior with other children to their experiences at home and in day care is that simple predictions from the extent of children's social experience with peers are rare. Mere exposure to other children is not sufficient to create a well-rounded repertoire of social skills that can be called upon in interactions with different children in different situations. The roles of adults and the physical environment for promoting children's social competence should not be underestimated.

Social Competence With an Unfamiliar Peer

The role of adults is particularly clear for the prediction of children's social competence with an unfamiliar peer. Children who were in day care, particularly those who had spent more time in day-care centers, were more socially competent with the unfamiliar peer. But this was not because they had more extensive and positive experience with other children there. These children did not spend their time in day care playing freely with peers; they did not interact with more different playmates. Socially competent children in centers interacted with fewer children. Socially competent children in home care spent less time interacting with other children. Socially competent children were less likely to have a sibling and, if they did have a sibling, their interactions at home at night tended to be less positive (more aggressive). Instead of learning social skills just from hanging around with other children, socially competent children apparently benefitted from some adult tutelage. In homes, in centers, and with their families at night, more socially competent children spent time in instructional activities with more educated caregivers. Combining these results, it seems that social competence with an unfamiliar peer is promoted by the opportunity to interact with a small number of older children in an educational context with an attentive caregiver, who can instruct children about the do's and don'ts of social interaction.

Interaction With a Friend

A different pattern was observed for children's interaction with a familiar playmate at home. This kind of sociability was predicted by more extensive and positive experience with other children—with siblings at dinnertime and with other children in the daytime. For predicting or promoting this kind of social competence, adults' behavior did not seem to be so important.

What was most beneficial, apparently, was a child-care arrangement that maximized the child's opportunity to form a friendship with another child: An arrangement in which the child could spend part of the day in a day-care center (nursery school) programs and part of the time at home. In brief, these results suggest, adults help children develop the social skills necessary to meet a new acquaintance and start a positive interaction, but it is practice with other children that helps them learn to be a good friend. When children form a friendship with a slightly older child this is also a help in demonstrating one's social abilities. Children who were more sociable with their friend had more older children to watch and interact with in the daytime; their social skill with the friend was correlated with the friend's age [$r = .24 \ (p < .01)$].

Negative Behavior With an Unfamiliar Peer

Children's negative behavior—avoiding, refusing, controlling—with the unfamiliar peer in the laboratory assessment was related to their experiences with both adults and peers.

In the first year assessment, children who acted more negative toward the peer had more educated parents; their mothers worked more hours, but were less satisfied with their lives. These more negative children had spent more time in poorer quality day care (less caregiver attention and responsiveness). They did not experience frequent intense, intimate interactions with peers—at home or in day care. Nor were their interactions with the caregiver intense and intimate: They received less frequent one-to-one conversation, physical contact, or teaching. Only discipline from the caregiver was more frequent.

This predominance of discipline over positive one-to-one attention was the only common thread between the two assessments of negative behavior to the unfamiliar peer made a year apart. More negative children received more discipline and less of other kinds of attention from their caregivers in both years. In addition, unlike the children who were more negative in Year 1, the children who were more negative in Year 2 had parents with lower levels of education and mothers who were less likely to be working. These more negative older children had spent less time in day care of high quality, especially center care, and interacted with fewer children.

Thus, it appears that children whose interactions with an unfamiliar peer contain frequent negative behaviors have not received the kinds of positive, intense, interpersonal experiences with other children (in day care or at home) that would help them interact with a new acquaintance. They were ignored by adults, except for demands and discipline, rather than being guided by them toward a repertoire of social skills with other children, and their interactions with other children were not sufficient for them to develop these social skills on their own.

Aggression

Children's aggressiveness was also predicted by qualities of the child's interactions with both adults and peers. Aggression toward familiar children in the daytime was increased by the adults' strict discipline, particularly by physical control and punishment exerted by fathers and daily caregivers. For children who were not in day care, aggression was most clearly predicted by physical discipline given by lower SES fathers. For children who were in day care, aggression was most closely predicted by physical discipline given by caregivers who had less training in child development and did not agree with the experts about appropriate strategies of discipline. These results demonstrate the well-known effect of punitive adult behavior on children's aggression (Larzelere, 1986; Parke & Slaby, 1983; Patterson, 1982). What is new is that they demonstrate the importance of non-parental caregivers as influences on the aggression of children who are in day care.

It is not that children in day care were more aggressive than those at home. Aggression was related to being in poor quality care, but it did not matter whether the care was in a home or a center. Children were more aggressive when they spent more hours a day in a messy, un-stimulating home setting. They were more aggressive if they were in a center class with fewer playmates, who were less likely to be older and more likely to be poor. They were more aggressive if they lived in messy, unstimulating homes. More aggressive children were involved in aggressive interactions not just in the daytime observations when their aggression was observed for this assessment but also in nighttime observations with their siblings.

13

Conclusion

A BROAD METHOD OF STUDY

The study we have described in this book extends existing research, adding to our knowledge about the relative effects of family and day-care experiences on young children. By exploring children's experiences in a wide variety of environments and examining how those experiences were related to children's development in a variety of domains, the study provided a broad view of the contexts of contemporary childhood and threw some light on the processes of child development. The breadth and variability of settings and measures and analyses included in the study were its major strengths.

Perhaps the most important source of variability in the study was the range of day-care environments observed. The study included day-care arrangements that ran the gamut from a single caregiver looking after one child at home to care by a team of teachers in an institution enrolling several hundred children. Within this range lay variability in the educational activities the day-care arrangement provided, the number and ages of children in the setting, and the backgrounds and qualifications of the care providers. Wide variability was also observed in the family environments represented in the study. We recorded this variability in detail using identical methods of data collection in both day-care and family settings. We then used the information gathered in these observations and interviews to predict a range of child development outcomes as diverse as reciting back numbers to a researcher and slugging it out with a peer, making social overtures to an adult stranger and initiating social play with a friend. By repeating both the observations of environments and the assessments of child development outcomes at two points during the study, it was possible to look for relations that were replicated across time, to address questions about cross-time predictions of development, and to go beyond analysis of simple differences in the level of outcomes to look at changes in outcome over time and increased exposure to day care.

In this concluding chapter, it is worth reiterating the unique advantages of using this variety of settings and methods and analyses. It was only by using such methods that we could document the natural flow and ecology of young children's lives and discover how much children's experiences depend on the physical setting and the presence of other children, as well as on the characteristics of their caregivers, which have more typically been the focus of research. Only by using such methods could we study children's development in the broadest context of their experiences rather than simply as a function of arbitrarily isolated interactions with their mothers and discover the parallel patterns of prediction from children's experiences in different settings and with different caregivers. Only by using such methods could we delve into the meaning of day-care quality and examine differences in prediction for different domains of development and, within domains, for different indexes of development. Only by using such methods could we uncover the distinctive links between children's experiences and specific abilities rather than simply documenting a generalized prediction of "good development" based on "good experiences." Only by using such methods and analyses could we isolate the experiences of individual children from the experiences of aggregated groups, test relations over time, separate the contributions to development of children's interactions with their mothers, their fathers, and their siblings, and identify aspects of experience that had both positive and negative effects on development.

Finally, only by using such methods and analyses could we answer the questions with which we began the study: Do mothers affect the development of children who are in day care as much as the development of children who are at home? Are children's experiences in day-care environments predictive of their development? Do the same kinds of experiences in day-care and home environments predict development? Does knowing about both family and day-care experiences increase the prediction of children's abilities? The observations and analyses carried out in this study suggest that the answer to all these questions is "yes."

NEW AND BETTER INFORMATION

Many of the findings in this study confirmed or strengthened what we already knew about children's development from a myriad of other studies. But, in addition, the findings pointed to the significance of aspects of children's experiences that have not received their due in previous research. In particular, the study underscored the importance for young children's development of interactions with their fathers, their brothers, and playmates who are older and more diverse. It highlighted the particular significance of

educational activities, like reading, at home and in day care. It demonstrated that even something good for development, like reading or day care,
can be detrimental if the child gets too much of it. And, most important, it
documented the contribution day care makes to children's development,
above and beyond the contributions of their families. In this concluding
chapter we discuss these new findings, as well as some tried and true
findings with some different twists.

THE CASE OF THE DISAPPEARING MOM

One of the new findings that appeared in the study was the finding that the
stereotype of mother as primary parent and shaper of children's development just doesn't hold up. This was not a historical study, so it is not
possible to say whether this represents a change from the "good old days"
when mother reigned supreme on the homefront, but it is clear that, in a
number of ways, the mother's role in these children's lives was less substantial than one might have expected. Evidence of the mother's diminished role came from a variety of analyses: observations of parents'
behavior at home at dinnertime, observations of the children's experiences
in the daytime, and empirical links between mothers' behavior and their
children's development.

Mother at Home at Dinnertime

One place we looked for the mother's influence was at home in the early
evening. This was a time when all mothers were faced with the same tasks
of preparing and eating dinner and getting the child to bed. It was therefore
an opportunity to observe the behavior of working mothers and nonworking mothers on an even playing field. It was also a time when mothers and
fathers and children were all together—so we could compare and contrast
the mother's interaction and influence with those of the father and siblings.

Frequency of Mother's Interaction.   What we found was that at home,
at the end of the day, during dinnertime and into bedtime, in a natural,
unstructured observation, mothers interacted with their children. But their
interaction was quite limited in frequency and content. On the average,
during the 2-hour period, mothers interacted with the target child for less
than 30 minutes, and the nature of their attention was most frequently
giving directions or demands. The rest of the time, the children were
interacting with the father, playing alone or with siblings, or watching TV.

Interaction With Dad.   The presence of the father made a significant
difference in children's experience at home at night. Because the father was
there, mothers interacted less with the children. Mothers did interact with

the children more frequently overall than fathers did (e.g., three times as many utterances), but apparently their behavior was not as salient or influential as the father's. For one thing, fathers interacted as much as mothers in two important ways (ways that turned out to be predictive of the child's development): reading and showing affection. They also were more likely than mothers to engage the child in physical play. Thus, the content of the mother's interaction appears to be relatively less educational and emotionally involving than father's. So the salience of mothers' interaction with the child was decreased by the presence of the father.

This was especially true for working mothers. Fathers were especially interactive and involved in child care in families of higher socioeconomic status and in families in which the mother was employed. Although the mother's work status did not affect the style or quality of mother's or father's behavior, it did make a difference in the *frequency* and *amount* of the father's behavior. Here, then, is a suggestion that the role of the mother is diminishing because more mothers are working, and as they increase their involvement in work, fathers become more active and influential participants in their children's lives and development.

Siblings as Playmates. What about when mothers do not work? Do these mothers, then, have more interaction with the children at the end of the day? Based on the results of this study, it appears that they do not. There was no difference in the frequency of mothers' interactions with children if they were or were not employed. Furthermore, when mothers were not involved in work (if they were less career oriented and their husbands were less involved in the child's care), there tended to be more children in the family. Then, children in these families spent more time at the end of the day playing with siblings—and less time interacting with either parent. The mother was not the key player for these children either.

As Children Get Older. There was also evidence in the study that the mother's interaction with the child at dinnertime diminished in frequency as the child got older. Attention of all kinds (from all adults) diminished as children got older. But what diminished especially was what might be considered the quintessential "maternal" care, that is "cuddly" care (physical contact, affection, and play)—by mothers and fathers. What increased was interaction with siblings, time alone, and teaching by father. The mother's role apparently decreases over time as the child is exposed to less of the kinds of behavior most associated with the traditional mother's care.

Mother's Influence on Child's Development

Another kind of evidence that the role of the mother is less significant than one might have expected came from the results of analyses predicting children's development from their mother's behavior. It turned out that in the study children's cognitive development was influenced by experiencing more interaction with father and with siblings, not by experiencing more interaction with the mother. In fact, the correlations between children's cognitive development and more frequent interaction with mother were significantly negative. This did not mean that interacting more with mother was detrimental to children's development; it seemed that mothers were responding to children's advanced development with less attention, not that less attention was causing advanced development. Nevertheless, there were not the strong positive links between development and more frequent or affectionate or responsive or didactic interaction with the mother that might have been expected (and that have been observed in other research—conducted at different times of day, without the father or siblings present). The mother's role as an influence on the child's development apparently took a back seat to the importance of both siblings and dad.

Mother in the Daytime

But perhaps the clearest evidence of the disappearing maternal role came from our observations of what was happening to these young children in the daytime. In this study and in the United States today, in the daytime the majority of mothers go to work and their children are in day care. In fact, in this study, data hinted that if the mother–child relationship had problems (was less close and reciprocal at age 2–3), mothers were more likely to put their children in day care (by age 3–4).

What Day Care Is Like.   Children in the study who were in center day care had experiences that were completely different from the experiences they had at home at dinnertime or the experiences they would have had if they stayed at home with mother during the day. The environment in day-care centers was more structured, and the children had more toys available and spent more time using academic materials and art supplies. They participated in more educational activities: reading and lessons, given by more professionally qualified caregivers. There were more other children for them to interact with—which they did. They received only half as much individual attention from an adult caregiver and much less affection than they would have at home. Even those children who went to a day-care home while their mother was at work had decidedly different experiences from children at home with their mothers. In day-care homes, there were more children to play with and each child got less attention and positive care (reading, responding, offering choices, not demanding) from the caregiver. Only those children who were with a sitter in their own home had experiences that were roughly comparable to what it was like to be with mother during the daytime.

Influence of Day Care.   Not only was the experience of children in day care different from the experience of children at home, so was their development. Children who were in day care, and more specifically in day-care centers, in this study, were consistently advanced in their development over children who were at home with their mothers. This advance showed up on all our measures of development: cognitive development, social competence with unfamiliar adults, independence from the mother in an unfamiliar situation, general obedience and competence at dinnertime, compliance with requests made by a researcher, social interaction with a peer friend, social competence with an unfamiliar peer, and negative behavior toward the unfamiliar peer.[1] Being in day care was positively linked with advanced development in all these ways. This finding of a consistent and powerful effect of day care on children's behavior provides further evidence of the mother's less-than-central role in shaping the child's development.

Hours of Day Care.   Not only did being in day care affect children's behavior and development (and reduce the mother's role) but how much time the children spent there made a difference too. Children who spent more time in day care (and less time with mother) were more independent from mother in the laboratory, more compliant with requests from researchers in the laboratory, more generally competent in the dinnertime observation at home, and more outgoing and cooperative with the unfamiliar peer. But for several measures, it seems, the relation with the amount of time the child spent in day care was more complex. For measures of cognitive development, social competence with unfamiliar adults, and sociability with a friend, the children who were most advanced were those who were in day care 10 to 30 hours a week. For these important outcomes, then, it seems that there is an optimal balance of day-care experience and time at home. Perhaps this indicates that although the mother's role may be less than total, it is still significant and that spending some relaxed time at home with mom is valuable for 2- and 3-year-old children. In addition, there are some ways in which the mother's role is unique in the child's development.

Unique Maternal Role

Despite the fact that mothers interacted less with their children and that their behavior had less influence on children's development than one might have expected, the results of this study also showed that mothers still have

---

[1]This relation was for negative behavior with the unfamiliar peer in Year 2, when scoring low on the measure was more clearly an index of developmental competence. The few outcome measures for which being in day care was not positively predictive—compliance with parents' requests at night, sociability with mother, aggression with peers—were not so clearly measures of development. They were not correlated with the child's age, and therefore may be indices of personal style rather than developmental outcomes. Moreover, although aggression was not related to being in day care, it was predicted by experiences in day care more strongly than by experiences at home.

an important and unique role in their children's development. For several aspects of the child's development, it was the mother's behavior and availability, in particular, that appeared to affect the child's development. This was true, first, for the quality of the child's relationship with the mother. Children had more positive, reciprocal, and cooperative interactions with their mothers in the laboratory when their mothers were more affectionate with them at home, had a more positive attitude toward them, and worked less. Even if the mother did work and the child was in day care, the child's relationship with her was related to these variables reflecting a positive mom. The mother's behavior was also related to the child's relationship with a familiar playmate. Children were more sociable with a playmate at home when their mothers were more affectionate and their fathers interacted with them less. Compliance was a third aspect of the child's behavior that was linked to the mother's role. Children were more compliant with the mother's requests at home at dinnertime when the mother did not work more than 40 hours per week. In these special ways, then, the child's development was affected by the mother. Perhaps it is no coincidence that the aspects of the child's behavior that were linked to the mother's behavior all involve "feminine" behavior—close relationships and compliant responses—whereas the influence of fathers and brothers and schools was in the domain of competence—knowledge and independence.

Family Influence Continues

Although it is true that the mother's role is less than all-encompassing and that children learn a lot in day care, it is important not to overlook the fact that this does not mean that their experience at home is irrelevant—even for measures of competence like knowledge and independence. In this study, both family features and day-care experience—independently—affected children's cognitive development, social competence with adults, social competence with unfamiliar peers, negative behavior with unfamiliar peers, and general competence at dinnertime. Children's development, according to our analyses, was affected by the sum of their experiences at home and in day care. In fact, when we conducted analyses that controlled the two sets of experiences, there was some small difference favoring family predictors of cognition and a larger one favoring family predictors of compliance. Moreover, correlations of cognitive development with family characteristics (stimulating home, mother's discipline, father's teaching) were higher for children in day care than for children at home with mother all day, so the effect of the family does not disappear just because the child is in day care.

Of course, this is just one study, and its results concerning the relative importance of mothers, fathers, siblings, and experiences outside of the family, however suggestive, can only take us one step along in our quest for an understanding of the dynamics of contemporary child development. The methods and analyses used here have provided some new and provocative findings, but these findings demand further investigation and inquiry before we can be sure of their truth. We are perhaps on less speculative ground when we consider the findings of the study related to the direct effects of different aspects of the day-care experience on children's development; research on this topic is more plentiful. We consider these findings next.

REPLACING OR SUPPLEMENTING MOM WITH GOOD QUALITY CARE

If mother is disappearing, it is especially important to scrutinize her replacement. If mother's care is being supplemented by day care we need to find out all about it. What is important about the alternative care that children receive? What are the qualities of care that predict children's development? Are the same qualities important in day care as in the family? Other research has most often focused on regulable indices of day-care "quality": the caregiver's qualifications, the adult–child ratio and class size, the presence of an educational or developmental curriculum, a stimulating and safe physical environment. In the present study we were able to ask whether, considered within a broader spectrum of measures, these qualities were indeed predictive of children's development and to establish whether the same qualities were predictive in different day-care settings and in the family.

Caregiver Qualifications

In other research it has been found that the educational "qualifications" of day-care teachers are related to both their behavior and the development of children in their care. In this study we also found some links between children's development and their day-care caregivers' backgrounds (their level of schooling and their knowledge and training in child development)—but the links were weak and indirect. In day-care centers, although the teacher's educational background was related to children's cognitive development, it did not have an independent effect beyond what was contributed by her actual behavior, and it was not strongly related to other aspects of the child's development. There was no association between the caregiver's education and her own behavior. In home day care, more qualified caregivers gave children more attention and positive caregiving, and the children in their care were more competent, but, again, the caregiver's educational background did not have an *independent* effect on children's development. For day-care caregivers, then, the effects of educational background were only indirect.

In contrast, *parents'* educational backgrounds (education, socioeconomic status, knowledge and training in child development) were related to children's development independent of the parents' behavior. Direct links were found with children's cognitive development, social competence with an unfamiliar peer, compliance with requests, and negative behavior with unfamiliar peers (positive in Year 1 and negative in Year 2). Parents' educational level was not related to children's sociability to mother, sociability with a friend, aggression, or compliance at home—measures of behavior that were less developmental in nature.

Thus, although there are superficial similarities between the predictors of development found in day care and in the family—at the level of simple correlations—these similarities are deceptive. Caregiver's education and training did not have the same strong direct effects on children as did parents' education and training. We assume that the reason for the direct links with the parents' educational backgrounds is the genetic connection underlying such associations. In this way, then, day-care caregivers are not replacing mothers and never will.

Educational Curriculum

One way in which day care may be supplanting or at least supplementing mom, however, is by offering children educational experiences that they do not have at home. Children in our study spent substantially more of their time in formal and informal educational activities when they were in day care than when they were at home with their families. These educational activities in day-care homes or day-care centers—being read to, hearing a lesson, being taught, being given an explanation, engaging in structured activities— we found, promoted children's cognitive development and social competence with adults and peers. The amount of reading children heard proved to be a particularly strong and consistent predictor of their cognitive development, a predictor that had an independent effect beyond the contributions of all other factors. The effects of these educational activities were particularly strong for children who spent the most time in the day-care setting and for boys.

But the associations with these educational activities also showed that it was possible to have too much of a good thing. Some children in day-care centers spent more than half of the time we observed them in lessons, singing, or being read to. At this level, the benefits of educational activities dwindled: Associations between cognitive development and reading and lessons in day-care centers were curvilinear. An unrelenting regimen of structured academic activities, this suggests, can lead to too much pressure on children and not promote even the development of the cognitive abilities that presumably are their goal.

Although formal educational activities were more common and time-consuming in day care than at home, they did occur when the children were with their parents, as well. More than half of the children in the study heard some reading at home at night from their parents. And, as was true in the daytime, how much reading the children heard was a key predictor of their cognitive development. Cognitive development was related to the amount of reading by both the mother and the father (this was the one maternal behavior of which greater frequency predicted children's cognitive development). It was related to cognitive development for both children with siblings and children with no siblings. It had an independent effect on cognitive development beyond the contributions of the parents' other behaviors and characteristics.

In this domain of educational activities, then, we see parallels between what happens to children at home and in day care. Mother's replacement in this arena has the same effect as mom, but more so. Both parents and day-care providers are educating today's children.

Individual Attention

In addition to educating children, one of the things that mothers provide to their children is close, intimate, one-to-one attention. As we have pointed out, in the present study, when we visited the children at home at dinnertime and bedtime, the influence of this aspect of the mother's role had been eliminated by the presence and participation of the father. What about in the daytime? Were children getting one-to-one attention from another adult in the daytime, and did that one-to-one attention benefit their development?

As it turned out, children got less individual attention in day care than they did with their parents at home, and the relations with individual attention for the sample as a whole were not significant. This lack of association occurred because children in centers, with less individual attention, were developmentally advanced over children in homes. Within the two kinds of daytime setting, homes and centers, there were small positive correlations between cognitive and social competence with one-to-one talk with the child, and in homes in the daytime, there were positive correlations with one-to-one physical contact (hugging and touching) as well. In day-care centers, however, one-to-one physical contact was related to lower cognitive development and social competence.

Individual attention by day-care caregivers, especially day-care center teachers, is not a prime influence on children's development or a substitute for contact with the mother.

Importance of Discipline

More important than the amount of one-to-one attention from caregivers was their disciplinary style. Strong associations were observed between children's development and the discipline they received from their caregivers. These associations occurred for daytime caregivers in the children's homes, in day-care homes, and in day-care centers. They appeared consistently in assessments 1 year apart, and remained significant even with the child's demands partialled out. Children who received less discipline (less demanding, controlling, punishing; more choices, responses) had advanced cognitive development, were less aggressive with playmates and less negative toward the unfamiliar peer, and were more compliant. For social competence with adults, authoritative discipline—a combination of a demanding style and more positive behavior (affectionate and not punishing or physically controlling)—predicted children's development.

Cross-time analyses suggested that a nonauthoritarian style of interaction (less discipline) encouraged children's cognitive development; that strict, especially physically controlling, discipline led to increased aggression and negative behavior toward an unfamiliar peer; that increased compliance led to decreased discipline; and that social competence was promoted by adults' positive behavior and attitude. Thus, it appeared that how day-care caregivers managed children was related to development in a variety of ways. Discipline was not a simple package. Physical punishment and control were unequivocally negative in their effects. But pushing kids in a demanding but not punitive way, although it led to lower cognitive development, promoted more outgoing social skills in an unfamiliar situation and enhanced the child's ability to deal with a strange adult in a strange place.

These associations between caregivers' discipline and children's development were completely parallel to the associations found for mothers and fathers at home. Both sources of discipline had independent effects on children's development. Moreover, parents who were more authoritarian had selected day-care caregivers who were also relatively authoritarian. Mothers' disciplinary efforts, thus, are echoed by those of fathers and day-care caregivers. It is not the mother's responsibility or role alone to discipline the child; all adults work together.

Importance of Interaction With Other Children

Beyond the importance of the these adults, the child is also influenced by contacts with other children. At home with siblings or in day care with a group of peers, the child's life is changed and enriched by the presence of other children. In our study, only six children were never observed to have another child present during our observations. Our analyses suggested that it is good for children's development to have some such experience with other children. It is even better when those children are older than the child. With older children, interactions were more verbal and positive; with younger children, interactions were more aggressive and negative. The opportunity to interact with more older children, in the present study, benefited children's cognitive development and social competence with peers (with friends and unfamiliar peers, these children were more positive and less negative and aggressive). Spending the daytime in a home with a younger child (including a younger sibling) was negatively related to children's cognitive development.

But although it is valuable to have some experience with peers, it is not necessarily better to spend more time interacting with them. Social competence with peers, which you might expect would be predicted by more frequent interaction with other children, was not so related. It was not related to the amount of time the child spent interacting with siblings, and it was related to less, not more, interaction with peers in day care. The other measures of child development were more positively related to the child's interaction with other children. More interaction with siblings was positively related to cognitive development and the child's ability to interact positively with a friend. But relations of these and other outcomes to the amount of time the child spent interacting with peers in day care were curvilinear. For cognitive development, sociability with a friend, and social competence with adults, a moderate amount of interaction with peers in day care was best. This moderate amount of interaction offered children the best of two worlds: an adequate opportunity to learn about peers by interacting freely with them, without at the same time losing the benefits of frequent interactions with an adult caregiver.

The kind of interaction children had with their peers mattered too. Children did better in terms of their cognitive development and sociability if their interactions with peers (in day care or at home) were at a higher level (pretend play rather than parallel play) and were more positive (characterized by positive affect rather than aggression).

It is clear that peers play an important role in the lives of contemporary preschool children.

Class Size, Adult–Child Ratio

In day care, how much time children spend interacting with their peers is related to the number of children in the class and the ratio of adult caregivers to children. Past research has suggested that children do better in day-care settings with smaller classes, with fewer children and more adults to go around. In this study, however, associations between children's development and the number of children in their daytime setting were often observed to be positive. This was because being with more children was associated with being in a center as opposed to a home setting. When class sizes and adult–child ratios were examined within the two types of settings, different patterns in the two settings were found.

In homes, whether in home day care in the daytime or the child's own home at night, when there were more children in the setting, adults were less available and interacted with the individual child less. Nevertheless, the number of children present was linked to better social development for the child. Children with more other children to play with in their home setting were more socially competent with unfamiliar adults and peers in the laboratory and less aggressive toward the other children in the setting.

In day-care centers, the number of children in the class did not affect the caregiver's behavior. It did, however, affect the children's development. Children in classes with more children per caregiver made smaller gains in cognitive development, were less socially skilled with unfamiliar peers, and were less compliant. On the other hand, these children were also less aggressive in the day-care setting and less negative (in Year 2) with an unfamiliar peer. There are apparently some benefits of being in a class with a low adult–child ratio; these children learn to curb their aggressive behavior.

Putting together the results of the home and day-care center analyses suggests that for fostering children's cognitive and social development an ideal day-care arrangement, whether in a home setting or a center, is one that offers the child opportunities to interact with a moderate number of diverse other children —four or five—under the supervision of one adult.

Stimulating Physical Setting

The final dimension of day care that was shown to be important in predicting children's development in the present study was the stimulation provided by the physical environment. Here, again, associations in day care paralleled those found in the child's own home. Being in a more stimulating home environment in the daytime, with more toys and decorations and less mess and hazards, improved children's cognitive development even beyond the contributions made by parents' or caregivers' backgrounds or behavior. It also promoted children's ability to interact positively with unfamiliar peers in the laboratory and led to less aggressive interactions among the children in the home. Spending more time in the home during the day watching TV was detrimental for development; It had a negative effect on cognitive development and also was related to more negative behavior with the unfamiliar peer (in Year 2).

Being in a day-care center was of even greater value because centers offered children more stimulating objects to look at and play with than homes did. But in most day-care centers there was enough stimulation in the environment, and increases in the variety of materials and decorations did not increase children's cognitive development. Only in large classes, where there was a need for more materials to go around, were associations with the number and variety of materials and decorations found.

A PARENTS' EYE VIEW OF DAY CARE

Now that we have discussed the patterns of day-care experience that seem to promote children's development, in closing, it is interesting to look at day care from the parent's perspective, rather than the researcher's or the child's.

Selecting Similarities

As we discussed earlier, parents select day care that is compatible with their own characteristics. In this study, there were similarities between the physical features of the family's home and the day-care setting: parents chose day-care centers or day-care homes which, like their own homes, had more toys and were less messy and unsafe. There were similarities in knowledge and attitudes: Parents who were more knowledgeable about child development chose caregivers who were more knowledgeable in the same ways; parents who held traditional family values selected caregivers who felt the same as they did.[2] There were similarities in behavior: Less authoritarian parents chose day care in which caregivers were less demanding and controlling; parents who spent more time teaching their children chose day-care centers with more structured programs; children whose parents who gave them more individual attention at home were given more teacher attention at the day-care center.

Satisfied Consumers

The more similar were the parents' and day-care characteristics, the greater was the parents' satisfaction with the day-care arrangement they had selected (and the better their children did developmentally). This compatibility was more important to parents, apparently, than how well the day-care arrangement met the standards that experts believe or that we found in this study index high-quality care: high levels of staff training, favorable adult–child ratios, nonauthoritarian discipline, and a safe and stimulating physical environment. Regardless of its characteristics, however, most parents, claimed to be satisfied with their child's day-care arrangement. This finding is consistent with other surveys of day-care consumers. In general, parents who are using day care do not claim to be dissatisfied, either about the particular day-care arrangement they have selected or about using day care for their children rather than having the mother stay at home. Mothers' role as primary caregiver may be diminishing in this day and age, but mothers apparently are not unhappy about it. In this study, in fact, the mothers who were most satisfied with their day-care arrangement were those who were least involved in it (when what they didn't know couldn't hurt them, perhaps).

Most mothers who use day care apparently believe that their children are learning more in day care than they would staying home and are convinced their children benefit from day care because it is educational, contributes to the child's personal development, and builds up social

---

[2]Correlation between parents' and caregivers' traditional values = .39 ($p < .001$).

skills (Cadden, 1993). They believe that their children are more ready for school, smarter, more independent, and more outgoing than they would be if they were not in day care. "The outstanding impression that emerged from [a] survey [of readers of *Working Mother*] is that working mothers with children in quality child care believe their youngsters are getting the best of two worlds. As a woman with a 2-year-old and a 6-year-old puts it: My children are growing up seeing Mom and Dad as their base, but also having the ability to branch out in relationships and experiences they would not have readily received staying at home with me all day" (Cadden, 1993, p. 61).

Not surprisingly, then, mothers in our study were happiest if their children were in full-time centers, with experienced teachers and a structured program—a day-care arrangement with practical benefits for the mother and educational benefits for the child. Only fathers preferred to keep children at home, with mother or nanny. In the *Working Mother* survey, too, mothers preferred center-based care as a learning environment and believed that one-on-one care, whether by a nanny, a relative, or the mother herself, was of lesser educational value than group care; on every question dealing with the educational value of care, centers come out on top. As these mothers said:

> The day-care center doesn't have to worry about washing clothes, cleaning house, running errands, and getting distracted.

> I feel teachers are better geared to educate a small child. After all, that's what they went to college for.

> Our children have gained insight into many facets of life, which I believe they would not have experienced if they had stayed home with me: exposure to many different types of adults and children; a wide variety of toys, games, books and activities; learning about cooperation and sharing; being able to giggle and act silly with lots of friends one day and being alone in a cozy corner with a book the next day; being in a physical environment that supports children's needs instead of placing limitations on them; being in a place where children are not pushed to learn but where they learn and discover because it's fun and they want to do it (Cadden, 1993, pp. 60–61).

The words of this insightful mother can serve as a suitable conclusion to our study. Out of the mouths of these mothers come the same conclusions as we have reached after arduous analyses: Children do benefit from the opportunities afforded by a day-care environment that is rich in toys and educational activities, with a group of stimulating and diverse peers. Without detracting from what their families offer, these opportunities enrich the lives and development of today's children and set them on the road to further adventures in school.

Appendix

TABLE A.1

Variables Measuring the Environment and the Child's Experiences

Adult affection

The number of physically affectionate gestures made by the adult to the child during the observation: hugs, kisses, cuddles, caresses, comforts ($r^a = .65$).

Adult control

The number of 10-second periods during the observation in which the adult physically controlled, forced, or punished the child ($r = .61$).

Adult demanding

The proportion of the adult 's utterances to the child during the observation that were demands ($r = .74$).

Adult demands

The number of verbal demands made by the adult to the child during the observation ($r = .98$).

Adult giving lesson

The number of 10-second periods during the observation in which the adult was giving the child a lesson, a nonplayful interaction in which the focus was on teaching something. Over half of the lessons observed were "academic" (about letters, colors, counting, science), about one quarter were about arts, crafts, music, sports, toys; the remainder focused on everyday knowledge or socialization rules ($r = .54$).

Adult giving object

The number of times the adult gave an object to the child during the observation ($r = .76$).

Adult helping child

The number of times the adult helped the child during the observation, not in response to a direct request by the child ($r = .85$).

Adult making appropriate response

The number of times the adult made an appropriate response during the observation, including helping, to the child's request, demand, or offer ($r = .59$).

Adult offering choice

The number of times the adult offered the child a choice (of an activity, object, etc.) during the observation ($r = .68$).

Adult one-to-one talk

The number of utterances by the adult that were directed to the child alone during the observation ($r = .70$).

(continued)

[a]Interobserver reliability coefficients.

TABLE A.1 *(continued)*

Adult play
> The number of 10-second periods during the observation in which the adult played with the child (play may be physical, social, cooperative, dramatic, or a game) ($r = .85$).

Adult reading or singing
> The number of 10-second periods during the observation in which the adult read, sang, or recited rhymes to the child (reciting occurred half as often as reading or singing; $r = .90$).

Adult talk
> The number of utterances to the child made by the adult during the observation ($r = .82$).

Adult talk to group
> The number of utterances by the adult that were directed to the child during the observation when the child was part of a group ($r = .81$).

Adult teaching
> The number of utterances directed to the child during the observation that were informative, didactic, or explanatory in content ($r = .84$).

Adult teaching (proportion)
> The proportion of the adult's utterances to the child during the observation that were didactic in content ($r = .75$).

Adult teaching group
> The number of didactic utterances that were directed to the child during the observation when the child was part of a group ($r = .81$).

Adult teaching one-to-one
> The number of didactic utterances to the child during the observation that were directed to the child alone ($r = .88$).

Adult touching
> The number of times the adult initiated physical contact with the child (touching, holding) during the observation ($r = .83$).

Adult touching, proportion
> The proportion of the adult's social interaction with the child during the observation that involved physical contact ($r = .82$).

Adult verbal responsiveness
> The proportion of the adult's utterances to the child during the observation that were responses to something the child had said or done ($r = .73$).

Adult's age
> The age of the child's primary caregiver (mother, head teacher, sitter). (Information collected during interview with the adult.)

Adult's education
> The level of education of the mother, father, sitter, head teacher in day-care center class on a scale from 1 = junior high school to 6 = postgraduate degree. (Information collected during interview with the adult.)

Adult's expectations for child
> The level of expectation that the parent or caregiver has for the child, based on the number of items in a questionnaire that the adult believes the child will know before he or she starts school; for example, his or her own name and address, the name of the president, what a pomegranate is, how to answer the phone and take a message; 20 items; Cronbach's alpha = .76).

Adult's experience in child care
> The level of experience with children or in child care that the adult has, 1 = none; 2 = informal; 3 = professional child-care experience. (Information collected during interview with the adult.

(continued)

TABLE A.1 *(continued)*

Adult's knowledge of child development

The amount or degree to which the adult has read about child care or child development, values the child-care arrangement for educational reasons, is aware of individual differences among children, and agrees with experts' solutions to 16 hypothetical child-care problems concerning how and when to discipline children (maximum possible score = 60; Cronbach's alpha = 70). (Information collected during interview with the adult and by questionnaire.)

Adult's positive attitude toward child

The adult's ratings of the child on a questionnaire as bright, loving, lively, fun (9-point rating scales; maximum possible = 36; Cronbach's alpha = .94).

Adult's traditional values

The caregiver, the mother, or the father endorses traditional family values like the family does things together (eating, going to church, taking vacations), lives in the same town as the grandparents; the father takes the sons to football games and makes decisions, the mother and daughters stay home, and do the cooking; the family is large. The adult sees day care as responsible for the disintegration of families, thinks mothers and fathers should have the greatest influence on children, believes home offers children better care than day care, is opposed to women's liberation and employment (maximum possible = 44; Cronbach's alpha = 76). (Information collected during interview with the adult.)

Adult's training in child care

The number of courses in child care or child development taken by the mother, the caregiver, or the head teacher, on a scale: 1 = none; 2 = 1 - 3 courses; 3 = 4 - 6 courses; 4 = more than 6 courses. (Information collected during interview with the adult.)

Caregiver stability

The length of time the caregiver or head teacher has been in the day-care setting. (Information collected during interview with the caregiver.)

Child-adult ratio

The number of children enrolled in the child's class divided by the number of adults who are regularly there. (Information collected during interview with the caregiver.)

Child alone

The number of 10-second periods during the observation in which the child was alone, out of another person's sight ($r = .82$).

Child imitating

The number of times the child imitated the action of an adult or a peer during the observation ($r = .76$).

Child playing with object

The number of 10-second periods during the observation in which the child played alone with an object in a focussed, concentrated manner ($r = .95$).

Child watching adult

The number of 10-second periods during the observation in which the child watched an adult or adults intently and noninteractively ($r = .46$).

Child watching interactions

The number of 10-second periods in which the child watched and listened to interactions between other people but did not participate during the observation ($r = .89$).

Child watching peers

The number of 10-second periods during the observation in which the child watched another child or children intently and noninteractively ($r = .52$).

Child watching TV

The number of 10-second periods during the observation in which the child watched television and was not interacting with anyone ($r = .90$).

(continued)

TABLE A.1 *(continued)*

Child's satisfaction with day care
Ratings by the parent and the caregiver of how much the child likes the care arrangement and the frequency of distress upon separation from parent (maximum = 35). (Information collected during interview with the adult.)

Child's social activities (with adults, with children)
The child's social activities with nonrelated adults and children, not including experiences in regular day-care arrangement (frequency and number of different people; maximum possible = 20). (Information collected during interview with the mother.)

Children in center
The number of children in the nursery school or day-care center. (Information collected during interview with the caregiver.)

Children in class
The number of children in the child's class, core group, or home-care arrangement. (Information collected during interview with the caregiver.)

Decoration
Decorative elements in the home or center: rugs, ornaments, books, plants, pictures, lamps, piano, curtains, TV, fireplace, etc. (Total possible = 40; based on checklist completed at the observation.)

Diversity
The opportunity the day-care arrangement offers for the child to interact with people of different ages, sexes, races, ethnicities, and social backgrounds from his or her own and from each other (maximum possible = 36). (Information collected during interview with caregiver.)

Pretend play
The amount of dramatic play, make believe, pretend during the observation ($r = .64$).

Extended family
Number of people in household, in extended family; frequency of activities together, and amount of participation in child care (maximum possible = 100). (Information collected during interview with mother.)

Family changes
The number of changes in the family over the course of the year of the study: moving, change in father's or mother's job, work status, increase or decrease in number of people in the household, marital separation, financial change, significant parent-child separation, etc. (maximum possible = 16). (Information collected during interviews with mother and father.)

Geographic stability
Parents' length of time in Chicago, the midwest, their present home, neighborhood, and marriage (maximum possible = 58). (Information collected during interviews with mother and father.)

Hazards
Number of physical hazards observed in the setting (e.g., unprotected heights, sharp objects, cleaning supplies, medicines). (Total possible = 12; based on checklist completed at the observation.)

Hours in day care
The number of hours the child is in day care per week: 1 = none, 2 = less than 30 hours, 3 = 30 - 40 hours, 4 = more than 40 hours. (Information collected during interview with mother.)

(continued)

TABLE A.1 *(continued)*

Household help

The amount of help with housework there is in the household: cleaning person, housekeeper, dishwasher, washer/drier, eating out, convenience meals, husband does chores regularly without nagging (maximum possible = 25). (Information collected during interview with mother.)

Mesh between home and day care

Agreement between parents and caregiver on solutions to hypothetical child-care problems and on the importance of discipline, teaching, affection, and opportunities for the child to learn in the child-care arrangement. Similarity between parents and caregiver in socioeconomic and ethnic background and in level of expectations for the child. The degree to which the parents are involved in the child-care arrangement (maximum possible = 94). (Information collected during interviews with adults and on questionnaires.)

Mess

Dirty and disorganized aspects of the environment (e.g., scattered toys, food, strewn clothes, dead plants, pet food, ashtrays, stained carpet, dirty floor, peeling paint). (Total possible = 40; based on checklist completed at the observation.)

Middle-class peers

The proportion of children in the day-care group who are of middle or professional class SES (scale 1 - 4). (Information collected during interview with caregiver.)

Money for day care (monthly)

The amount of money spent by parents on child care per month (range 0 - $700). (Information collected during interview with mother.)

Money for day care (hourly)

The amount paid by parents for day care on an hourly basis, calculated by dividing the monthly amount for child care by full-time/part-time day-care status. (Information collected during interview with mother.)

Months in day care

The number of months the child has been in day care. (Information collected during interviews with mother.)

Mother's career orientation

The degree to which the mother wishes she were working or is glad she is working; liked or likes working because of the type of work, career, job; prefers work activities; thinks work activities are important, enjoyable; chose child-care arrangement in order to work (maximum possible = 47; Cronbach's alpha = .73). (Information collected during interviews with mother.)

Mother's feeling of alienation

Total of responses to a 78-item alienation questionnaire in which mother agree with questions like the following: "Most of my life is spent doing meaningless things." "I feel no need to try my best for it makes no difference anyhow." "Everyone is out to manipulate you toward his own ends." And responses to a 56-item preference questionnaire, in which mother indicated that she prefers to spend her time alone, in selfish pursuits rather than with the family or on work.

Mother's overall role satisfaction

Mother's satisfaction and enjoyment of overall role, including juggling job and motherhood, satisfaction with time for self, with accomplishments (20 5-point scales). (Information collected on questionnaire.)

(continued)

TABLE A.1 *(continued)*

Mother's satisfaction with maternal role

Mother's satisfaction with her role as mother, including child care, teaching, playing with child, sharing child care with husband (15 5-point scales). (Information collected by questionnaire.)

Mother's work hours

Amount of time mother has worked in the past year: weeks x hours per week. (Information collected during interviews with mother.)

Negative affect

The number of expressions of negative affect observed during the observation: insults, scolding, criticism, refusals, reprimands, whining, fretting, crying ($r = .63$).

Number of caregivers

The number of different caregivers in the child's class or home day care arrangement who are in regular contact with the child. (Information collected during interviews with caregiver and in 15-minute checklist observations.)

Number of children interacting

Number of different children interacting with child during the observation. (Range = 0 - 29; based on checklists completed at the observation.)

Older children present

Number of children in the class or group who are more than one year older than the child. (Information collected during interview with caregiver.)

Parallel play

The amount of parallel play with peers, focussed on an object, during the observation.

Parent in day care as child

Length and amount of time parent spent in day care, nursery school, kindergarten as a child (maximum possible = 50). (Information collected during interviews with parents.)

Parent's involvement in child care

For father: The amount of time the child spends with the father (dinner, outings, physical care, playing, learning, bedtime) when the father is responsible for the child's care; how involved was the father in making decisions about the child's care arrangement (maximum possible = 50).

For mother: The amount of time the mother spends in the day-care arrangement, has contact with the day-care staff, how much she says she knows what goes on in the day-care setting (maximum possible = 40). (Information collected during interviews with parents.)

Parent's satisfaction with child care

The mother's and the father's satisfaction with the child-care arrangement: overall rating of satisfaction; positive evaluation of features in the child-care arrangement that the parent thinks are most important; number of features parent would change (reverse coded; maximum possible = 30). (Information collected during interviews with parents.)

Peer aggression

The proportion of 10-second periods of interaction with another child or children during the observation in which aggression was observed: hitting, kicking, threatening, grabbing toy away ($r = .64$).

Peer interaction

The number of 10-second periods during the observation in which the child interacted with another child or children (including touching, playing, talking, helping, responding; inter$r = .40 - .81$ $M = .60$; $r = .95$).

(continued)

TABLE A.1 *(continued)*

Peer play
The number of 10-second periods during the observation in which peer played with the child (play may be physical, social, cooperative, dramatic, or a game; $r = .85$).

Peer talk
The number of utterances by a peer directed toward the child during the observation ($r = 1.0$).

Positive affect
The number of expressions of positive affect observed during the observation: praise, smile, laugh, kiss, hug, use positive tone of voice ($r = .51$).

Program
The extent to which the caregiver describes the day care program as being high in structure, schedule, group activities, individual activities, teacher direction (maximum possible = 24). (Information collected during interview with caregiver.)

Showing object
The number of times an adult or peer showed an object to the child during the observation ($r = .37$).

Siblings (older, younger, brothers, sisters)
The number and kind of siblings the child has. (Information collected during interview with mother.)

SES
A composite measure consisting of the sum of mother's occupation (1 = unskilled, 2 = skilled, 3 = blue collar, 4 = white collar [sales], 5 = white collar [management], 6 = professional/executive), father's occupation (X 2), mother's father's occupation; mother's education (1 = junior high school to 6 = postgraduate), father's education (X 2); mother's highest wage (1 = < \$2/hour to 13 = >\$10/hour), family income (1 = < \$400/month to 10 = > \$2,000/month). (Information collected during interviews with mother and father.)

Structure
Clearly defined activity areas in the home or center, specific routines for each area, children assigned to areas, planned activities for the class, for groups of children, for individual children, by-the-clock schedule. (Total possible = 8; based on checklist completed at the observation.)

Toys
Numbers of different types of toys and educational equipment in the home or center: stuffed animals, trucks and cars, story books, puzzles, instructive games, wheel toys, dress-up clothes, animals, math activities, record player, sandbox, jungle gym, etc. (Total possible = 34; based on checklist completed at the observation.)

Younger children present
Number of children in child's care arrangement who are more than 1 year younger than the child. (Information collected during interview with caregiver.)

TABLE A.2
Family Variables: Mean Values and Correlations with Child's Age

Independent Variables	Mean	(SD)	Maximum[a]	r^b with age
Family Variables				
Extended family[c]	73.9	(26.9)	90.	•
Household help	9.9	(3.8)	25.	•
SES	44.9	(12.1)	65.	•
Geographic stability	43.0	(6.3)	58.	•
Family changes	2.9	(0.9)	5.	•
Parent Variables[d]				
Parent giving lesson[e]	15.1	(27.1)	164.1	•
Parent giving object	14.5	(10.6)	69.5	−.37***
Parent offering choice	.04	(.03)	.22	−.28***
Parent helping child	15.4	(15.2)	71.6	−.35***
Parent appropriate response	25.6	(27.0)	186.2	−.30***
Parent verbal responsiveness	.54	(.14)	1.58	.20*
Child Activity at Home Variables				
Child alone	84.7	(92.8)	483.7	.31***
Child playing with object	95.5	(75.0)	389.4	•
Child watching TV	56.0	(89.9)	431.4	•
Child watching parent	4.0	(6.7)	43.1	•
Child's activities with adults	4.6	(3.9)	16.	•
Child's activities with children	6.1	(4.2)	19.	•
Sibling Variables				
Siblings : 64 children had 1 sibling; 13 had 2; 4 had 3				•
Brothers : 41 children had 1 brother; 5 had 2				•
Sisters : 33 children had 1 sister; 6 had 2; 2 had 3				•
Older siblings : 25 children had 1; 7 had 2; 2 had 3				•
Younger siblings : 31 children had 1; 1 had 2				.26**
Sibling interaction	75.0	(95.0)	423.1	.30***
Sibling talk	62.7	(84.2)	370.0	.26**
Sibling aggression	.04	(.16)	1.8	.20*
Negative affect	25.4	(24.7)	138.1	−.22**
Positive affect	92.6	(55.0)	299.3	•
Father Variables				
Father's education	4.6	(2.0)	6.	•
Father's knowledge of child develpmnt	41.9	(6.2)	60.	•
Father's traditional values	13.8	(5.1)	28.	•
Father's expectations for child	12.4	(2.9)	18.	•
Father's positive attitude toward child	34.2	(2.0)	36.	•
Father's involvement in child care	19.3	7.8	35.	•
Father's satisfaction with child care	20.5	(10.6)	28.	•
Father touching	7.8	(7.1)	35.1	−.23**
Father touching, proportion	.06	(.05)	.36	−.28***
Father playing	20.9	(45.1)	433.6	•
Father affection	1.6	(2.4)	14.7	−.18*
Father talking	181.6	(144.3)	856.4	•
Father demands	26.7	(28.8)	256.7	•

(continued)

TABLE A.2 *(continued)*

Independent Variables	Mean	(SD)	Maximum[a]	r[b] with age
Father demanding	.20	(.10)	.73	•
Father control	.40	(.93)	8.2	•
Father teaching	11.4	(15.7)	100.4	.20*
Father teaching, proportion	.06	(.06)	.38	.19*
Father reading or singing	6.7	(21.2)	151.5	•
Father in day care as child	11.0	(4.5)	25.	•
Mother Variables				
Mother's education	4.4	(2.3)	6.	•
Mother's training in child care	2.9	(1.4)	4.	•
Mother's knowledge of child develpmnt	42.3	(5.9)	60.	•
Mother's experience in child care[f]	1.4	(1.1)	3.	•
Mother's traditional values	15.0	(7.0)	29.	•
Mother's expectations for child	13.2	(3.1)	19.	•
Mother's positive attitude toward child	30.2	(4.0)	36.	•
Mother's involvement in child care	37.2	(6.9)	50.	•
Mother's satisfaction with child care	20.7	(6.8)	30.	•
Mother's work hours	1040.[g]	(598.)	2250.	•
Mother's career orientation	15.1	(5.3)	30.	•
Mother's overall satisfaction with role	71.6	(15.3)	100.	•
Mother's satisfactn with maternal role	63.8	(9.1)	81.	•
Mother's feeling of alienation	64.1	(23.1)	103.	•
Mother touching	10.1	(8.6)	48.1	−.41***
Mother touching, proportion	.05	(.04)	.24	−.30***
Mother playing	9.8	(24.6)	199.4	−.17*
Mother affection	2.0	(3.2)	20.6	−.25**
Mother talking	254.9	(149.3)	859.0	−.26**
Mother demands	39.8	(29.6)	173.2	−.22**
Mother demanding	.18	(.11)	.68	•
Mother control	.80	(1.8)	16.4	−.20*
Mother teaching	20.4	(24.1)	200.6	−.28***
Mother teaching, proportion	.08	(.07)	.37	−.18*
Mother reading or singing	5.2	(14.8)	93.1	•
Mother in day care as child	15.0	(4.3)	35.	•
Home Variables				
Home decoration	20.9	(4.6)	40.	•
Home toys	11.6	(5.2)	25.	•
Home mess	5.0	(4.0)	19.	−.21**
Home hazards	0.6	(0.9)	10.	•

[a]The minimum value for all observed behaviors was 0.

[b]Table shows all significant rs, $p < .05$.

[c]32 families had a nonparental adult living in the house.

[d]Mother + father.

[e]Numbers for observation variables reflect the frequency of occurrence or the number of 10-second periods in which behavior occurred in a two-hour observation (maximum = 720).

[f]29 had none; 31 had professional child-care experience.

[g]For mothers who were working.

*$p < .05$. ** $p < .01$. *** $p < .001$.

TABLE A.3
Daytime Variables: Mean Values and Correlations with Child's Age

Independent Variables	Mean	(SD)	Maximum[a]	r^b with age
Day Variables[c]				
Caregiver Variables				
Caregiver's age	36.0	(11.9)	76.	●
Caregiver's training in child care	2.8	(1.5)	4.	●
Caregiver's education	3.2	(2.6)	6.	●
Caregiver's experience in child care	2.0	(0.6)	3.	.32***
Caregiver's knowledge of child development	49.2	(5.5)	60.	●
Caregiver's traditional values	11.6	(5.9)	20.	●
Caregiver's positive attitude toward child	28.1	(5.6)	36.	●
Caregiver's expectations for child	13.3	(2.2)	19.	●
Caregiver stability	3.1	(1.6)	20.	●
Number of caregivers	2.9	(1.8)	10.	●
Caregiver touching[d]	47.2	(55.6)	303.0	− .43***
Caregiver playing	21.2	(48.5)	373.0	− .22**
Caregiver affection	1.9	(3.4)	18.8	− .33***
Caregiver talking	294.0	(175.5)	894.9	− -.25**
Caregiver one-to-one talk	245.4	(187.8)	894.9	− .30***
Caregiver talk to group	27.7	(38.0)	217.7	.16*
Caregiver demands	47.1	(33.6)	199.3	− .23**
Caregiver demanding	.21	(.13)	.81	− .13 +
Caregiver teaching	24.0	(30.3)	264.4	− .27**
Caregiver teaching one-to-one	21.2	(30.4)	246.4	− .26**
Caregiver teaching group	2.8	(5.7)	48.2	●
Caregiver teaching, proportion	.08	(.07)	.36	− .16*
Caregiver reading or singing	4.0	(32.3)	181.9	●
Caregiver giving lesson	19.0	(42.8)	550.5	●
Caregiver giving object	11.8	(12.1)	169.5	− .21**
Caregiver offering choice	12.7	(12.0)	84.8	− .21**
Caregiver helping child	12.8	(16.3)	137.0	− .41**
Caregiver appropriate response	18.4	(25.6)	369.0	− .25**
Caregiver verbal responsiveness	.49	(.19)	2.49	●
Caregiver control	.60	(.83)	15.8	− .38***
Peer Variables				
Children in care arrangement	53.4	(52.8)	500.	.33***
Children in class	13.9	(7.0)	33.	.38***
Child–adult ratio	6.2	(4.3)	23.	.33***
Number of children interacting	7.0	(4.9)	29.	.40***
Older children present	1.8	(3.7)	22.	− .21 **
in Year 1, 28 had an older child; in Year 2, 22 had older child				
Younger children present	.58	(2.0)	10.	.19*
Middle-class peers	2.2	(0.6)	4.4	●
Child watching peers	5.9	(8.5)	61.3	− .23**
Peer interaction	125.0	(99.9)	540.8	●
Peer talk	95.7	(89.5)	552.4	.25**
Child imitating peer	2.2	(3.7)	46.6	●
Peer aggression	.06	(.26)	3.89	− .23**

(continued)

TABLE A.3 *(continued)*

Independent Variables	Mean	(SD)	Maximum[a]	r^{b} with age
Setting Variables				
Decoration	13.6	(5.0)	32.	•
Toys	12.6	(5.1)	25.	.24**
Mess	3.5	(2.2)	12.	•
Hazards	1.4	(1.7)	12.	− .16*
Program Variables				
Program			22.	.40***
Structure	1.6	(1.0)	8.	.29***
Money for day care, monthly	21.8	(73.0)	669.4	•
Child's satisfaction with day care	26.0	(3.8)	39.	.21**
Mesh between home and day care	55.0	(14.3)	92.	•
Diversity	15.3	(8.0)	36.	.26**
Child watching adult	5.0	(9.4)	102.7	-.28***
Child imitating adult	2.7	(8.1)	74.8	− .14+
Child watching interactions	19.1	(26.9)	176.5	•
Child alone	69.2	(104.0)	569.0	•
Child playing with object	128.6	(91.5)	618.1	•
Child watching TV	42.6	(86.2)	507.7	•
Showing object	4.5	(10.0)	154.9	•
Negative affect	19.7	(23.2)	167.5	− .26**
Positive affect	84.3	(52.6)	320.7	•
Pretend play	14.6	(38.9)	386.1	•
Parallel play	9.1	(24.0)	232.1	•
Length Variables				
Months in day care	9.5	(7.9)	24.	.31***
Hours in day care	2.5	(1.3)	4.	•

[a]The minimum value for all observed behaviors was 0.

[b]Table shows all significant rs, $p < .05$.

[c]For children who were at home with mother during the day, the caregiver in the daytime observation was the mother.

[d]Numbers for observation variables reflect the frequency of occurrence or number of 10-second periods in which behavior occurred in a 2-hour observation (720 periods).

+ $p < .10$. * $p < .05$. ** $p < .01$. *** $p < .001$.

TABLE A.4
Variables Assessing the Child's Behavior and Development

Aggression toward peers
The frequency of aggressive acts by the child directed toward peers during the observation: hitting, kicking, threatening, grabbing toy away ($r = .99$).

Avoiding adult
The number of times during the observation that the child avoided physical contact with an adult ($r = .66$).

Compliance with parents
The proportion of parents' demands during the dinnertime observation with which the child complied ($r = .50$).

Compliance with requests
Compliance with requests by mother or researcher in the laboratory assessment or the home assessment. (Measured during structured assessments in the laboratory playroom and in the home.) Plus, the sum of thefollowing ratings made by mothers and by fathers on 9-point scales: obedient, cooperative, always does what he/she is told; quiet, peaceful, no trouble; and, scored in negative direction, likes doing things by himself/herself, assertive, has a mind of his/her own, stands up for his/her rights; adventurous, outgoing; disobedient to parents; inter$rs = .38$ to $.49$; mean $r = .42$; Cronbach's alpha $= .74$). (Information collected by questionnaires given to parents.)

Complying with caregiver
The proportion of the caregivers' demands during the daytime observation with which the child complied ($r = .50$).

Demanding
The proportion of the child's utterances during the observation that were demanding ($r = .90$).

Demands
The number of verbal or nonverbal demands (for objects, food, help, attention, etc.) that the child directed to an adult, including the observer, during the observation ($r = .59$).

Difficult temperament
The parent's responses to questions on the Carey Temperament Questionnaire indicating that the child has a difficult temperament (1 = hardly ever; 7 = almost always), for example, When upset or annoyed with a task, my child may throw it down, cry, yell, or slam the door. When playing with other children my child often argues with them. When my child gets angry about something it is difficult to sidetrack him or her. My child has difficulty in adjusting to the rules of another household if they are different from those at home (Cronbach's alpha $= .84$).

General competence
The sum of eight scales, reflecting the child's obedience, self confidence, sociability, autonomy, assertiveness, playfulness, cheerfulness, and nonaggression. Each of these scales was based on a 7-point behavioral checklist with +, -, and 0 ratings for each item, collected during the observations (Cronbach's alpha $= .81$).

Independence from mother
Physical contact and proximity to mother during play when mother and child were alone or with another mother and child in the laboratory, when the researcher was present, and following brief separations from the mother; inter$rs = .30$ to $.38$; Cronbach's alpha $= .65$). (Measured during semistructured assessments in the laboratory playroom.)

Intellectual ability
Digit-span memory; language comprehension; verbal fluency; object recognition; knowledge of concepts; inter$rs = .47$ to $.55$; Cronbach's alpha $= .79$). (Measured during structured assessments in the home.)

(continued)

TABLE A.4 *(continued)*

Negative behavior with unfamiliar peer

Negative physical or verbal actions toward the unfamiliar peer in the laboratory, including controlling, refusing, avoiding, during free play and in cooperation tasks. (Measured during semistructured assessments in the laboratory playroom.)

Negativity

The amount of negative behavior from the child during the observation: fretting, crying, whining, complaining ($r = .73$).

Refusing

The proportion of requests with which the child refused to comply during the observation ($r = .79$).

Sociability with mother

Positive, reciprocal, cooperative social interaction with mother during free play and in a structured task in the laboratory; positive interaction and greeting after brief mother-child separations; prosocial interaction when mother is "hurt"; inter$r$s = .29 to .41; Cronbach's alpha = .55). (Measured during semistructured assessments in the laboratory playroom.)

Social cognitive ability

Visual and conceptual perspective taking; ability to communicate nonegocentrically; knowledge of gender roles; ability to label emotions and solve hypothetical emotional problems; inter$r$s = .24 to .72; Cronbach's alpha = .82). (Measured during structured assessments in the laboratory playroom.)

Social competence with familiar peer

Positive social interaction during free play and cooperation in a semi-structured task with a familiar playmate ($r = .38$). (Measured during semistructured assessments in the home.)

Social competence with strangers

Friendliness toward the researchers in the laboratory; cooperation in joint tasks; prosocial behavior when the researcher needs help or comfort; trust of the researcher in "dangerous" situations; and ratings of the child's likability and social competence; inter$r$s = .29 to .65; Cronbach's alpha = .84). (Measured during semistructured assessments in the laboratory playroom.)

Social competence with unfamiliar peer

Positive interaction with an unfamiliar peer during free play in the laboratory with toys and without toys; cooperation with the unfamiliar peer in joint tasks; inter$r$s = .33 to .37; Cronbach's alpha = .52). (Measured during semistructured assessments in the laboratory playroom.)

Social competence with visitor

Friendliness toward the researcher visiting the home; cooperation in joint tasks; prosocial behavior when the researcher needs help or comfort; trust of the researcher in "dangerous" situations; and appropriate and competent responses to requests; inter$r$s = .19 to .44; Cronbach's alpha = .63). (Measured during semistructured assessments in the home.)

Talking

The number of utterances by the child during the observation directed toward mother, father, etc. ($r = .79$).

Touching adult

The amount of touching of an adult initiated by the child during the observation ($r = .80$).

REFERENCES

Ackerman-Ross, S., & Khanna, P. (1989). The relationship of high quality day care to middle-class 3-year-olds' language performance. *Early Childhood Research Quarterly, 4,* 97–116.

Allen, G. B., & Masling, J. M. (1957). An evaluation of the effects of nursery school training on children in the kindergarten, first, and second grades. *Journal of Educational Research, 51,* 285–296.

Allhusen, V. D. (1992). *Differences in day care experiences of infants in three different teacher–child ratio groups: Variations in caregiving quality.* Unpublished doctoral dissertation, Cornell University, Ithaca, NY.

Anderson, K. E., Lytton, H., & Romney, D. M. (1986). Mothers' interaction with normal and conduct-disordered boys: Who affects whom? *Developmental Psychology, 22,* 604–609.

Andersson, B.-E. (1989). Effects of public day care: A longitudinal study. *Child Development, 60,* 857–866.

Arnett, J. (1989). Caregivers in day-care centers: Does training matter? *Journal of Applied Developmental Psychology, 10,* 541–552.

Asher, K. N., & Erickson, M. T. (1979). Effects of varying child–teacher ratio and group size on day care children's and teachers' behavior. *American Journal of Orthopsychiatry, 49,* 518–521.

Azmitia, M., & Hesser, J. (1993). Why siblings are important agents of cognitive development: A comparison of siblings and peers. *Child Development, 64,* 430–444.

Barnard, K. E., Bee, H. L., & Hammond, M. A. (1984). Home environment and cognitive development in a healthy, low-risk sample: The Seattle study. In A. W. Gottfried (Ed.), *Home environment and early cognitive development* (pp. 117–149). Orlando, FL: Academic Press.

Barocas, R., Seifer, R., Sameroff, A. J., Andrews, T., Croft, R. T., & Ostrow, E. (1991). Social and interpersonal determinants of developmental risk. *Developmental Psychology, 27,* 479–488.

Barton, M. E., & Tomasello, M. (1991). Joint attention and conversation in mother–infant–sibling triads. *Child Development, 62,* 517–529.

Bates, J. E., Marvinney, D., Bennett, D. S., Dodge, K. A., Kelly, T., & Pettit, G. S. (1991, April). *Children's daycare history and kindergarten adjustment.* Paper presented at the biennial meetings of the Society for Research in Child Development, Seattle, WA.

Bates, J., Maslin, C., & Frankel, K. (1985). Attachment security, mother–child interaction, and temperament as predictors of behavior-problem ratings at age three years. *Monographs of the Society for Research in Child Development, 50*, 1–2, Serial No. 209, 167–193.

Baumrind, D. (1967). Child care practices anteceding three patterns of preschool behavior. *Genetic Psychology Monographs, 75*, 43–88.

Baumrind, D., & Black, A. E. (1967). Socialization practices associated with dimensions of competence in preschool boys and girls. *Child Development, 38*, 291–327.

Baydar, N., & Brooks-Gunn, J. (1991). Effects of maternal employment and child-care arrangements on preschoolers' cognitive and behavioral outcomes: Evidence from the children of the National Longitudinal Survey of Youth. *Developmental Psychology, 27*, 932–945.

Beller, E. K. (1974). *Infant day care: A longitudinal study* (Final Report to the Office of Child Development, Washington, DC [OCD -CB- 310]).

Belsky, J. (1984). Two waves of day care research: Developmental effects and conditions of quality. In R. C. Ainslie (Ed.), *The child and the day care setting* (pp. 1–34). New York: Praeger.

Belsky, J. (1988). The "effects" of infant day care reconsidered. *Early Childhood Research Quarterly, 3*, 235–272.

Belsky, J., Rovine, M., & Taylor, D. G. (1984). The Pennsylvania Infant and Family Development Project, III: The origins of individual differences in infant–mother attachment: Maternal and infant contributions. *Child Development, 55*, 718–728.

Berk, L. (1985). Relationship of educational attainment, child oriented attitude, job satisfaction, and career commitment to caregiver behavior toward children. *Child Care Quarterly, 14*, 103–129.

Berndt, T. J., & Bulleit, T. N. (1985). Effects of sibling relationships on preschoolers' behavior at home and at school. *Developmental Psychology, 21*, 761–767.

Biller, H. B. (1974). Paternal and sex-role factors in cognitive and academic functioning. In J. K. Cole & R. Diestbier (Eds.), *Nebraska Symposium on Motivation 1973* (pp. 84–123). Lincoln, NE: University of Nebraska Press.

Bizman, A., Yinon, Y., Mivtzari, E., & Shavit, R. (1978). Effects of the age structure of the kindergarten on altruistic behavior. *Journal of School Psychology, 16*, 154–160.

Blurton Jones, N. G. (1972). Categories of child–child interaction. In N. Blurton Jones (Ed.), *Ethological studies of child behaviour* (pp. 97–127). Cambridge: Cambridge University Press.

Blurton Jones, N. G., Ferreira, M. C. R., Brown, M. F., & Macdonald, L. (1980). *Behaviour of one year old children that predicted the age at which they started pre-school: An illustration of the perils of self-selected samples.* Unpublished manuscript, University of London, Institute of Child Health, England.

Borke, H. (1971). Interpersonal perception of young children: Egocentrism or empathy. *Developmental Psychology, 5*, 263–269.

Bradley, R. H. (1986). Play material and intellectual development. In A. W. Gottfried & C. C. Brown (Eds.), *Play interactions* (pp. 227–251). Lexington, MA: Lexington Books.

Bradley, R. H., & Caldwell, B. M. (1984). 174 children: A study of the relationship between home environment and cognitive development during the first 5 years. In A. W. Gottfried (Ed.), *Home environment and early cognitive development* (pp. 5–56). Orlando, FL: Academic Press.

Bradley, R. H., Caldwell, B. M., Rock, S. L., Ramey, C. T., Barnard, K. E., Gray, C., Hammond, M. A., Mitchell, S., Gottfried, A. W., Siegel, L., & Johnson, D. L. (1989). Home environment and cognitive development in the first 3 years of life: A collaborative study involving six sites and three ethnic groups in North America. *Developmental Psychology, 25,* 217–235.

Broberg, A. G., Hwang, C.-P., Lamb M. E., & Bookstein, F. L. (1990). Factors related to verbal abilities in Swedish preschoolers. *British Journal of Developmental Psychology, 8,* 335–349.

Bryant, B., Harris, M., & Newton, D. (1980). *Children and minders.* London: Grant McIntyre.

Burchinal, M., Lee, M., & Ramey, C. (1989). Type of day care and preschool intellectual development in disadvantaged children. *Child Development, 60,* 128–137.

Busse, T. V., Ree, M., Gatride, M., & Alexander, T. (1972). Environmentally enriched classrooms and the cognitive and perceptual development of Negro preschool children. *Journal of Educational Psychology, 63,* 15–21.

Cadden, V. (1993, April). How kids benefit from child care. *Working Mother,* pp. 58–61.

Carew, J. (1980). Experience and the development of intelligence in young children. *Monographs of the Society for Research in Child Development, 45* (6–7, Serial No. 187).

Carey, W. B., & McDevitt, S. C. (1978). Revision of the Infant Temperament Questionnaire. *Pediatrics, 61,* 735–739.

Cicirelli, V. G. (1967). Sibling constellation, creativity, IQ, and academic achievement. *Child Development, 38,* 481–490.

Cicirelli, V. G. (1975). Effects of mother and older sibling on the problem-solving behavior of the younger child. *Developmental Psychology, 11,* 749–756.

Clarke-Stewart, K. A. (1973). Interactions between mothers and their young children: Characteristics and consequences. *Monographs of the Society for Research in Child Development, 38* (6–7, Serial No. 153).

Clarke-Stewart, K. A. (1978). And daddy makes three: The father's impact on mother and young child. *Child Development, 49,* 466–478.

Clarke-Stewart, K. A. (1980). The father's contribution to child development. In F. A. Pedersen (Ed.), *The father–infant relationship: Observational studies in a family context* (pp. 116–146). New York: Praeger.

Clarke-Stewart, K. A. (1988). Parents' effects on children's development: A decade of progress? *Journal of Applied Developmental Psychology, 9,* 41–84.

Clarke-Stewart, K. A. (1989). Infant day care: Maligned or malignant? *American Psychologist, 44,* 266–273.

Clarke-Stewart, K. A., & Apfel, N. (1979). Evaluating parental effects on child development. In L. S. Shulman (Ed.), *Review of research in education* (Vol. 2, pp. 47–119). Itasca, IL: Peacock.

Clarke-Stewart, K. A., & Fein, G. G. (1983). Early childhood programs. In P. H. Mussen, M. Haith, & J. Campos (Eds.), *Handbook of child psychology* (Vol. 2, pp. 917–1000). New York: Wiley.

Clarke-Stewart, K. A., & Hevey, C. M. (1981). Longitudinal relations in repeated observations of mother–child interaction from 1 to 2 1/2 years. *Developmental Psychology, 17,* 127–145.

Clarke-Stewart, K. A., Umeh, B. J., Snow, M. E., & Pederson, J. A. (1980). Development and prediction of children's sociability from 1 to 2 1/2 years of age. *Developmental Psychology, 16,* 290–302.

Clerkx, L. E., & Van IJzendoorn, M. H. (1992). Child care in a Dutch context: On the history, current status, and evaluation of nonmaternal child care in the Netherlands. In M. E. Lamb, K. J. Sternberg, C.-P. Hwang, & Broberg, A. G. (Eds.), *Child care in context: Cross-cultural perspectives* (pp. 55–79). Hillsdale, NJ: Lawrence Erlbaum Associates.

Cochran, M.M. (1977a). A comparison of group day and family child-rearing patterns in Sweden. *Child Development, 48,* 702–707.

Cochran, M. M. (1977b). *Group day care and family childrearing patterns in Sweden.* Unpublished report to the Foundation for Child Development, Cornell University, Ithaca, NY.

Connolly, K. J., & Smith, P. K. (1978). Experimental studies of the preschool environment. *International Journal of Early Childhood, 10,* 86–95.

Coon, H., Fulker, D. W., DeFries, J. C., & Plomin, R. (1990). Home environment and cognitive ability of 7-year-old children in the Colorado Adoption Project: Genetic and environmental etiologies. *Developmental Psychology, 26,* 459–468.

Crockenberg, S. (1981). Infant irritability, mother responsiveness, and social support influences on the security of infant–mother attachment. *Child Development, 52,* 857-869.

Crockenberg, S. (1991, April). *Conceptual issues in the study of child compliance, noncompliance and parental control.* Paper presented at the biennial meetings of the Society for Research in Child Development, Seattle, WA.

Crockenberg, S., & Litman, C. (1990). Autonomy as competence in 2-year-olds: Maternal correlates of child defiance, compliance, and self-assertion. *Developmental Psychology, 26,* 961–971.

Cryan, J. R., Sheehan, R., Wiechel, J., & Bandy-Hedden, I. G. (1992). Success outcomes of full-day kindergarten: More positive behavior and increased achievement in the years after. *Early Childhood Research Quarterly, 7,* 187-203.

DeHart, G. (1987, April). *Social functions of language in sibling and mother–child conversation.* Paper presented at the biennial meetings of the Society for Research in Child Development, Baltimore, MD.

Desai, S., Chase-Lansdale, P. L., & Michael, R. T. (1989). Mother or market? Effects of maternal employment on the intellectual ability of four-year-old children. *Demography, 26,* 545–561.

Easterbrooks, M A., & Lamb, M. E. (1979). The relationship between quality of infant–mother attachment and infant competence in initial encounters with peers. *Child Development, 50,* 380-387.

Eckerman, C. O., Whatley, J. L., & Kutz, S. L. (1975). Growth of social play with peers during the second year of life. *Developmental Psychology, 11,* 42-49.

Edwards, C.P., Logue, M.E., Loehr, S., & Roth, S. (1987).The effects of day care participation on parent–infant interaction at home. *American Journal of Orthopsychiatry, 57,* 116–119.

Egeland, B., & Farber, E. A. (1984). Infant–mother attachment: Factors related to its development and changes over time. *Child Development, 55,* 753–771.

Epstein, A. S., & Radin, N. (1975). Motivational components related to father behavior and cognitive functioning in preschoolers. *Child Development, 46,* 831–839.

Estrada, P., Arsenio, W. F., Hess, R. D., & Holloway, S. D. (1987). Affective quality of the mother–child relationship: Longitudinal consequences for children's school-relevant cognitive functioning. *Developmental Psychology, 23,* 210–215.

Fagot, B. I. (1973). Influence of teacher behavior in the preschool. *Developmental Psychology, 9*, 198–206.

Fagot, B. I. (1991, April). *Parent influences on behavior of toddler play groups.* Paper presented at the biennial meetings of the Society for Research in Child Development, Seattle, WA.

Ferri, E. (1980). Combined nursery centres. *Concern*, National Children's Bureau, No. 37.

Flavell, J. H. (1968). *The development of role-taking and communication skills in children.* New York: Wiley.

Fosburg, S., Hawkins, P. D., Singer, J. D., Goodson, B. D., Smith, J. M., & Brush, L. R. (1980). *National Day Care Home Study.* Cambridge: Abt.

Fowler, W. (1978). *Day care and its effects on early development: A study of group and home care in multi-ethnic, working-class families.* Toronto: Ontario Institute for Studies in Education.

Gadberry, S. (1980). Effects of restricting first graders' TV-viewing on leisure time use, IQ change, and cognitive style. *Journal of Applied Developmental Psychology, 1*, 45–57.

Gaensbauer, T.J., Harmon, R.J., Culp, A.M., Schultz, L.A., Van Doorninck, W.J., & Dawson, P. (1985). Relationships between attachment behavior in the laboratory and the caretaking environment. *Infant Behavior and Development, 8*, 355–369.

Garber, H. L., & Heber, R. (1980, April). *Modification of predicted cognitive development in high-risk children through early intervention.* Paper presented at the annual meeting of the American Educational Research Association, Boston.

Garber, H. L., & Hodge, J. D. (1989). Risk for deceleration in the rate of mental development. *Developmental Review, 9*, 259–300.

Garvey, C. (1974). Some properties of social play. *Merrill-Palmer Quarterly, 20*, 163–180.

Goelman, H., & Pence, A. R. (1987a). Effects of child care, family, and individual characteristics on children's language development: The Victoria Day Care Research Project. In D. A. Phillips (Ed.), *Quality in child care: What does research tell us?* (pp. 89–104). Washington, DC: National Association for the Education of Young Children.

Goelman, H., & Pence, A. R. (1987b). Some aspects of the relationship between family structure and child language in three types of day care. In I. E. Sigel, D. L. Peters, & S. Kontos (Eds.), *Annual advances in applied developmental psychology* (Vol. 2, pp. 129–149). Norwood, NJ: Ablex.

Golden, M., Rosenbluth, L., Grossi, M. T., Policare, H. J., Freeman, H., & Brownlee, E. M. (1978). *The New York City Infant Day Care Study.* New York: Medical and Health Research Association of New York City.

Goodman, N., & Andrews, J. (1981). Cognitive development of children in family and group day care. *American Journal of Orthopsychiatry, 51*, 271–284.

Gordon, I., Lally, J. R., Yarrow, L., & Beller, E. K. (1973). *Studies in socioemotional development in infancy: A final report* (Final Report to the Office of Child Development). Gainesville, FL: University of Florida

Gottfried, A. E., Gottfried, A. W., & Bathurst, K. (1987, April). *Physical and social environmental influences in traditional and nontraditional families.* Paper presented at the biennial meetings of the Society for Research in Child Development, Baltimore, MD.

Gottfried, A. E., Gottfried, A. W., & Bathurst, K. (1988). Maternal employment, family environment, and children's development: Infancy through the school years. In A. E. Gottfried & A. W. Gottfried (Eds.), *Maternal employment and children's development: Longitudinal research.* New York: Plenum.

Gottfried, A. W. (1984). Home environment and early cognitive development: Integration, meta-analyses, and conclusions. In A. W. Gottfried (Ed.), *Home environment and early cognitive development* (pp. 329–342). Orlando, FL: Academic Press.

Gottfried, A. W., & Gottfried, A. E. (1984). Home environment and cognitive development in young children of middle-socioeconomic-status families. In A. W. Gottfried (Ed.), *Home environment and early cognitive development* (pp. 57–116). Orlando, FL: Academic Press.

Grossmann, K., Grossmann, K. E., Spangler, G., Suess, G., & Unzner, L. (1985). Maternal sensitivity and newborns' orientation responses as related to quality of attachment in Northern Germany. *Monographs of the Society for Research in Child Development, 50* (1–2, Serial No. 209, pp. 233–256).

Gullo, D. F., & Burton, C. B. (1992). Age of entry, preschool experience, and sex as antecedents of academic readiness in kindergarten. *Early Childhood Research Quarterly, 7,* 175–186.

Harper, L. V., & Huie, K. S. (1987). The effects of prior group experience, age, and familiarity on the quality and organization of preschoolers' social relationships. *Child Development, 56,* 704–717.

Haskins, R. (1985). Public school aggression among children with varying day-care experience. *Child Development, 56,* 689–703.

Hayes, C. D., Palmer, J. L., & Zaslow, M. J. (1990). *Who cares for America's children?* Washington, DC: National Academy Press.

Hayes, W.A., Massey, G.C., Thomas, E.A.C., David, J., Milbrath, C., Buchanan, A., & Lieberman, A. (1983). *Analytical and technical report of the National Infant Care Study.* San Mateo, CA: The Urban Institute for Human Services.

Hegland, S. M., & Rix, M. K. (1990). Aggression and assertiveness in kindergarten children differing in day care experiences. *Early Childhood Research Quarterly, 5,* 105–116.

Herwig, J. E. (1989, April). *Longitudinal effects of preschool experience on social and cognitive play behaviors of preschoolers.* Paper presented at the biennial meetings of the Society for Research in Child Development, Kansas City, MO.

Hess, R. D., & McDevitt, T. M. (1984). Some cognitive consequences of maternal intervention techniques: A longitudinal study. *Child Development, 55,* 2017–2030.

Hess, R. D., Price, G. G., Dickson, W. P., & Conroy, M. (1981). Different roles for mothers and teachers: Contrasting styles of child care. In S. Kilmer (Ed.), *Advances in early education and day care* (Vol. 2, pp. 1–28). Greenwich, CT.: JAI Press.

Hinde, R. A., & Stevenson-Hinde, J. (1986). Relating childhood relationships to individual characteristics. In W. W. Hartup & Z. Rubin (Eds.), *Relationships and development* (pp. 27–50). Hillsdale, NJ: Lawrence Erlbaum Associates.

Hirsh-Pasek, K., Hyson, M. C., & Rescorla, L. (1990). Academic environments in preschool: Do they pressure or challenge young children? *Early Education and Development, 1,* 401–423.

Hoffman, L. W. (1984). Maternal employment and the young child. In M. Perlmutter (Ed.), *Parent–child interaction and parent–child relations in child development. The Minnesota Symposia on Child Psychology* (Vol. 17, pp. 101–128). Hillsdale, NJ: Lawrence Erlbaum Associates.

Hoffman, L. W. (1986). Work, family, and the child. In M. S. Pallak & R. O. Perloff (Eds.), *Psychology and work: Productivity, change, and employment* (pp. 173–220). Washington, DC: American Psychological Association.

Hoffman, L. W. (1989). Effects of maternal employment in the two-parent family. *American Psychologist, 44*, 283–292.

Holloway, S. D., & Reichhart-Erickson, M. (1988). The relationship of day care quality to children's free-play behavior and social problem-solving skills. *Early Childhood Research Quarterly, 3*, 39–53.

Holloway, S. D., & Reichhart-Erickson, M. (1989). Child-care quality, family structure, and maternal expectations: Relationship to preschool children's peer relations. *Journal of Applied Developmental Psychology, 10*, 281–298.

Honzik, M. P. (1967). Environmental correlates of mental growth: Prediction from the family setting at 21 months. *Child Development, 38*, 337–364.

Howes, C. (1983). Caregiver behavior in centers and family day care. *Journal of Applied Developmental Psychology, 4*, 99–107.

Howes, C. (1987). Social competency with peers: Contributions from child care. *Early Childhood Research Quarterly, 2*, 155–167.

Howes, C. (1988). Relations between early child care and schooling. *Developmental Psychology, 24*, 53–57.

Howes, C. (1990). Current research on early day care. In S. S. Chehrazi (Ed.), *Psychosocial issues in day care* (pp. 21–35). Washington, DC: American Psychiatric Press.

Howes, C., & Olenick, M. (1986). Family and child care influences on toddler's compliance. *Child Development, 57*, 202–216.

Howes, C., Rodning, C., Galluzzo, D. C., & Myers, L. (1988). Attachment and child care: Relationships with mother and caregiver. *Early Childhood Research Quarterly, 3*, 403–416.

Howes, C., & Rubenstein, J. L. (1981). Toddler peer behavior in two types of day care. *Infant Behavior and Development, 4*, 387–394.

Howes, C., & Rubenstein, J. L. (1985). Determinants of toddlers' experience in day care: Age of entry and quality of setting. *Child Care Quarterly, 14*, 140–151.

Howes, C., & Stewart, P. (1987). Child's play with adults, toys, and peers: An examination of family and child-care influences. *Developmental Psychology, 23*, 423–430.

Huston-Stein, A., Friedrich, L. K., & Susman, E. J. (1977). The relation of classroom structure to social behavior, imaginative play, and self-regulation of economically disadvantaged children. *Child Development, 48*, 908–916.

Huttenlocher, J., Haight, W., Bryk, A., Seltzer, M., & Lyons, T. (1991). Early vocabulary growth: Relation to language input and gender. *Developmental Psychology, 27*, 236–248.

Huttenlocher, J., & Levine, S. (1990). *Primary test of cognitive skills*. Monterey, CA: CTB–McGraw Hill.

Iannotti, R. J., Cummings, E. M., Pierrehumbert, B., Zahn-Waxler, C., & Milano, J. J. (1989, April). *Parental influences on prosocial behavior and empathy in early childhood*. Paper presented at the biennial meetings of the Society for Research in Child Development, Kansas City, MO.

Jarvis, C. H. (1987, August). *Kindergarten days: Too much, too soon?* Paper presented at the annual convention of the American Psychological Association, New York.

Jennings, K. E., & Connors, R. E. (1989). Mothers' interactional style and children's competence at 3 years. *International Journal of Behavioral Development, 12*, 155–175.

Johnson, J. E., Ershler, J., & Bell, C. (1980). Play behavior in a discovery-based and a formal-education program. *Child Development, 51,* 271–274.

Jordan, B. E., Radin, N., & Epstein, A. (1975). Paternal behavior and intellectual functioning in preschool boys and girls. *Developmental Psychology, 11,* 407–408.

Kagan, J., Kearsley, R. B., & Zelazo, P. R. (1978). *Infancy: Its place in human development.* Cambridge, MA: Harvard University Press.

Kagan, S., & Madsen, M. C. (1971). Cooperation and competition of Mexican, Mexican–American, and Anglo-American children of two ages under four instructional sets. *Developmental Psychology, 5,* 32–39.

Kagan, S. L. (1991). Examining profit and nonprofit child care: An odyssey of quality and auspices. *Journal of Social Issues, 47,* 87–104.

Kinney, P. F. (1988). *Antecedents of caregiver involvement with infants and toddlers in group care.* Unpublished doctoral dissertation, University of Maryland, College Park, MD.

Kisker, E. E., Hofferth, S. L., Phillips, D. A., & Farquhar, E. (1991). *A profile of child care settings: Early education and care in 1990* (Final report for U.S. Department of Education, No. LC88090001). Princeton, NJ: Mathematica.

Klinzing, D. G., & Klinzing, D. R. (1974). An examination of the verbal behavior, knowledge, and attitudes of day care teachers. *Education, 95,* 65–71.

Koch, H. L. (1955). Some personality correlates of sex, sibling position, and spacing among five- and six-year-old children. *Genetic Psychology Monographs, 52,* 3–50.

Koch, H. L. (1956). Attitudes of young children toward their peers as related to certain characteristics of their siblings. *Psychological Monographs, 70* (19, Serial No. 426).

Kontos, S. (1992). *Family day care: Out of the shadows and into the limelight.* Washington, DC: National Association for the Education of Young Children.

Kontos, S. (1993, March). *The ecology of family day care.* Paper presented at the biennial meetings of the Society for Research in Child Development, New Orleans, LA.

Kontos, S., & Dunn, L. (1993, March). *Children's cognitive and social competence in child care centers and family day care homes.* Paper presented at the biennial meetings of the Society for Research in Child Development, New Orleans, LA.

Kontos, S., & Fiene, R. (1987). Child care quality, compliance with regulations, and children's development: The Pennsylvania Study. In D. A. Phillips (Ed.), *Quality in child care: What does research tell us?* (pp. 57–80). Washington, DC: National Association for the Education of Young Children.

Krauss, R. M., & Glucksberg, S. (1969). The development of communicative competence as a function of age. *Child Development, 42,* 255–266.

Lally, J. R., & Honig, A. S. (1977). *The Family Development Research Program* (Final Report, No. OCD-CB-100). Syracuse, NY: University of Syracuse.

Lamb, M. E. (1975). Fathers: Forgotten contributors to child development. *Human Development, 18,* 245–266.

Lamb, M. E., Hwang, C-P., Broberg, A., & Bookstein, F. L. (1988). The effects of out-of-home care on the development of social competence in Sweden: A longitudinal study. *Early Childhood Research Quarterly, 3,* 379–402.

Lamb, M. E., Sternberg, K. J., Knuth, N., Hwang, C.-P., & Broberg, A. G. (1991). In H. Goelman (Ed.), *Play and child care.* Albany: State University of New York Press.

Laosa, L. M. (1982). Families as facilitators of children's intellectual development at 3 years of age: A causal analysis. In L. M. Laosa & I. E. Sigel (Eds.), *Families as learning environments for children* (pp. 1–46). New York: Plenum.

Larner, M., Gunnarsson, L., Cochran, M., & Hagglund, S. (1989, April). *The peer relations of children reared in day care centers or home settings.* Paper presented at the biennial meetings of the Society for Research in Child Development, Kansas City, MO.

Larsen, J. M., & Robinson, C. C. (1987, April). *Later effects of preschool on low-risk children.* Paper presented at the biennial meetings of the Society for Research in Child Development, Baltimore, MD.

Larsen, J.M., & Robinson, C. C. (1989). Later effects of preschool on low-risk children. *Early Childhood Research Quarterly, 4,* 133–144.

Larzelere, R. E. (1986). Moderate spanking: Model or deterrent of children's aggression in the family? *Journal of Family Violence, 1,* 27–36.

Lay, K.-L., Waters, E., & Park, K. A. (1989). Maternal responsiveness and child compliance: The role of mood as a mediator. *Child Development, 60,* 1405–1411.

Lazar, I., Darlington, R. B., Murray, H., Royce, J., & Snipper, A. (1982). Lasting effects of early education. *Monographs of the Society for Research in Child Development, 47* (2–3, Serial No. 195).

Lazar, I., Hubbell, R., Murray, H., Rosche, M., & Royce, J. (1977). *The persistence of preschool effects: A long-term follow-up of fourteen infant and preschool experiments* (Final Report to Office of Human Development Services, Grant No. 18-76-07843). Ithaca, NY: Cornell University.

Levenstein, P. (1986). Mother–child play interaction and children's educational achievement. In A. W. Gottfried & C. C. Brown (Eds.), *Play interactions* (pp. 293–303). Lexington, MA: Lexington Books.

Lewis, C. C. (1981). The effects of parental firm control: A reinterpretation of findings. *Psychological Bulletin, 90,* 547–563.

Lieberman, A. F. (1977). Preschoolers' competence with a peer: Relations with attachment and peer experience. *Child Development, 48,* 1277–1287.

Logue, M. E. (1989, April). *Social behavior of toddlers and preschoolers in same-age and multi-age daycare settings.* Paper presented at the biennial meetings of the Society for Research in Child Development, Kansas City, MO.

Londerville, S., & Main, M. (1981). Security of attachment, compliance, and maternal training methods in the second year of life. *Developmental Psychology, 17,* 289–299.

Long, F., Peters, D. L., & Garduque, L. (1985). Continuity between home and day care: A model for defining relevant dimensions of child care. In I. E. Sigel (Ed.), *Advances in applied developmental psychology* (pp. 131–170). Norwood, NJ: Ablex.

MacDonald, K., & Parke, R. D. (1984). Bridging the gap: Parent–child play interaction and peer interactive competence. *Child Development, 55,* 1265–1277.

Mackinnon, C. E., Brody, G. H., & Stoneman, Z. (1982). The effects of divorce and maternal employment on the home environments of preschool children. *Child Development, 53,* 1392–1399.

Maddi, S. R. (1971). The search for meaning. In M. Page (Ed.), *Nebraska Symposium on Motivation 1970* (pp. 137–186). Lincoln, NE: University of Nebraska Press.

Marjoribanks, K. (1976). Birth order, family environment, and mental abilities: A regression surface analysis. *Psychological Reports, 39,* 759–765.

Marvin, R. B., Greenberg, M. T., & Mossler, D. G. (1976). The early development of conceptual perspective taking: Distinguishing among multiple perspectives. *Child Development, 47,* 511–514.

Mason, K. O., & Duberstein, L. (1992). Consequences of child care for parents' well-being. In A. Booth (Ed.), *Child care in the 1990s: Trends and consequences* (pp. 127–158). Hillsdale, NJ: Lawrence Erlbaum Associates.

Masur, E. F., & Gleason, J. B. (1980). Parent–child interaction and the acquisition of lexical information during play. *Developmental Psychology, 16,* 404–409.

McCartney, K. (1984). Effect of quality of day care environment on children's language development. *Developmental Psychology, 20,* 244–260.

Melhuish, E. C., Lloyd, E., Martin, S., & Mooney, A. (1990). Type of child care at 18 months–II. Relations with cognitive and language development. *Journal of Child Psychology and Psychiatry, 31,* 861–870.

Melhuish, E. C., Moss, P., Mooney, A., & Martin, S. (1991). How similar are day care groups before the start of day care? *Journal of Applied Developmental Psychology, 12,* 331–335.

Miller, L. B, & Dyer, J. L. (1975). Four preschool programs: Their dimensions and effects. *Monographs of the Society for Research in Child Development, 40* (5–6, Serial No. 162).

Miller, L. B., Bugbee, M. R., & Hybertson, D. W. (1985). Dimensions of preschool: The effects of individual experience. In I. E. Sigel (Ed.), *Advances in applied developmental psychology* (Vol. 1, pp. 25–90). Norwood, NJ: Ablex.

Milner, E. (1951). A study of the relationship between reading readiness in grade one school children and patterns of parent–child interaction. *Child Development, 22,* 95–112.

Moskowitz, D. W., Schwarz, J. C., & Corsini, D. A. (1977). Initiating day care at three years of age: Effects on attachment. *Child Development, 48,* 1271–1276.

Moss, H. A., & Kagan, J. (1958). Maternal influences on early IQ scores. *Psychological Reports, 4,* 655–661.

National Center for Education Statistics. (1992). *Home activities of 3- to 8-year olds.* Washington, DC: U.S. Department of Education, Office of Educational Research and Improvement (NCES 92–004).

Nelson, K. (1973). Structure and strategy in learning to talk. *Monographs of the Society for Research in Child Development, 38,* (1–2, Serial No. 149).

Olson, S. L., Bates, J. E., & Bayles, K. (1984). Mother–infant interaction and the development of individual differences in children's cognitive competence. *Developmental Psychology, 20,* 166–179.

Olson, S. L., Bayles, K., & Bates, J. E. (1986). Mother–child interaction and children's speech progress: A longitudinal study of the first two years. *Merrill-Palmer Quarterly, 32,* 1–20.

Olson, S. L., Bates, J. E., & Kaskie, B. (1992). Caregiver–infant interaction antecedents of children's school-age cognitive ability. *Merrill-Palmer Quarterly, 38,* 309–330.

Osborn, A. F., & Milbank, J. E. (1987). *The effects of early education.* Oxford: Clarendon Press.

Owen, M. T., & Cox, M. J. (1988). Maternal employment and the transition to parenthood. In A. E. Gottfried & A. W. Gottfried (Eds.), *Maternal employment and children's development: Longitudinal research.* New York: Plenum.

Owen, M. T., & Henderson, V. K. (1989, April). *Relations between child care qualities and child behavior at age 4: Do parent–child interactions play a role?* Paper presented at the biennial meetings of the Society for Research in Child Development, Kansas City, MO.

Park, K. J., & Honig, A. S. (1991, August). *Infant child care patterns and later ratings of preschool behaviors.* Paper presented at the annual convention of the American Psychological Association, San Francisco, CA.

Parke, R. D. (1979). Perspectives on father–infant interaction. In J. D. Osofsky (Ed.), *Handbook of infant development* (pp. 549–590). New York: Wiley.

Parke, R. D., & Slaby, R. G. (1983). The development of aggression. In P. H. Mussen & E. M. Hetherington (Eds.), *Handbook of child psychology* (Vol. 4, pp. 547–641). New York: Wiley.

Parpal, M., & Maccoby, E. E. (1985). Maternal responsiveness and subsequent child compliance. *Child Development, 56,* 1326–1334.

Patterson, G. R. (1982). *Coercive family process.* Eugene, OR: Castalia Publishing.

Peaslee, M. V. (1976). The development of competency in 2-year-old infants in day care and home reared environments (Doctoral dissertation, Florida State University). *Dissertation Abstracts International, 37,* 4218A.

Pedersen, F. A. (Ed.). (1980). *The father–infant relationship: Observational studies in a family context.* New York: Praeger.

Pedersen, F. A., Cain, R. L., Jr., Zaslow, M. J., & Anderson, B. J. (1982). Variation in infant experience associated with alternative family roles. In L. M. Laosa & I. E. Sigel (Eds.), *Families as learning environments for children* (pp. 203–222). New York: Plenum.

Pence, A. R., & Goelman, H. (1987). Silent partners: Parents of children in three types of day care. *Early Childhood Research Quarterly, 2,* 103–118.

Pepler, D., Corter, C., & Abramovitch, R. (1982). Social relations among children: Comparison of sibling and peer interaction. In K. H. Rubin & H. S. Ross (Eds.), *Peer relationships and social skills in childhood* (pp. 209–228). New York: Springer-Verlag.

Pettit, G. S. (1991, April). *Family interaction style and children's subsequent social–behavioral competence: A six-month longitudinal investigation.* Paper presented at the biennial meetings of the Society for Research in Child Development, Seattle, WA.

Phillips, D. A., McCartney, K., & Scarr, S. (1987). Child-care quality and children's social development. *Developmental Psychology, 23,* 537–543.

Phillips, D. A., Scarr, S., & McCartney, K. (1987). Dimensions and effects of child care quality: The Bermuda study. In D. A. Phillips (Ed.), *Quality in child care: What does research tell us?* (pp. 43–56). Washington, DC: National Association for the Education of Young Children.

Phyfe-Perkins, E. (1980). Children's behavior in preschool settings: A review of research concerning the influence of physical environment. In L. Katz (Ed.), *Current topics in early childhood education* (Vol. 3, pp. 91–124). Norwood, NJ: Ablex.

Phyfe-Perkins, E. (1981). *Effects of teacher behavior on preschool children: Review of research.* Washington, DC: National Institute of Education (ERIC Document Reproduction Service No. ED 211 176).

Prescott, E. (1973). *A comparison of three types of day care and nursery school–home care.* Washington, DC: National Institute of Education (ERIC Document Reproduction Service No. ED 078 910).

Prescott, E., & David, T. G. (1976). *Concept paper on the effects of the physical environment on day care* (prepared for the U.S. Office of Child Development). Pasadena, CA: Pacific Oaks College.

Prodromidis, M., Lamb, M. E., Sternberg, K. J., Hwang, C.-P., & Broberg, A. G. (1993). *Aggression and noncompliance among Swedish children in center-based care, family day-care and home care.* Manuscript submitted for review.

Rabinovich, B. A., Zaslow, M. J., Berman, P. W., & Heyman, R. (1987, April). *Employed and homemaker mothers' perceptions of their toddlers' compliance behavior in the home.* Paper presented at the biennial meetings of the Society for Research in Child Development, Baltimore, MD.

Radin, N. (1973). Observed paternal behaviors as antecedents of intellectual functioning in young boys. *Developmental Psychology, 8,* 369–376.

Radin, N. (1976). The role of the father in cognitive, academic, and intellectual development. In M. E. Lamb (Ed.), *The role of the father in child development* (pp. 237–276). New York: Wiley.

Ramey, C. T., Farran, D. D., & Campbell, F. A. (1979). Predicting IQ from mother–infant interactions. *Child Development, 50,* 804–814.

Reis, M., & Gold, D. (1977). Relations of paternal availability to problem solving and sex-role orientation in young boys. *Psychological Reports, 40,* 823–829.

Rheingold, H. L., & Eckerman, C. O. (1971). Departures from the mother. In H. R. Schaffer (Ed.), *The origins of human social relations* (pp. 73–82). London: Academic Press.

Roberts, W. L. (1986). Nonlinear models of development: An example from the socialization of competence. *Child Development, 57,* 1166–1178.

Robertson, J., & Robertson, J. (1971). Young children in brief separation: A fresh look. *Psychoanalytic Study of the Child, 26,* 264–315.

Robinson, H. B., & Robinson, N. M. (1971). Longitudinal development of very young children in a comprehensive day care program. *Child Development, 42,* 1673–1683.

Robinson, J., & Corley, R. (1989, April). *The effects of day care participation: sex differences in early and middle childhood.* Paper presented at the biennial meetings of the Society for Research in Child Development, Kansas City, MO.

Roopnarine, J. L., & Johnson, J. E. (1984). Socialization in a mixed-age experimental program. *Developmental Psychology, 20,* 828–832.

Rosenberg, B. G., & Sutton-Smith, B. (1966). Sibling association, family size and cognitive abilities. *Journal of Genetic Psychology, 109,* 271–279.

Rosenthal, S. (1993, March). *The social ecology of early maternal employment: Effects on verbal intelligence and behavior problems in a national sample.* Paper presented at the biennial meetings of the Society for Research in Child Development, New Orleans, LA.

Rothstein-Fisch, C., & Howes, C. (1988). Toddler peer interaction in mixed-age groups. *Journal of Applied Developmental Psychology, 9,* 211–218.

Rubenstein, J. L., & Howes, C. (1979) Caregiving and infant behavior in day care and in homes. *Developmental Psychology, 15,* 1-24.

Rubenstein, J. L., & Howes, C. (1983). Social–emotional development of toddlers in day care: The role of peers and of individual differences. In S. Kilmer (Ed.), *Advances in early education and day care* (Vol. 3, pp. 13–45). Greenwich, CT: JAI Press.

Rubenstein, J. L., Howes, C., & Boyle, P. (1981). A two-year follow-up of infants in community based infant day care. *Journal of Child Psychology and Psychiatry, 22,* 209–218.

Rubenstein, J. L., Pedersen, F.A., & Yarrow, L. J. (1977). What happens when mother is away: A comparison of mothers and substitute caregivers. *Developmental Psychology, 13,* 529–530.

Ruopp, R., Travers, J., Glantz, F., & Coelen, C. (1979). *Children at the center.* Cambridge, MA: Abt Associates.

Scarr, S. (1993). *The effects of maternal employment and nonmaternal infant care on development at two and four years.* Unpublished manuscript, University of Virginia.

Scarr, S., Lande, J., & McCartney, K. (1989). Child care and the family. In J. Lande, S. Scarr, & N. Gunzenhauser (Eds.), *Caring for children: Challenge to America* (pp. 1–21). Hillsdale, NJ: Lawrence Erlbaum Associates.

Schachter, F. F. (1981). Toddlers with employed mothers. *Child Development, 52*, 958–964.

Schenk, V. M., & Grusec, J. E. (1987). A comparison of prosocial behavior of children with and without day care experience. *Merrill-Palmer Quarterly, 33*, 231–240.

Schlieker, E., White, D. R., & Jacobs, E. (1989–1990). Does day care quality contribute to language development? *Concordia University Research Bulletins, 8*, No. 010.

Schlieker, E., White, D. R., & Jacobs, E. (1991). The role of day care quality in the prediction of children's vocabulary. *Canadian Journal of Behavioural Science, 23*, 12–24.

Schwarz, J. C., Krolick, G., & Strickland, R. G. (1973). Effects of early day care experience on adjustment to a new environment. *American Journal of Orthopsychiatry, 43*, 340–346.

Schweinhart, L. J., Weikart, D. P., & Larner, M. D. (1986). Consequences of three preschool curriculum models through age 15. *Early Childhood Research Quarterly, 1*, 15–45.

Siegal, M., & Storey, R. M. (1985). Day care and children's conceptions of moral and social rules. *Child Development, 56*, 1001–1008.

Siegel-Gorelick, B., Ambron, S. R., & Everson, M. D. (1981a, April). *Direction of influence and intensity of affect in caregiver–child interactions in day care and at home.* Paper presented at the biennial meetings of the Society for Research in Child Development, Boston.

Siegel-Gorelick, B., Ambron, S. R., & Everson, M. D. (1981b, April). *Day care as a learning environment: The relation between environmental characteristics and social development in family day care.* Paper presented at AERA, Los Angeles.

Silverman, I., W., & Ragusa, D. M. (1990). Child and maternal correlates of impulse control in 24-month-old children. *Genetic, Social, & General Psychology Monographs, 116*, 435–473.

Smith, P., & Pederson, D. (1983, April). *Maternal sensitivity and patterns of infant–mother attachment.* Paper presented at the meetings of the Society for Research in Child Development, Detroit.

Smith, P. K., & Connolly, K. J. (1972). Patterns of play and social interaction in preschool children. In N. Blurton Jones (Ed.), *Ecological studies of child behaviour* (pp. 65–95). London: Cambridge University Press.

Smith, P. K., & Connolly, K. J. (1980). *The ecology of preschool behaviour.* Cambridge: Cambridge University Press.

Smith, P. K., & Connolly, K. J. (1986). Experimental studies of the preschool environment: The Sheffield Project. In S. Kilmer (Eds), *Advances in early education and day care* (Vol. 4, pp. 27–66). Greenwich, CT: JAI press.

Snow, M. E., Jacklin, C. N., & Maccoby, E. E. (1981). Birth-order differences in peer sociability at thirty-three months. *Child Development, 52*, 589–595.

Sonenstein, F. L. (1990). The child care preferences of parents with young children: How little is known. In J. S. Hyde & M. J. Essex (Eds.), *Parental leave and child care: Setting a research and policy agenda* (pp. 337–353). Philadelphia: Temple University Press.

Sonenstein, F. L., & Wolf, D. A. (1991). Satisfaction with child care: Perspectives of welfare mothers. *Journal of Social Issues, 47*, 15–31.

Spitz, R. A. (1946). Hospitalism. *Psychoanalytic Study of the Child, 2*, 113–117.

Spitz, R. A., & Wolf, K. J. (1946). Anaclitic depression. *Psychoanalytic Study of the Child, 2*, 313–342.

Stallings, J. A. (1980). An observation study of family day care. In J. C. Colberg (Ed.), *Home day care: A perspective* (pp. 25–47). Chicago: Roosevelt University.

Steiger, J. H. (1989). *EzPATH causal modeling.* Evanston, IL: SYSTAT.

Sternberg, K. J., Lamb, M. E., Hwang, C.-P., Broberg, A., Ketterlinus, R. D., & Bookstein, F. L. (1991). Does out-of-home care affect compliance in preschoolers? *International Journal of Behavioral Development, 14,* 45–65.

Stevenson-Hinde, J., Hinde, R. A., & Simpson, A. E. (1986). Behavior at home and friendly or hostile behavior in preschool. In D. Olweus, J. Block, & M. Radke-Yarrow (Eds.), *Development of antisocial and prosocial behavior* (pp. 127–145). Orlando, FL: Academic Press.

Stith, S. M., & Davis, A. J. (1984). Employed mothers and family day-care substitute caregivers: A comparative analysis of infant care. *Child Development, 55,* 1340–1348.

Sylva, K., Roy, C., & Painter, M. (1980). *Child watching at playgroup and nursery school.* London: Grant McIntyre.

Taylor, L. J. (1976). Outcome and process evaluation of a day care centre. *Canadian Journal of Behavioural Science, 8,* 410–413.

Thomas, J. H., Due, K. M., & Wigger, D. M. (1987). Effects of the competence and sex of peer models on children's imitative behavior. *Journal of Genetic Psychology, 148,* 324–332.

Thornburg, K. R., Pearl, P., Crompton, D., & Ispa, J. M. (1990). Development of kindergarten children based on child care arrangements. *Early Childhood Research Quarterly, 5,* 27–42.

Tizard, B., Philips, J., & Plewis, I. (1976). Play in preschool centres—II. Effects on play of the child's social class and of the educational orientation of the centre. *Journal of Child Psychology and Psychiatry, 17,* 265–274.

Tizard, B., Carmichael, H., Hughes, M., & Pinkerton, B. (1980). Four-year-olds talking to mothers and teachers. In L. A. Hersov & M. Berger (Eds.), *Language and language disorders in childhood* (pp. 49–76). London: Pergamon Press.

Tyler, B., & Dittman, L. (1980). Meeting the toddler more than halfway: The behavior of toddlers and their caregivers. *Young Child, 35,* 39–46.

Urberg, K. A., & Docherty, E. M. (1976). Development of role-taking skills in young children. *Developmental Psychology, 12,* 198–203.

U.S. Bureau of the Census. (1982). *Trends in child care arrangements of working mothers* (Current Population Reports, Series P-23, No. 117). Washington, DC: U.S. Government Printing Office.

U.S. Bureau of the Census. (1990). *Who's minding the kids? Child care arrangements, 1986–87* (Current Population Reports, Series P-70, No. 20). Washington, DC: U.S. Government Printing Office.

U.S. Bureau of the Census. (1992). *How we're changing. Demographic state of the nation: 1992* (Current Population Reports, Special Studies, Series P-23, No. 177). Washington, DC: U.S. Government Printing Office.

Vandell, D. L., & Corasaniti, M. A. (1990). Variations in early child care: Do they predict subsequent social, emotional, and cognitive differences? *Early Childhood Research Quarterly, 5,* 555–572.

Vandell, D. L., Henderson, V. K., & Wilson, K. S. (1988). A longitudinal study of children with day-care experiences of varying quality. *Child Development, 59,* 1286–1292.

Vandell, D. L., & Ramanan, J. (1992). Effects of early and recent maternal employment on children from low-income families. *Child Development, 63,* 938–949.

Wadsworth, M. E. J. (1986). Effects of parenting style and preschool experience on children's verbal attainment: Results of a British longitudinal study. *Early Childhood Research Quarterly, 1,* 237–248.

Wasik, B. H., Ramey, C. T., Bryant, D. M., & Sparling, J. J. (1990). A longitudinal study of two early intervention strategies: Project CARE. *Child Development, 61,* 1682–1696.

Weiss, B., Dodge, K. A., Bates, J. E., & Pettit, G. S. (1992). Some consequences of early harsh discipline: Child aggression and a maladaptive social information processing style. *Child Development, 63,* 1321–1335.

Whitebook, M., Howes, C., & Phillips, D. (1990). *Who cares? Child care teachers and the quality of care in America. Final Report. National Child Care Staffing Study.* Oakland CA: Child Care Employee Project.

Wille, D. E., & Jacobson, J. L. (1984, April). *The influence of maternal employment, attachment pattern, extrafamilial child care, and previous experience with peers on early peer interaction.* Paper presented at the International Conference on Infancy Studies, Beverly Hills, CA.

Winnett, R. A., Fuchs, W. L., Moffatt, S., & Nerviano, V. J. (1977). A cross-sectional study of children and their families in different child care environments. *Journal of Community Psychology, 5,* 149–159.

Wittmer, D., & Honig, A. (1989, April). *Convergent or divergent? Teachers' questions to three-year-old children in day care.* Paper presented at the biennial meetings of the Society for Research in Child Development, Kansas City, MO.

Wittmer, D. S., & Honig, A. S. (1988). Teacher re-creation of negative interactions with toddlers. *Early Child Development and Care, 33,* 77–88.

Woollett, A. (1986). The influence of older siblings on the language environment of young children. *British Journal of Developmental Psychology, 4,* 235–245.

Wynn, R. L. (1979, March). *The effect of a playmate on day-care and home-reared toddlers in a strange situation.* Paper presented at the biennial meetings of the Society for Research in Child Development, San Francisco, CA.

Yankelovich, Skelly, & White, Inc. (1977). *Raising children in a changing society* (General Mills American Family Report, 1976–77). Minneapolis, MN: General Mills.

Yeates, K. W., MacPhee, D., Campbell, F. A., & Ramey, C. T. (1983). Maternal IQ and home environment as determinants of early childhood intellectual competence: A developmental analysis. *Developmental Psychology, 19,* 731–739.

Yogman, M. W. (1981). Games fathers and mothers play with their infants. *Infant Mental Health Journal, 2,* 241–248.

Zahn-Waxler, C., Radke-Yarrow, M., & Brady-Smith, J. (1977). Perspective-taking and prosocial behavior. *Developmental Psychology, 13,* 87–88.

Zahn-Waxler, C., Radke-Yarrow, M., & King, R. A. (1979). Child rearing and children's prosocial initiations toward victims of distress. *Child Development, 50,* 319–330.).

Zaslow, M. J., Pedersen, F.A., Suwalsky, J. T. D., Cain, R. L., & Fivel, M. (1985). The early resumption of employment by mothers: Implications for parent–infant interaction. *Journal of Applied Developmental Psychology, 6,* 1–16.

Author Index

Subject Index